MW00513076

TALK ABOUT ASSESSMENT

HIGH SCHOOL STRATEGIES AND TOOLS

Author

Damian Cooper

Contributing Author

Jeff Catania

Reviewers

Phil Davison, Ontario
James L. Falcone, Nova Scotia
John Ford, Ontario
Barb Isaak, Manitoba
Jill Reid, British Columbia
Mili Rowse, Alberta
Ron Smith, Newfoundland
Lisa Spicer, Alberta
Gerry Varty, Alberta
Mike Ward, British Columbia

NELSON EDUCATION

NELSON EDUCATION

Talk About Assessment: High School Strategies and Tools

Author
Damian Cooper

Contributing Author
Jeff Catania

Vice President, Publishing
Janice Schoening

Executive Publisher, Literacy and Reference
Michelle Kelly

Managing Editor, Development
Lara Caplan

Product Manager
Doug Morrow

Senior Program Manager
Ann Downar

Project Manager
Adam Rennie

Developmental Editor
Kathy Evans

Editorial Assistant
Hannah Gifford

Senior Content Production Manager
Sujata Singh

Senior Content Production Editor
Nicasio G. Punto

Copyeditor
Rebecca Rosenblum

Proofreader
Heather Sangster

Indexer
Noeline Bridge

Production Coordinator
Susan Ure

Design Director
Ken Phipps

Cover Image
Christopher Drost

Asset Coordinators
Renée Forde
Suzanne Peden

Compositor
GEX Publishing Services

Photo Shoot Coordinator
CFA Communications Ltd.

Photo/Permissions Researcher
Joanne Tang

Printer
RR Donnelley

COPYRIGHT © 2010 by
Nelson Education Ltd.

ISBN-13: 978-0-17-635712-2
ISBN-10: 0-17-635712-2

Printed and bound in the
United States
5 6 7 8 13 12 11 10

For more information contact
Nelson Education Ltd.,
1120 Birchmount Road, Toronto,
Ontario M1K 5G4. Or you can visit
our Internet site at
http://www.nelson.com.

ALL RIGHTS RESERVED. No part of
this work covered by the copyright
herein may be reproduced,
transcribed, or used in any form or
by any means—graphic, electronic,
or mechanical, including
photocopying, recording, taping,
Web distribution, or information
storage and retrieval systems—
without the written permission of
the publisher.

For permission to use material
from this text or product, submit
all requests online at
www.cengage.com/permissions.
Further questions about
permissions can be e-mailed to
permissionrequest@cengage.com.

Every effort has been made to
trace ownership of all copyrighted
material and to secure permission
from copyright holders. In the
event of any question arising as
to the use of any material, we will
be pleased to make the necessary
corrections in future printings.

Reproduction of DVD tools
is permitted for classroom/
instruction purposes only and only
to the purchaser of this product.

Dedication

To the memory of my dear mother, Alice Cooper, and to the ongoing inspiration of my father, Doug Cooper, who taught me to always strive for the summit.

Author Acknowledgments

I wish to thank everyone who has contributed to the writing of this book, as well as to the production of the accompanying DVD. To Jeff Catania, I owe a huge debt of gratitude for his superb contributions to the text and graphics, as well as for assistance in locating schools for the DVD shoot. To Jennifer Adams, Julia Cale, Joe Stafford, and Darlene Bowles, thank you for your significant contributions to the text.

Thank you, Jay McTighe, for so graciously agreeing to write the Foreword to *Talk About Assessment: High School Strategies and Tools.* Your support and commendation are invaluable.

I continue to draw inspiration from the wisdom of Grant Wiggins and Carl Bereiter. I am indebted to the assessment and grading expertise of Ken O'Connor, Tom Guskey, Rick Stiggins, Carol Ann Tomlinson, Dylan Wiliam, Paul Black, Andy Hargreaves, Doug Reeves, Michael Fullan, Ruth Sutton, and Bob Marzano. I also wish to thank the staff and students at Walkden High School for showing me what is possible!

To Doug Mohun, David Steele, Stubby McLean, George MacRae, and Joni Heard, thanks for your ongoing support.

My life partner, Nanci Wakeman, has been involved in this project from start to finish. She has made significant contributions to both the text and the DVD, as well as providing constant support and advice. And yes, on numerous occasions, has demanded that I take some time off. Thank you!

I am indebted to the editorial, publishing, and sales staff at Nelson Education, especially Kathy Evans, Adam Rennie, Ann Downar, Audrey Wearn, Michelle Kelly, and Lara Caplan.

In locating classrooms to shoot the DVD, I returned to my teaching roots at the Halton District School Board, Ontario, where I began my career in 1979. Each school welcomed me with the same infectious warmth and enthusiasm that is evident throughout the video. Production of the DVD required a veritable army of dedicated troops. Behind the scenes, Frances Petruccelli and Nanci Wakeman worked tirelessly. I am most grateful to Jacqueline Newton, Deb Robinson, and John Stieva, who invited us into their schools. To the teachers and students, a huge "Thank you" for making it real. They include the classes of Andrew Bigham, Jeff Boulton, Meg Carey, Krista Caron, Brenda Celi, Mike Gallant, Monique Gazan, Samantha Goodwin, Jennifer Houslander, Jennifer Jenkins, Aimmie Kellar, Leigh Macklin, Kristen McCoy, Amber Mitchell, Barb Porecki, Jacqueline Schettler, Amanda Udit, and Scott Williamson. A special note of thanks is due to Andrew Bigham, Brenda Celi, and Mike Gallant for ensuring that each shoot went off without a hitch at each of their schools.

Thanks also to the team at CFA Communications and especially to Cliff Rawnsley and his superb crew. And to Chris Smith, thanks for the music. You're the best.

I wish to thank Rod Bohm and his staff at Preble High School, Green Bay, Wisconsin, as well as Eve Minuk and the staff at A. R. MacNeill Secondary School in Richmond, British Columbia for contributing many of the photographs appearing in the text.

And finally, I want to thank all of the teachers who take the time to learn with me as we explore how curriculum, instruction, and assessment can work together to ensure that all students reach their potential.

Contents

Contents

Foreword

Damian Cooper has written the book that I didn't know I needed as a beginning teacher but now wished that I had. Like many educators of my era, my pre-service preparation in the assessment arena consisted of a course in Tests and Measurement, focused on large-scale testing theory and statistics. Consequently, I began my teaching career completely unprepared for, and indeed unaware of, the basics of effective classroom assessment practices.

Thankfully, today's educators, both beginner and veteran, have access to *Talk About Assessment: High School Strategies and Tools*—a treasure trove of practical information to inform and guide the use of assessments by secondary teachers. The book explores the key principles of classroom assessment, framed around eight "big ideas." These abstractions are brought to life through engaging case studies and memorable stories featuring recognizable students and familiar teaching situations.

The book would be worth the read if it simply concentrated on summative assessments *of* learning. It clearly delineates the principles and practices needed to ensure that evaluative assessments and concomitant grades provide fair and valid measures of targeted goals. But *Talk About Assessment* goes further in exploring the rich terrain of assessing *for* learning. Cooper makes the case for the importance of diagnostic (pre-assessments) and formative (ongoing) assessments and their benefits to teaching and learning. He offers tried and true, manageable methods by which secondary teachers can use assessments to enhance, not simply evaluate, the performance of their students.

Unlike some books on the topic, *Talk About Assessment* does not shy away from confronting the vexing issues of assessment and grading at the secondary level. Indeed, Cooper unearths virtually every salient challenge that a secondary teacher is likely to encounter, including the grading of "missed" work and differentiation for students with learning difficulties and language limitations.

Moreover, the book is refreshingly confrontational in addressing the "Yes, buts ..." commonly heard at in-service workshops and in faculty rooms; e.g., "Giving kids a second chance won't prepare them for the real world." After reading this work, one would be hard pressed to justify many of the prevailing assessment and grading habits (e.g., averaging all the grades collected during a marking period) so common in secondary schools.

Talk About Assessment: High School Strategies and Tools is scholarly without being "ivory tower"; practical without being simplistic. Cooper cites relevant research with the authority and assurance of an academic, while offering no-nonsense advice with the clarity and confidence of the veteran educator he is. Simply put, *Talk About Assessment: High School Strategies and Tools* speaks the truth. Accordingly, it deserves a careful read and a special place on the bookshelf for ready and frequent access.

Jay McTighe
Co-author of *Understanding by Design*
2009

Introduction

The times they are a-changing! Certainly for secondary teachers and administrators, the words of the song ring true. *Talk About Assessment: High School Strategies and Tools* is designed to help educators navigate the turbulent waters of assessment, grading, and reporting in today's high schools. My goal is the same as it was when I wrote *Talk About Assessment: Strategies and Tools to Improve Learning*—to present teachers with a common sense, accessible guide to best practice that ensures all students are well served and that teachers are not overwhelmed by assessment and grading procedures. While this resource is founded upon the same eight Big Ideas as the preceding volume, the examples, case studies, video clips, and tools focus exclusively on the secondary school context.

While I have not shied away from the controversial issues—how to respond to missed and late work, questioning our continued reliance on percentage grades, separating achievement from behaviour—*Talk About Assessment: High School Strategies and Tools* is first and foremost an invitation to examine your current practice through the lens of our fast-changing world. Marc Prensky describes today's students as "digital natives" who find themselves being taught, for the most part, by "digital immigrants." During my frequent school visits, time-on-task behaviour, task completion, attendance, discipline referrals, learning climate, and achievement all vary according to the degree to which teachers are willing to engage with students in *their* world, while maintaining a clear sense of those habits of mind, key concepts, and essential skills that are timeless—respect for self and others, honesty, perseverance, pride in one's work, craftsmanship, the wisdom of experience, and so on.

My plea to you as you explore *Talk About Assessment: High School Strategies and Tools* is to maintain an open mind. I certainly don't ask or expect you to agree with all that I suggest. Just as is the case in my workshops, my intent is to provide you with plenty to think about and push against as you reflect upon your current practice. But as professionals, we have a responsibility to think, to learn, to reflect, and to constantly strive to improve our practice. I hope this resource will assist you in each of these tasks.

Section 1 sets the context by presenting the eight Big Ideas of assessment and exploring the most significant changes that we face as secondary educators. Section 2 explains the importance of planning assessment with the end in mind. Chapter 3 specifically focuses on the planning process, while Chapter 4 focuses on assessment designed to measure learning at the end of an instructional period, i.e., assessment *of* learning. Section 3 presents a case for the vital role played by assessment that promotes learning—assessment *for* learning. Specifically, Chapter 5 examines the critical connection between assessment and differentiated instruction;

Chapter 6 describes the vital role of assessment *for* learning in supporting all students to achieve success; and Chapter 7 deals with assessment of students with special needs as well as second language learners. Section 4 is concerned with recording and communicating information about learning to students and parents. And so in Chapter 8, we examine the various kinds of assessment tools required by today's teachers, including the increasing role of digital technology. Chapter 9 focuses on grading and communicating about achievement with students and parents. Section 5—Chapter 10—speaks to district staff, school administrators, and teachers about strategies for implementing change.

As you read *Talk About Assessment: High School Strategies and Tools,* I invite you to follow the icons when they suggest viewing a video clip from the accompanying DVD (see the full table of contents below). Each clip provides a real classroom example of teachers and students implementing the strategies described in the text. As well, the DVD contains a sample of exemplary planning and assessment tools to support the practices advocated in this resource.

Let me know what you find useful, what you don't like, and especially what you modify so that it works better! And finally, keep "talking about assessment" with your colleagues, your students, and their parents. That's how we improve our practice, make it more transparent, and, most importantly, improve learning for our students.

Damian Cooper
Clarkson, Ontario
2009

DVD Video Clips Table of Contents

1. Assessment serves different purposes at different times: it may be used to find out what students already know and can do; it may be used to help students improve their learning; or it may be used to let students and their parents know how much they have learned within a prescribed period of time.

Section 1

ASSESSMENT FOR THE 21ST CENTURY

Chapter 1: The Big Ideas of Assessment introduces two goals that should guide assessment reform, and the eight Big Ideas that are the foundation of *Talk About Assessment: High School Strategies and Tools*. This chapter also introduces and defines some key assessment terms.

Chapter 2: Changes in Education—Changes in Assessment explains why we all need to re-examine the purposes of assessment and grading in the digital age. Issues include the changing role of the teacher and the shift from norm-referenced to criterion-referenced assessment systems.

CHAPTER ONE

THE BIG IDEAS OF ASSESSMENT

I begin workshops by informing teachers that I have two goals in the work that I do:

Goal 1: To ensure that assessment benefits all students.
Goal 2: To assist teachers in making their assessment practices more effective and more efficient.

What do these goals mean in practice? Assessment that benefits all students has several characteristics. It must:

- promote learning
- avoid bias
- be flexible in order to meet the needs of all students

For assessment to be both more effective and more efficient for teachers, it must:

- be planned
- sample performance, rather than attempt to assess all students on everything, all of the time
- equip students with the skills and tools to assess their own work and the work of their peers
- be designed to cause students to think about how to improve their work

As I have worked with teachers and students to achieve these goals during the past decade, eight "Big Ideas" have evolved. Big Ideas, by their very nature, are applicable in many contexts. Big Ideas in assessment apply to all secondary grades, as well as to all subjects. They are useful because they help educators to better understand the bigger picture of assessment. They enable the faculty of an entire high school to talk a common language with reference to best practice, regardless of the grade or subject. Big Ideas in assessment enable teachers in the same department, in the same school, in the same board or district, and even in the same province or state to ensure that students benefit optimally from assessment practices.

Let's examine these Big Ideas in the context of the secondary school.

For other discussions on assessment that benefits all students, see Rick Stiggins et al., Classroom Assessment for Student Learning: Doing It Right— Using It Well.

As you work your way through Talk About Assessment: High School Strategies and Tools, *you'll find the Big Ideas reflected in the text, in the assessment strategies and tools, and in the DVD clips. A given Big Idea is not specifically "covered" in a given chapter; in the spirit of Grant Wiggins (co-author with Jay McTighe of* Understanding by Design), *they are progressively "uncovered" throughout the resource.*

THE BIG IDEAS

> Assessment serves different purposes at different times; it may be used to find out what students already know and can do; it may be used to help students improve their learning; or it may be used to let students, and their parents, know how much they have learned within a prescribed period of time.

BIG IDEA 1

Assessment has two overriding functions: to inform instruction and to communicate information about achievement. The first function includes diagnostic or initial assessment, which enables the teacher to ascertain what students currently know and can do, as well as formative assessment, which provides students with feedback to help them improve their learning. The second function informs students and their parents how well the students have learned. This involves judging the quality of student work and using letter grades, scores, or achievement levels to describe that quality.

> Assessment must be planned, purposeful, and accurate. Planning must ensure that assessment is aligned with curriculum, instruction, grading, and reporting.

BIG IDEA 2

In the past, programs and lesson plans clearly identified teaching objectives, instructional approaches, and resources, but offered little in terms of assessment strategies and tools to judge the quality of student work. During my own teaching career, I saw nothing wrong with leaving the "Evaluation" column of my program plans blank until I had taught a course for a couple of years! Times have changed, though, and outcomes-based learning and backward design (Wiggins, 1998) have clarified the questions that must be posed *before* teaching begins:

- What do I expect students to know and be able to do at the end of this unit, term, or year? (curriculum question)
- How will I determine whether they have learned these things? (assessment question)
- What series of lessons will be most effective in enabling students to demonstrate they have learned these things? (instruction question)

> Assessment must be balanced, including oral and performance as well as written tasks, and be flexible in order to improve learning for all students.

BIG IDEA 3

All curriculum documents include a broad range of learning outcomes. These outcomes, or learning targets, prescribe knowledge and understanding, skills, and attitudes or dispositions.

To adequately assess whether students have acquired these learning targets, a broad range of assessment strategies must be used. This means that some of the assessments you select or design will require students to perform or demonstrate their skills; some will require students to speak and present; and others will require students to write about what they know and understand. Balanced assessment plans contain all three kinds of tasks—what *Talk About Assessment: High School Strategies and Tools* refers to as "write, do, and say tasks."

Flexibility is also essential in assessment because you may need to adapt or modify your planned assessment approach for any number of reasons. For example, some students may require an alternative approach to compensate for a particular exceptionality. Other students may just be learning English or French, so a flexible approach will be necessary to prevent a language bias from interfering with the assessment information you gather. Flexibility could also take the form of an extended deadline for a student experiencing extenuating circumstances at home.

Flexibility does not mean a lack of clear expectations. Effective teachers provide their students with succinct guidelines about assessment. Flexibility is reflected in the professional judgment that such teachers demonstrate when applying these guidelines to an individual student, a group of students, or sometimes to the whole class when a specific situation demands it.

BIG IDEA 4

Assessment and instruction are inseparable because effective assessment informs learning.

Effective teachers are constantly assessing their students' learning in informal ways—by listening to them, observing them, and conferencing with them. Teachers can then use the information they gather to adjust instruction to maximize learning. When more formal assessment has occurred, such as a major project or a test, effective teachers carefully analyze the results and adjust subsequent instruction to address the learning gaps.

BIG IDEA 5

For assessment to be helpful to students, it must inform them in words, not numerical scores or letter grades, what they have done well, what they have done poorly, and what they need to do next in order to improve.

Marks, scores, and letter grades alone do not provide students with the information they need to improve their work. They are merely symbols that represent degrees of quality. Too often, however, these symbols become the sole focus of assessment. Assessment information that improves learning provides students with clear and specific direction about what to do differently to improve the quality of their work.

> **BIG IDEA 6**
>
> Assessment is a collaborative process that is most effective when it involves self-, peer, and teacher assessment and when it helps students to be reflective learners who take ownership of their own learning.

Assessment is not something that teachers *do* to students; it is a collaborative process involving students, teachers, and parents. Everyone has a role to play if the quality of students' learning is to improve. Teachers can initiate collaborative assessment by generating the criteria for assessing an upcoming task with students. For example, begin class by saying, "We're going to use Think-Pair-Share to identify the criteria for assessing next week's debate." (Kagan, 1994) Assessment strategies such as student work portfolios and three-way conferencing with parents are highly effective because they maximize the potential for collaboration and help students plan for future learning.

> **BIG IDEA 7**
>
> Performance standards are an essential component of effective assessment. In a standards-based system they must be criterion-referenced (absolute), not norm-referenced (relative).

Whether assessment is being used to further student learning or to describe the quality of polished work, teachers, students, and parents need to know the standards being used to identify quality work. During the past decade, most provinces and states have moved away from norm-referenced standards, by which student work was judged against how other students performed. Instead, criterion-referenced standards are being used. For each assessment, predetermined performance criteria are identified and student achievement is measured against those criteria. The use of rubrics and student exemplars are indicative of jurisdictions where criterion-referenced standards are in place.

> **BIG IDEA 8**
>
> Grading and reporting student achievement is a responsive, human process that requires teachers to exercise their professional judgment.

Someone once said that any teacher who could be replaced by a computer ought to be! But we all know that effective teachers will never be replaced by computers, because one of the essential characteristics of the teaching–learning process is the human interaction that occurs between students and a caring, sensitive, skilled teacher.

That same care, sensitivity, and skill must come into play when teachers determine report card grades. The summary of learning that appears on a report

See A Repair Kit for Grading: 15 Fixes for Broken Grades *by Ken O'Connor for a detailed discussion of grading.*

card should not come as a surprise to the student, teacher, or parents. It should simply confirm the trend in achievement that a student has demonstrated over time. Surprises tend to occur only when the trend in a student's achievement is overridden by faulty methods used to compute a final grade. *Talk About Assessment* will steer you away from those pitfalls and allow you to report achievement with confidence.

SOME KEY ASSESSMENT TERMS

A glossary of terms is provided on page 253. However, some of these terms are defined by curriculum documents in idiosyncratic ways. For example, the term *evaluation* is defined quite differently in various Canadian provinces. Similarly, the definition of *diagnostic assessment* varies widely as one travels across the country. Although there are no absolute definitions for any of these terms in *Talk About Assessment*, the following definitions are used.

Key Assessment Terms	
assessment	gathering data about student knowledge and/or skills, either through informal methods such as observation, or formal methods such as testing
assessment *for* learning	assessment designed primarily to promote learning. Assessment *for* learning includes both initial, or diagnostic, assessment and formative assessment. Early drafts, first tries, and practice assignments are all examples of assessment *for* learning.
assessment *of* learning	assessment designed primarily to determine student achievement at a given point in time. Summative assessments are assessments *of* learning. Report card grades should be based on a summary of data from assessments of learning.
evaluation	making judgments about student-demonstrated knowledge and/or skills
grading	summarizing assessment data for reporting purposes in the form of a letter or numerical grade
diagnostic assessment	assessment to determine appropriate starting points for instruction. Described as "initial assessment" in some jurisdictions.
formative assessment	assessment that occurs during the learning process and provides feedback to both students and teachers to help improve learning
summative assessment	assessment that occurs at the end of a significant period of learning and summarizes student achievement of that learning

Some of the terms—specifically *grading, assessment*, and *evaluation*—cause some confusion. The distinction among these terms is very important.

GRADING

The term *grade* is used less frequently in Canada than in the United States. In Canada, the term *mark* is used more frequently. Unfortunately, it can be confusing when *mark* is used to refer both to the scores assigned to individual pieces of student work and to the overall score on a report card. For example, one may say, "Damian earned a mark of 18 out of 25 on the quiz" but also, "I have to do my report card marks tonight."

Ken O'Connor (2002) urges educators to use *grade* to denote exclusively the summary score on a report card. In this sense, *grade* is recognized as the summary of a set of marks that explains where the student stands with respect to a set of achievement standards. And, while report card grades assume more importance for students and parents as time goes on, O'Connor cautions that "…grading is not essential to teaching and learning" (p. 17).

ASSESSMENT AND EVALUATION

Although related, assessment and evaluation are two distinct processes. Assessment involves feedback, and its primary purpose is to promote learning for students (Wiggins, 1998). Evaluation is the process of judging work against a standard. It should occur only after a particular performance has been practised and the student has received feedback and had a chance to improve the skills.

Teachers must both assess (provide feedback) and evaluate (pass judgment), but sometimes it is hard to differentiate between the feedback and evaluative functions of assessment. At times, they are fused into a single process. However, once the distinction between assessment and evaluation is understood, the role that each plays in teaching and learning becomes much clearer. Assessment plays an essential role in helping students learn and improve their work. Evaluation informs students about the quality of a given task or piece of work they have done, relative to a known standard.

ASSESSMENT *FOR* LEARNING AND ASSESSMENT *OF* LEARNING

Educators are now using the terms *assessment for learning* and *assessment of learning* to differentiate between the coaching and judging functions of assessment. Assessment *for* learning encompasses both diagnostic (initial) and formative assessment; it is assessment that occurs during the instructional process and is primarily intended to help students improve their learning. Assessment *of* learning includes all summative assessment; it occurs when a teacher deems it necessary to determine the extent of a student's achievement in relation to an established standard. The following chart compares the purposes and characteristics of the two types of assessment.

Comparing Assessment *for* Learning and Assessment *of* Learning

Assessment *for* Learning	Assessment *of* Learning
• designed to assist teachers and students by checking learning to decide what to do next	• designed to provide information to parents, school, and board-level administration, as well as students
• used in conferencing	• presented in a periodic report
• uses detailed, specific, descriptive feedback in words, not scores	• summarizes information with numbers or letter grades
• focuses on improvement of student's previous best performance	• compares student achievement with established standards

SOURCE: ADAPTED FROM RUTH SUTTON, 2001

▲ Effective teachers are constantly assessing their students' learning in informal ways.

Summary

This chapter has introduced eight Big Ideas that are the foundation of this resource and of my main goals: to help ensure that assessment benefits all students and to assist teachers in making their assessment practices more efficient and more effective. The Big Ideas are principles that capture the broad picture of assessment, and provide some common ground for guiding educators' practice. The chapter also introduces and explains some key assessment terms that are used throughout the book.

End-of-Chapter Activity

At this point, I invite you to reflect on the Big Ideas in the context of your own classes or the whole school. To do this, you could work either on your own or with a group to complete the checklist below. You will be gathering data that will identify your own areas of strength and areas needing improvement. You can also identify colleagues who have strengths in those areas where you need to improve, and how, in turn, you can help them.

Another activity for teachers and principal to do together at this point is the Human Bar Graph. Have the eight Big Ideas available for reference. Post the numbers 1 to 8 on the wall of the gym or other large, open area. Ask teachers to line up in front of the Big Idea number that is *least* evident in their current practice. Invite a sampling of teachers to explain why they lined up where they did, while one of the group records the number of teachers in front of each Big Idea. This part of the activity helps the principal and staff identify the Big Ideas needing the most attention in terms of professional development.

Then ask teachers to line up in front of the Big Idea that is *most* evident in their current practice. Again, have a sampling of teachers explain their choice, and have the recorder note the numbers. This part of the activity helps the principal and staff identify current areas of strength related to the Big Ideas. Also, on the basis of these two sets of data, the principal can identify possible coaching partners to work on particular Big Ideas.

Big Ideas: Self-Assessment Checklist		
Big Idea	Self/Team Assessment (Strengths, Weaknesses)	Plan of Action (What I/we plan to do, individually or collectively, to improve practice in this area)
Big Idea 1 Assessment serves different purposes at different times; it may be used to find out what students already know and can do; it may be used to help students improve their learning; or it may be used to let students, and their parents, know how much they have learned within a prescribed period of time.		
Big Idea 2 Assessment must be planned, purposeful, and accurate. Planning must ensure that assessment is aligned with curriculum, instruction, grading, and reporting.		
Big Idea 3 Assessment must be balanced, including oral and performance as well as written tasks, and be flexible in order to improve learning for all students.		
Big Idea 4 Assessment and instruction are inseparable because effective assessment informs learning.		
Big Idea 5 For assessment to be helpful to students, it must inform them in words, not numerical scores or letter grades, what they have done well, what they have		

TOOL 1.1

Big Ideas: Self-Assessment Checklist

A modifiable version of this tool can be found on the DVD.

CHAPTER TWO

CHANGES IN EDUCATION— CHANGES IN ASSESSMENT

BIG IDEA 1

Assessment serves different purposes at different times; it may be used to find out what students already know and can do; it may be used to help students improve their learning; or it may be used to let students, and their parents, know how much they have learned within a prescribed period of time.

CHANGES IN LEARNING

This chapter addresses these frequently asked questions:

- *If we have to give students repeated opportunities to demonstrate learning, what are we teaching them about being responsible in the real world?*
- *How is it fair to give extra opportunities to one student who has missed many days of school, and none to the student who has attended regularly?*

How the world is changing, and at such speed! It's no wonder that the teachers I work with across Canada, the United States, and beyond are struggling to engage students in learning. Increasingly, students are "hijacking" education because they're finding that school is not relevant to their needs, nor to an increasingly plugged-in world.

We are experiencing some fundamental shifts in secondary education—its purpose, the teacher's role, approaches to teaching and learning, and, of course, assessment. Two incidents highlight the new reality facing teachers in this digital age.

In the first case, a high-school English teacher had covered two chalkboards with notes about a piece of literature and then instructed her students to copy the notes into their notebooks. One student refused, only to be told by the teacher that everyone had to copy the notes or there would be serious consequences! At that point, the student walked to the front of the class, flipped open a cellphone, and photographed the two chalkboards.

In the second case, it was a Friday afternoon and as I was packing up after facilitating a workshop, a young teacher asked if I would look at a unit she had designed. As she flipped open her laptop, it chimed, indicating new mail. "Look at this," she said. "Emily has just sent me a draft of her position paper and is desperate for feedback! Guess I'd better respond before I go home."

▲ The sheer volume of information available today, as well as the rate at which information is increasing and being replaced by current and better information, cannot all possibly be captured and transmitted by teachers and textbooks.

THE ROLE OF THE TEACHER IN THE DIGITAL AGE

The English class example calls into question the role of the teacher in today's information age. Students have figured out for themselves that it no longer makes sense for school to serve as the primary source of knowledge. The sheer volume of information available today, as well as the rate at which information is increasing and being replaced by current and better information, cannot all possibly be captured and transmitted by teachers and textbooks. Information must increasingly be accessed through digital/electronic media.

Emily's request for immediate feedback could be seen as an added burden for her teacher; when I raised this concern, the teacher explained, "This is my job. When I see this kind of eagerness from my students, it's so rewarding that I just have to help them improve."

So what implications do new technologies have for today's secondary teacher? While the teacher's role has changed, it is as crucial as ever. But instead of serving as the source of all knowledge, the teacher must now help students develop the skills and "habits of mind" (Marzano, 1993) to function effectively in the information age.

INQUIRY-BASED LEARNING

What does this look like? Here's an example: For a unit called "Democracy," instead of relying heavily on a textbook and presenting information about democracies in general, and Canada as a democracy in particular, the teacher helps the students structure their own inquiries into democracy. These inquiries are initiated with a series of "essential questions" (Wiggins, 1999) such as "What is democracy?"; "Do democracies serve people better than other forms of government do?"; "Is Canada a democracy?" Students then conduct their own inquiries into one or more of these questions by accessing a wide variety of resources: digital, print, and human. As they undertake the inquiries, students will learn a great deal about democracy in general and Canadian democracy specifically, but it will be learned in the context of their own inquiries.

Why isn't such inquiry-based learning more prevalent in our schools? The most likely reason is teachers' reluctance to place learning in the hands of students. As long as the teacher controls what is learned and how it is learned, then there will be fewer surprises for the teacher. But increasingly we are hearing students say, "I don't learn the way you teach, so I'm going to teach myself." My own son is typical in this regard. After a very successful elementary school career, he went on to struggle significantly in high school. While a good deal of his difficulties stemmed from typical adolescent angst, the fact is that he was bored in many of his classes. The notable exceptions were classes in which the learning was student-centred and project-based.

In our democracy example, most of the learning in the more traditional approach focused on facts and examples (taken mainly from the teacher's notes and the textbook) to be memorized. In the inquiry-based approach, the learning includes a large set of research and communication skills, as well as conceptual understanding and simpler factual knowledge. The role of the teacher has shifted from being the source of knowledge to being the facilitator of learning.

And this leads us to changes in assessment. With the traditional approach, the unit on democracy would end with a written test to determine how much of the information presented has been learned—or, very often, has been remembered just long enough to write the test! Consider the mark breakdown for a final exam in Grade 10 History:

Part A: Multiple Choice   50 marks
Part B: Matching People and Events   20 marks
Part C: Matching People and Things   15 marks
Part D: Interpreting a Political Cartoon   7 marks
Part E: Essay Question   20 marks

Total: 112 marks

Of the 112 marks available to students, 85 are awarded for factual items and only 27 marks require students to engage in higher-order thinking (Parts D and E).

There's a joke about a Martian expedition that goes to Earth to conduct research about its schools. When the expedition returns to Mars, the Martian leader asks, "So what did you discover about these places Earthlings call 'schools'? What goes on in them?" "Well," says the expedition leader, "it appears that 'schools' are places where young Earthlings go to watch old Earthlings work."

In contrast, with the inquiry model and the democracy example, students would be required to demonstrate their skills, as well as their understanding, by responding to a previously unseen case study and determining to what extent the country or regime represented is or is not democratic. Assessment is designed to determine whether students can apply the skills they have learned in a new context. Granted, this type of work is not easy. It is challenging, but most students will willingly undertake work that challenges them, as long as it is engaging and relevant.

NORM-REFERENCED AND CRITERION-REFERENCED SYSTEMS

We are currently in the midst of a fundamental shift in the purpose of secondary education.

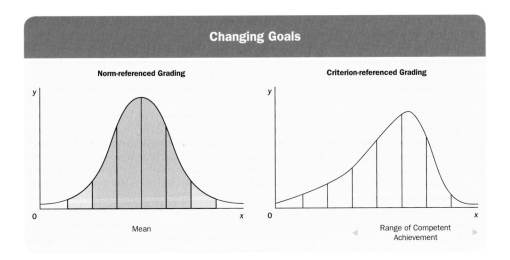

Historically, secondary schools have served to sift and sort students into high, average, and low achievers for purposes of post-secondary destinations. Norm-referenced assessment and grading procedures have been used to compare students' achievements with one another's. Teachers were deemed to have appropriately high standards if, at the end of a term, semester, or year, there were some, but not too many, "A's," more "B's," lots of "C's," fewer "D's," and a small number of "F's." Principals kept an eye on standards by requiring teachers to submit grading summaries and using the "Goldilocks Method" to see that class medians were neither too high nor too low but "just right."

Today, in school districts around the world, norm-referenced assessment systems are being replaced by criterion-referenced models. In other words, the goal is no longer to sift and sort students into winners and losers by comparing one student's achievement with others' in the class; instead, all students are expected to meet a clearly defined and publicly known standard. In other words, success for all is not a problem—it is the goal! But while increasing numbers of policies and procedures stipulate criterion-referenced practices, many teachers with whom I work are struggling with the implications of such a change. Let's consider the frequently asked questions introduced at the beginning of this chapter:

- If we have to give students repeated opportunities to demonstrate learning, what are we teaching them about being responsible in the real world?
- How is it fair to give extra opportunities to one student who has missed many days of school, and none to the student who has attended regularly?

Because norm-referenced systems were designed specifically to spread students' achievement across a full range of possible scores, teachers have usually mixed two types of data: data reflecting achievement, and data reflecting attendance, behaviour, and attitudes. Criterion-referenced systems, on the other hand, rely on clarity about what is to be learned and how well such learning is to be demonstrated. Think of learning how to drive a car. There is a body of knowledge to be acquired and a set of skills to be mastered. Some students will take longer than others to pass their driving test, but decisions about their proficiency are not affected by issues of time or effort. But herein lies a fundamental challenge to implementing criterion-referenced assessment and grading systems in secondary schools. Such systems hold the standard for achievement constant and allow time to be variable—some students pass their in-car test the first time, while others may try several times before meeting the standard. Our schools have traditionally held time constant—a term, semester, or academic year—while allowing the standard for achievement to vary.

Since I'm a keen cyclist, I like to use the following metaphor to illustrate the shift that teachers are being asked to make in how they think about their role. A norm-referenced approach to teaching and learning is like a stage in the Tour de France. There is a distance to be covered, and it will be covered once (a unit in Grade 9 Science, for example); there is a set time in which the stage (or unit) must be completed; it's every rider for himself, and only three riders will stand on the podium at the end of the stage (the "A" students). Along with the lead group, there is the peloton (the "B" and "C" students) that works extremely hard to keep up with the leaders. Inevitably, some riders will not make it to the end of the stage and will drop out of the Tour (the "F" students).

In contrast, a criterion-referenced approach to teaching and learning is like a Vermont Bicycle Tour. While the destination is the same for all riders—a beautiful country inn where everyone will enjoy a fine meal and celebrate their

▲ A norm-referenced approach to teaching and learning is like a stage in the Tour de France. There is a distance to be covered, and it will be covered once (a unit in Grade 9 Science, for example); there is a set time in which the stage (or unit) must be completed; it's every rider for himself, and only three riders will stand on the podium at the end of the stage (the "A" students).

achievement—some riders will take a longer, more challenging route than others (differentiated assessment). While the tour guide starts out by leading the group, she frequently circles back to check on the progress of all the riders in the group—what we call differentiated instruction.

What of the naysayers who claim that these practices don't prepare students for the rigours of university or the realities of the working world? High school is *preparation* for college, university, or work—it is *not* college, university, or the workplace. So, when teachers say to me, "Why should students get to do work over if it doesn't meet the standard? If an Airbus pilot blows a landing, he or she doesn't get to do it over"—I reply, "Actually, the pilot does get to repeat the landing—not once, but hundreds of times—in the flight simulator at flying school." In short, school is the flight simulator, not the Airbus.

ISSUES IN NORM- AND CRITERION-REFERENCED APPROACHES

Two issues are emerging here. One is the radically different purposes of norm-referenced and criterion-referenced approaches to assessment and grading. The other is the distinction between preparing students for the realities of life beyond high school and the belief that the best preparation is to throw students in at the deep end.

Changes in Education—Changes in Assessment

Issue 1: Different Purposes

As we have seen, norm-referenced systems are specifically designed to spread student achievement across the full range of possible scores or grades. They are designed to ensure that only a small percentage of students achieve mastery. For example, when a standardized, norm-referenced test is being developed, any questions that are answered correctly by most students in the norming sample are immediately omitted from the test. Such tests are built according to the statistical principles of the bell curve.

In other words, the numbers of students achieving at each percentage range on the test is set to reflect a "normal" distribution. The purpose of such tests is to sift and sort students into high, average, and low achievers.

Criterion-referenced systems, on the other hand, are designed to certify students as proficient with respect to specified knowledge and skills, or a combination. The goal is for all students to achieve proficiency; of course, some students will take more time, and/or may require different approaches before they are able to demonstrate proficiency.

Traditionally, high schools have functioned as norm-referenced systems, sifting and sorting students into three groups: university-bound, college-bound, and workplace-bound. Students' grades directed them toward the appropriate destination. So, teachers would speak of Helen as being an "A" student, with the expectation that she is "university material." Les, on the other hand, is a struggling student, with no hope for a college or university placement.

Today, as teachers adopt rubrics into their assessment routines, I hear Helen described as "one of my Level 4s" while "Les and my other Level 1s won't be able to handle this assignment." But there are no Level 1 students, just as there are no Level 4 students. There are only Level 1 and Level 4 *performances*. The most gratifying moments in my teaching career occurred when a previously struggling student suddenly "got it" and produced a Level 4 performance.

While most teachers I encounter are committed to doing their best for all their students, many of them are unaware of the extent to which their words and actions perpetuate a sifting-and-sorting philosophy of assessment and grading. The power of teachers to influence the self-images of their students cannot be over-emphasized. Students tend to live up to or down to the expectations that we have for them.

Let's consider the case of Keith.

Consider using wording such as the following on your criterion-referenced assessment tools (rubrics, checklists) for project-based learning:

Choose Your Own Mark.

Use the criteria below to assess the quality of your work. Feel free to improve your work to the level of your own choosing.

CASE STUDY 1 — Keith

I taught Keith for two of his four years at a composite high school. He was enrolled in the Basic Program, as it was then called. Keith was a surly young man with a chip on his shoulder. He had a short fuse and was easily provoked into violent outbursts. After one such altercation, I sat down with Keith and made it clear that fighting was not an acceptable way to deal with problems at school. I discussed with him strategies for resolving issues in non-violent ways.

At Parents' Night some weeks later, I met Keith's father, an arrogant, physically intimidating man who had no time for my conciliatory approach to conflict resolution. In fact, in front of a roomful of other parents, he made it clear to me that he had taught his sons to "hit the guy back hard enough so that he stays down!" Suddenly the troubles I was having with Keith made more sense. But I persevered. I demanded quality work from Keith and refused to collect some of the rubbish he attempted to pass off as the best he could do. When he was rude or bullied other students, I confronted him about his behaviour—out of sight and earshot of the rest of the class—and presented him with choices that would either see him re-enter the class, or do his work stationed just outside the classroom door. Gradually, Keith came around. Behaviour improved, the quality of his work improved, and we developed an excellent student–teacher relationship. And when his younger brother appeared in my class the following year, I went through the same process!

Many years later at a school reunion, a tall, good-looking young man approached me and said, "Mr. Cooper, remember me?" It was Keith. "Never guess what I'm doing now."

"Surprise me," I replied.

"I'm married and have a nice house—all paid for. I have my own tractor-trailer rig."

"That's great, Keith. I knew you could do it."

"Actually, the only reason I came here tonight is to say thanks. I know I was a bad kid, but you didn't give up on me. You made me work harder than any other teacher, but you're the only reason I didn't drop out. You were always firm but fair."

Issue 2: Preparing Students for After High School

The second issue arising from criterion-referenced versus norm-referenced approaches is this: how best to prepare high-school students for the rigours and competitiveness of post-secondary education and the workplace. I encounter many teachers who believe that the best way to prepare students for the frequently unfair and pedagogically unsound practices they might encounter in college and university is to routinely use similar practices in their high school classes. Let's explore some examples to illustrate the fallacy of this approach.

Mary and Desmond are both teaching the same university preparation English literature course. They both expect that the majority of their students will be going to university, with a significant number planning to take one or more English courses. They know that in first-year courses, the primary method of instruction is lecturing to large numbers of students in lecture halls that do not lend themselves to interaction between instructor and student.

▲ Using a range of instructional strategies, such as student interaction with digital technology, is an effective way to improve students' learning and prepare them for life after high school.

Although he is a skilled teacher who uses a range of instructional strategies in the lower grades, most days Desmond lectures to his senior students. Although his students regularly complain, Desmond assures them they will be grateful in the long run because he's preparing them for their university experience.

Mary, on the other hand, continues to use a full range of instructional strategies with her senior students, but every other Friday, she delivers a 40-minute lecture. During this time, students are not permitted to ask questions, but they are expected to take notes. Following each lecture, she collects a sample of notebooks and provides feedback to students on the quality of their note-taking. Both Mary and her students are relieved when each lecture is over—they all know that it is a largely ineffective way to learn. But as Mary has explained to her class, "I have a responsibility to prepare you for what you can expect next year. It's important that I train you to learn from your lectures, but that doesn't mean that I have to do it every day."

Mary's instructional approach is designed to prepare students for university, but she lectures only once in a 10-day cycle. Her formative assessment strategy— reading and responding to students' notes—is designed to monitor students' developing skills in being able to extract the most important points made during a lecture.

The next example is about Rebecca.

CASE STUDY 2 Rebecca's Art Class

Rebecca was 16 years old and had spent two years in British Columbia, living with her boyfriend and working at a variety of part-time jobs. Of her own volition, Rebecca decided to move back to Ontario so that she could graduate from high school. She lived in the basement apartment of a house owned by a friend's parents. While Rebecca was bright, likeable, and communicated well verbally, she always struggled with academic subjects. Her passion was art, and she had a particular talent for oil painting.

While it was unfortunate for Rebecca, a late-sleeper, that classes at the local high school began at 7:50 a.m., the first period of the day was art, her favourite subject. As well as teaching Rebecca in Learning Strategies, I also served as her mentor, and was responsible for overseeing her entire program and providing support. Rebecca came storming into my class one morning, in tears, and also yelling obscene epithets about her art teacher.

"Calm down, Rebecca," I urged. "What's wrong?"

"Look at this!" she screamed, hurling her grade printout at me. "I got 43 percent in art!"

When I managed to calm Rebecca sufficiently for us to talk, I examined her printout more closely:

Interim Report – Rebecca Pullham

Course	Gr. 11 Art		School	EODHS		
Code	AVI3M1-01		Teacher	Y. Jackson		
Date	12/10/2009		Phone	635-1212		

Item	Date	Mark	Out Of	%	Weight
Impression Expression	2009-09-09	0	20	0%	4
Early Renaissance Soc.	2009-09-15	4–	[Level]	83%	5
Cultural Art Ref.	2009-09-25	0	[Level]	0%	5
Applied Design Analysis	2009-09-30	8.5	10	85%	3
Figure in Tones	2009-10-05	4+	[Level]	95%	8
Figure Drawing	2009-10-07	0	[Level]	0%	8

Overall Average	**43%**		
Class Average	**68%**		

Comment

More regular attendance would help Rebecca complete important assignments. I look forward to Rebecca making up this work to the same high quality she has shown to date.

The printout clearly illustrated that Rebecca had excelled on the pieces of work that she had completed. However, she had failed to submit several pieces of work, and her teacher had assigned each of these a zero. As Rebecca and I talked, she acknowledged that she was frequently late for art class, and on several occasions had decided to skip it, since by the time she had arrived at school, the class was almost over. We talked about her struggle to get herself up on time and how she had the best of intentions but was finding it difficult to be independently responsible. I suggested that I would meet with her art teacher to discuss this problem.

When Mr. Jackson and I met over coffee, I pointed out the need to separate Rebecca's achievement in art from the difficulties she was having with tardiness and absence. While her art skills were clearly exceptional, she was having a great deal of difficulty getting herself back on track, having been out of school for two years. I suggested that, as educators, a major part of our role was to help students like Rebecca develop the responsibility that would enable her to be successful in school and beyond. "I agree completely," said Mr. Jackson. "And the way to do that is to show her what happens in the real world. If you don't produce, you suffer the consequences. At school, that means you get zero."

Before the first semester ended, Rebecca had dropped out of school—not because she was failing math or English, but because she was failing art, her best and favourite subject!

Mr. Jackson believed that school is the Airbus, not the flight simulator. I don't question his commitment to teaching and learning, or to his students. But I ask him this question: "How did your actions help Rebecca?" Clearly, Rebecca's tardiness and chronic absenteeism were serious problems and had to be dealt with as part of her education. But assigning a grade in art that suggested she was not skilled is not an appropriate course of action. What might have been an appropriate response?

1. Separate Rebecca's achievement from her behaviour when gathering assessment data.
2. Separate Rebecca's achievement from her behaviour when grading and reporting on the printout.
3. Use "Incomplete" or a similar designation on the interim report card, supported by a comment explaining that there is insufficient evidence of essential learning because of missed assignments.
4. Have classroom procedures that support students and increase the likelihood that they will complete all essential work.
5. Meet regularly with students, especially those who are struggling, to ensure they are completing tasks.
6. Provide a plan to get Rebecca back on track that specifies student and teacher responsibilities.

We shall explore each of these strategies elsewhere in *Talk About Assessment: High School Strategies and Tools*.

▲ School is the flight simulator, not the Airbus.

Summary

In this chapter, we have explored some of the changes that our education systems are facing today, and how these changes in teaching and learning necessitate changes in assessment practices. As you enter this book, you might keep in mind the learning from the case studies in this chapter that highlight the importance of being "firm but fair." It's a simple formula for setting high expectations for all students; holding them accountable for producing quality work—and behaviour—but then showing understanding and flexibility when, as young adults, they struggle to meet those expectations the first time, the second time, and, yes, even a third time. The trainee pilots often crash the flight simulator on their early landing attempts.

End-of-Chapter Activity

As a department or school staff, complete "The Times They Are a-Changing!" Checklist. Use the data as the basis for a department or staff meeting to inform improvement goals to better serve the needs of your students.

TOOL 1.2

"The Times They Are a-Changing!" Checklist

A modifiable version of this tool can be found on the DVD.

"The Times They Are a-Changing!" Checklist

Use the chart below to examine your current attitudes and practice with regard to digital technology in the classroom and related changes in education.

Convene a department or staff meeting for reflecting on the checklist and discussing the topic of changes in education and teachers' changing roles.

N = Not at all   S = Somewhat   V = Very

Am I?	N ✓	S ✓	V ✓	Notes on Maintaining/ Modifying/Changing Practice
1. Am I interested in the possibilities that digital technology holds for my classroom?				
2. Am I knowledgeable about digital sources of information and reference?				
3. Am I open to receiving students' work, and offering feedback, via e-mail?				
4. Am I currently using digital technology for planning and managing assessment?				
5. Am I comfortable with inquiry-based learning?				
6. Am I comfortable with the role of the teacher as being "facilitator of learning" rather than				

BIG IDEAS
in Section 2

1. Assessment serves different purposes at different times; it may be used to find out what students already know and can do; it may be used to help students improve their learning; or it may be used to let students, and their parents, know how much they have learned within a prescribed period of time.

2. Assessment must be planned, purposeful, and accurate. Planning must ensure that assessment is aligned with curriculum, instruction, grading, and reporting.

3. Assessment must be balanced, including oral and performance as well as written tasks, and be flexible in order to improve learning for all students.

Section 2

PLANNING ASSESSMENT *OF* LEARNING

A sound assessment plan depends upon a simple, logical process as well as strategic decision making by course teams.

Chapter 3: Planning with the End in Mind describes a three-stage "backward design" approach to unit planning that logically connects curriculum, assessment, and instruction. The chapter outlines each stage, using sample units of study and templates that are available on the DVD.

Chapter 4: Assessment *of* Learning focuses on summative assessment. The chapter emphasizes the need for balanced assessment—the inclusion of rich oral and performance tasks along with written tasks—and for matching tasks to curriculum targets. It also provides suggestions for motivating students to complete all of these assessments.

Planning with the End in Mind

BIG IDEA 2 Assessment must be planned, purposeful, and accurate. Planning must ensure that assessment is aligned with curriculum, instruction, grading, and reporting.

This chapter addresses these frequently asked questions:

- *I'm required to use a marks program in my school. How do I make changes to reflect new assessment practices?*
- *If I don't evaluate the specific outcomes, how do I know students have achieved the overall outcomes?*
- *How do I evaluate enduring understandings?*
- *Aren't enduring understandings simply overall outcomes?*
- *I redesign my tests every time I teach a course. Why should I have to spend more time creating more tasks to evaluate the same outcomes that are on my tests?*
- *If I'm preparing my summative assessments at the beginning of the course, will I not be just "teaching to the test"?*

A THREE-STAGE MODEL

Most teachers I work with say that lack of time is their biggest challenge. "I don't have time to cover everything in my curriculum"; "I don't have time to differentiate instruction for groups of students in my class"; "I don't have time to allow some students to redo unsatisfactory work"; "I don't have time to assess students individually"; "I don't have time to plan units with my colleagues"; "I don't have time to do all the marking I think I should be doing."

As the amount of information available to "be taught" expands exponentially, finding time to cover it all, as well as do all that teachers are expected to do, will become an ever-greater challenge. Strategic planning is paramount. In their 1998 groundbreaking resource, *Understanding by Design* (now in its second edition), Grant Wiggins and Jay McTighe provided teachers with a simple and logical approach to curriculum planning. Drawing on the work of Covey (1989), they described a three-stage model that flows from one simple question: "By the end of this unit, term, or semester, what is essential for students to understand and be able to do?"

◀ Strategic planning is paramount if teaching is to focus on essential learning.

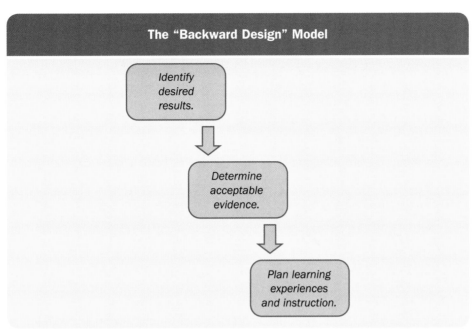

The "Backward Design" Model

Identify desired results.

Determine acceptable evidence.

Plan learning experiences and instruction.

Video Clip 2

Planning a Unit Through Backward Design (15:16)

SOURCE: Grant Wiggins & Jay McTighe, *Understanding by Design*, 1998

STAGE 1: IDENTIFYING ESSENTIAL LEARNING

Given the current information explosion, deciding what is essential for students to learn *must* be the starting point for curriculum planning. Consider, for example, high school chemistry. Is it essential for students to memorize the periodic table? And note that this isn't the same as asking whether the periodic table is important. Of course it is. But is it essential for students to spend a significant amount of time memorizing it? Can't copies of the periodic table be found everywhere that chemistry is being learned, from the classroom to the research laboratory? Wiggins and McTighe recommend the use of essential questions, initially posed by teachers but ideally, after modelling, generated by students, to drive the quest for understanding. So what essential understandings are related to the periodic table? For example, students may ask, "What determines the relative positions of elements on the periodic table?" Or, at a more basic level, "What does the periodic table tell us about elements?" Such questions can drive student-centred inquiry by actively engaging them in their own learning rather than simply absorbing subject content through teacher-directed instruction.

Whether through the use of enduring understandings or essential questions, this first stage in a backward design planning process is to identify, from all that *could* be learned, that which *must* be learned. Clearly, when making such decisions, teachers must work from their provincial, state, or local curriculum documents. Typically these resources imply that all the learning outcomes they contain must be taught and learned. I firmly believe that every curriculum-writing team at the secondary level should include a member who is *not* an expert or specialist in the given subject. Subject specialists customarily hold that all the content in their domain is important and so are usually unwilling to delete anything from existing documents

Do your assessment tools reflect essential learning? For example, consider this checklist. How does it relate to essential learning? In short, it doesn't!

Lab Report Checklist

¤ *date of experiment is included*

¤ *title is double underlined*

¤ *all materials are listed*

¤ *sentences are complete*

when conducting reviews and revisions. But if a social studies teacher becomes part of the mathematics curriculum revision team, he or she is far more likely to ask, "Do students really need to know how to 'express $y = ax^2 + bx + c$ in the form $y = a(x - h)^2 + k$ by completing the square in situations involving no fractions'?" The same teacher may point out that, instead, students may need to be able to "solve real-world problems involving quadratic relations" or simply "recognize that modelling real-world situations with quadratics is powerful."

Since many teachers are hesitant to pare down their curriculum into what is essential, when I conduct backward design workshops, I like to use a strategy I learned from Karen Greenham of Thames Valley District School Board, Ontario. I tell teachers, "You have only five weeks to teach your entire course. What learning outcomes would you address?" I then provide 20 minutes for discussing their curriculum decisions and recording them on chart paper. Each group then presents their curriculum plan to their colleagues from other subject areas, who are invited to ask questions for clarification and seek explanations about why the items are essential.

Grant Wiggins emphasizes that a peer-review process is a critical element in any program-writing exercise. It is all very well for a writing team to congratulate themselves after getting their ideas down on paper. Just like students, we often think our first draft is fine. But we need to seek input from "critical friends" in order to improve the quality of our initial work.

Let's now examine the question "What is essential learning?" in more detail. Wiggins and McTighe identify a curriculum hierarchy that is useful in examining curricula as a first step in unit design.

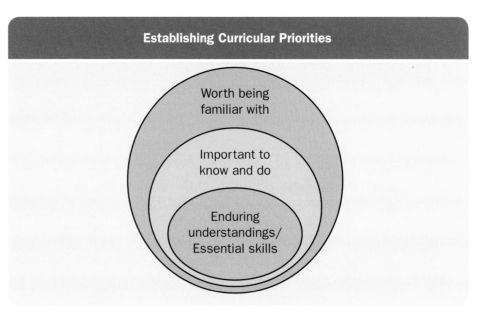

Establishing Curricular Priorities

Worth being familiar with

Important to know and do

Enduring understandings/ Essential skills

SOURCE: Adapted from Grant Wiggins & Jay McTighe, *Understanding by Design*, 1998

We will use a unit entitled "Conflict and Co-operation" from a Grade 11 World History course to explore the questions and issues related to Stage 1 curriculum planning.

Stage 1 Key Question: "What is essential for students to understand and be able to do at the end of this unit?" This unit necessarily contains plenty of factual content related to the two world wars, so it isn't surprising that, during planning sessions, when I ask teachers what essential knowledge and skills they want students to retain, they typically say "the causes of the two world wars." I then ask why—and the question is inevitably followed by a lengthy pause! And then I suggest that we consult the relevant curriculum guide. There we might find the following:

> ***Overall Learning Expectation***
> *– describe major global and regional conflicts and their consequences, as well as instances of international cooperation, since 1900;*
>
> ***Specific Learning Expectations***
> *– explain the causes, course, and results of World War I and World War II (e.g., alliance systems, rise of fascism; trench warfare, Blitzkrieg; Treaty of Versailles, economic dislocation);*
> *– explain the causes, course, and results of the Cold War (e.g., Stalinism, McCarthyism, Cuban Missile Crisis, Vietnam War, destruction of the Berlin Wall, collapse of the Soviet Union);*
> *– assess the local, regional, and/or global impact of selected local and regional conflicts since 1900 (e.g., Northern Ireland, Middle East, East Timor, Sri Lanka, India and Pakistan, Somalia, Rwanda);*
> *– evaluate the effectiveness of selected processes used to promote peace (e.g., the League of Nations' oil sanctions against Italy in 1935, Neville Chamberlain's diplomatic intervention at Munich, L.B. Pearson's intervention in the Suez Crisis, NATO military intervention in Kuwait, the Camp David Accord of 1978).*
>
> – Ontario Ministry of Education. *The Ontario Curriculum Grades 11 and 12: Canadian and World Studies*, 2005

Turning to the planning team, I ask, "Does the curriculum guide help us answer the question 'Why do students need to know this?'" This question is critical because these days students themselves are asking the question more than ever—although they tend to phrase it as "Why do I have to know this stuff?" or "What's this got to do with me?" Rather than regarding such questions as obstreperous, we can turn them into student-centred inquiry questions— "essential questions," in the language of Wiggins and McTighe. My own preference at this stage in a unit-planning workshop is to suggest to teachers the use of INTUs (Bereiter & Scardamalia, 1996).

INTU: I NEED TO UNDERSTAND

Many years ago, while I was studying at the Ontario Institute for Studies in Education, Carl Bereiter introduced our graduate studies class to the concept of student-formulated inquiries. He maintained that students become far more

INTU ARTICLE

Integrating Assessment with Instruction through Student-Directed Research Projects can be found on page 246.

engaged in the research process if, instead of being assigned questions, they have to formulate their own. Bereiter called these student-generated questions INTUs. The acronym stands for "I need to understand," and students complete the sentence by listing their own topic of interest. INTUs ensure that students undertake their inquiry with a clearly focused question that they truly want to answer. This leads to much more sophisticated research since, armed with an INTU, students no longer fill their projects with the first information they find about their topic. Rather, they make critical and thoughtful decisions about which resources, from all that are available, help them to answer their INTUs.

So what INTUs might students generate at the start of the "Conflict and Co-operation" unit? Here are some examples:

- I need to understand why we need to study wars.
- I need to understand why countries go to war.
- I need to understand why Germany didn't learn from its defeat in WWI.
- I need to understand what was cold about the Cold War.
- I need to understand why killing seems to be acceptable in wartime.

The INTU approach is powerful because it is intrinsically relevant to students. It begins with the very questions that students so often want to ask but are either afraid or not permitted to ask. Instead of students asking the teacher, "Why do I have to know this?" the teacher asks the student, "Do you need to know this to answer your INTU?" The locus of control has shifted from teacher to student; the teacher acts in the critical role of facilitator of learning.

In my classrooms, depending on students' age and maturity, I have had to provide some students with plenty of scaffolding just to enable them to formulate

◀ Equipped with an INTU question, students no longer fill their projects with the first information they find about their topic. Rather, they make critical and thoughtful decisions about which resources help them answer that question.

a workable INTU. Others have leapt at the opportunity to formulate their own research question and haven't looked back!

Many teachers may worry that much of what they view as important content may not be learned if students are in charge of their own learning. For example, with the "Conflict and Co-operation" unit, teachers may want to ensure that topics such as alliance systems, the rise of fascism, trench warfare, the Blitzkrieg, the Treaty of Versailles, and economic dislocation are specifically addressed. There are two solutions to this concern: the teacher can simply monitor whether students are learning important specific facts as they conduct their research; alternatively, the teacher can intersperse student research time with timely, teacher-directed mini-lessons that present important facts. If such mini-lessons can be presented in response to questions that arise naturally from students' INTUs, then so much the better.

Let's return to the question of whether knowing the causes of the two world wars is, in fact, essential learning for the "Conflict and Co-operation" unit. I would answer that it is, but only insofar as it helps students answer their INTU questions. Take the example of the student who posed the INTU "I need to understand why Germany didn't learn from its defeat in WWI." Perhaps the student can explain how events in Europe differed in the lead-up to each of the world wars and how these differences explain why history often repeats itself. Therein lies the essential learning. And note that the essential learning has shifted from a focus on facts as important in and of themselves to a focus on reasoning skills.

ESSENTIAL QUESTIONS AND ESSENTIAL SKILLS

Recently, I was working with two high school teachers as they planned units of study based on the Grade 9 Social Studies curriculum for Manitoba. They had identified essential skills such as researching, summarizing, and critical thinking, and they had also identified the following topics to provide a focus for the units: Democracy, the Legal System, and the Canadian Bill of Rights. I asked them, "What effect might there be on students' demonstrations of critical thinking if you changed each of these topics into an essential question? For example, 'Is Canada a democracy?'; 'Does Canada's legal system ensure order within society?'; 'Does the Canadian Bill of Rights ensure that the rights of all Canadians are protected?'" The teachers quickly saw how this change had the potential to dramatically increase the level of critical thinking occurring in their classes in the following ways:

- students see that there are multiple perspectives to any issue
- subject content is seen as a series of issues to be discussed rather than simply a list of facts to be memorized
- students learn the importance of recognizing that there are multiple points of view, depending on varying perspectives
- enabling and culminating assessment tasks can be created that will allow for the assessment of these skills rather than simple mastery of content

The teachers also became really excited by the potential this change had for making learning in the social studies class more interesting and, therefore, more engaging for students. Essential questions provide for richer teaching and lead to greater understanding because they always point to a relationship between two or more things, as opposed to a topic that is one-dimensional. For example, the question "Is Canada a democracy?" sets up the possibility for debate, while the topic "Democracy" does not.

ENDURING UNDERSTANDINGS AND ESSENTIAL SKILLS

The Manitoba example illustrates the importance of both subject content and skills. I frequently hear teachers, and even consultants, say, "I'm not concerned with the content; it's the process and skills that are important." This is a fallacy. In all subjects there is important content to be learned as well as skills to be acquired. Unfortunately, many curriculum documents—particularly, it seems, those for mathematics and English—contain only skills. Without their corresponding "enduring understandings," students may have no idea *why* they need to master these skills. Consider the following broad learning outcomes from the Writing and Representing strand of a Grade 10 English curriculum guide:

- *Students will be expected to use writing and other forms of representation to explore, clarify, and reflect on their thoughts, feelings, experiences, and learnings; and to use their imaginations.*
- *Students will be expected to create texts collaboratively and independently, using a variety of forms for a range of audiences and purposes.*
- *Students will be expected to use a range of strategies to develop effective writing and other ways of representing and to enhance their clarity, precision, and effectiveness.*

– Nova Scotia Department of Education and Culture. *Atlantic Canada English Language Arts Curriculum Guide, Grades 10–12,* 1997

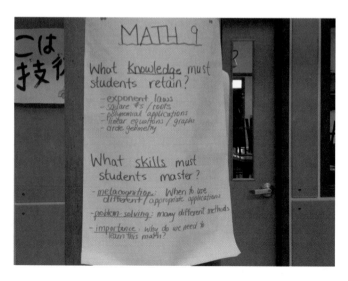

▲ In team planning sessions, identify enduring understandings as well as skills.

Many students, especially reluctant learners, will respond to these outcomes with a resounding "Why do I have to be able to do these things?" But if we balance these essential skills with corresponding enduring understandings, students are reminded of the purpose for developing these skills. For example, consider the way the following enduring understandings relate to the essential skills listed on the preceding page:

■ Before beginning to write, effective writers identify their audience and purpose for writing, and choose a form that matches their audience and purpose.

■ Writers constantly revise their work so that the message they want to communicate is clear and effective.

During a recent backward design workshop, I asked the planning teams to identify one or two essential skills and one or two enduring understandings for the units they were developing. The English team had completed the following details on their Stage 1 template:

TOOLS 4.1–4.5

Program Planning Templates

This set of modifiable tools can be found on the DVD.

Template 2: Unit Curriculum and Assessment Plan

Unit/Strand: Grade 9 English

Focus for Learning: Reading and writing expository texts

Enduring Understandings:
1. Summarizing
2. Reading for meaning
3. Identifying main ideas

Essential Skills:

Title/Description of Culminating Task

Enabling and/or Other Assessment Tasks

Learning Habits:	Title: Diagnostic/Formative Write/Do/Say	Curriculum Outcomes/Content Standards:
Learning Habits:	Title: Diagnostic/Formative Write/Do/Say	Curriculum Outcomes/Content Standards:
Learning Habits:	Title: Diagnostic/Formative Write/Do/Say	Curriculum Outcomes/Content Standards:
Learning Habits:	Title: Diagnostic/Formative Write/Do/Say	Curriculum Outcomes/Content Standards:

Planning with the End in Mind

Here is part of the conversation that ensued as I sat down at their table:

> *Damian:* So what have you identified as the essential learning for this unit?
>
> *Megan:* Summarizing, reading for meaning, and identifying main ideas.
>
> *Damian:* I see that you've entered them as enduring understandings. Are you sure about that?
>
> *Andrew:* I guess they are really skills, right?
>
> *Damian:* Okay, then what might be an enduring understanding? Something you want your students to understand about summarizing, for example, by the end of this unit?
>
> *[No response from the group.]*
>
> *Damian:* Think about the most reluctant learner in your class, who would challenge you on the first day of the unit by saying, "Why do we need to summarize stuff anyway?" How would you respond?
>
> *Megan:* I'd probably explain that we sometimes need to make things shorter.
>
> *Damian:* Yes, but why do we need to do that?
>
> *Andrew:* Well, think how deadly it is if a friend stops you in the staff room and asks if you've seen the new Batman movie. Then when you say you haven't, she proceeds to tell you every single detail of the movie, from start to finish! That's why summarizing is important!
>
> *Damian:* Great example! Now, how can we phrase that concept as an Enduring Understanding that will provide students with a rationale for learning the skills of summarizing?
>
> *Megan:* Maybe something like "People often need to write or say things in a shortened form to save time."
>
> *Andrew:* Sounds good to me, Megan.

An enduring understanding will often serve to explain to students *why* a given skill or set of skills are essential to master. Granted, in a subject such as mathematics, especially at the senior high school level, identifying enduring understandings can be a challenging task. And while it is not my intent to launch a large-scale examination of senior mathematics curricula in terms of relevance to students not planning to study university-level math, I do implore mathematics teachers to identify enduring understandings whenever possible.

Here are some samples of enduring understandings from a senior math curriculum:

■ We can powerfully and efficiently understand many real-world situations by modelling them using a function (e.g., linear, quadratic, exponential, trigonometric).

- Probabilities can help us understand and predict possible outcomes in complex situations.
- Being able to analyze, interpret, and draw conclusions from single-variable and two-variable data will help us assess the validity of much information in the media.

STAGE 2: ASSESSING ESSENTIAL LEARNING

With the curriculum targets in place, teachers can progress to the next stage: assessment planning.

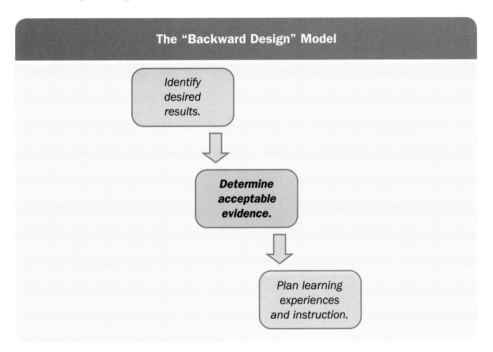

The "Backward Design" Model

Identify desired results.

Determine acceptable evidence.

Plan learning experiences and instruction.

SOURCE: Grant Wiggins & Jay McTighe, *Understanding by Design*, 1998

Before the emergence of backward design, many teachers began their course or unit design process by asking, "What do I need to teach, and what activities should I have students complete?" In contrast, by using the backward design model and beginning with the end, teachers ensure that all decisions related to assessment and instruction logically develop from a clear vision of the desired destination—the essential understandings and skills. Consider the following case study in which an experienced history teacher re-examines an existing unit on "Canadian History Since World War I" and revises it using the backward design model.

Joseph Stafford—Using the Backward Design Model

History teacher Joseph Stafford wrote the following:

For years I have used a popular re-enactment I call the "1920s Nightclub." For this activity the students completed research projects, as well as organized the entire day with a complete meal, vaudeville acts, music, and dance shows. All the students were in period costume. The students loved the activity, enjoyed history, and most importantly, many of them enrolled in the optional Grade 11 History course! A simple formula was used to develop a vibrant history course: interesting content, student-centred activities, and research/essay skills. Despite the success of the activity, the teachers in the department, me included, were unaware of some serious flaws in curriculum design. Indeed curriculum design was not even a concern. No overall plan existed. No serious effort was made to connect what the students learned in the activity with the history of 20ᵗʰ century Canada beyond the 1920s. It did not even matter if the students remembered the content that they had researched. No serious thought was given to assessment. The projects were graded without any precise scoring system, and extra marks were assigned to those students who either organized the day or participated in the various acts. A fun and engaging classroom activity remained only that—a fun activity!

Yet with the benefit of recent research, this activity became much more.... Wiggins and McTighe (1998) emphasize that teachers must reverse what they have traditionally done: that is, design daily lesson plans first, and only consider assessment at the end of a particular unit, with little thought given to organizing an overall curriculum plan.... Wiggins and McTighe begin at what is traditionally tackled at the end: assessment and overall learning goals....

A major problem with the nightclub activity, then, was in connecting it to important content, to the enduring understandings.... For this course, "Canadian History Since World War I," ten enduring understandings were therefore developed...for example, the understanding dealing with the powerful dynamics of regionalism in Canada and the emergence of a new assertive Western Canada.... Each of these understandings is accompanied by a list of statements indicating how the understanding is linked to specific content or skills throughout the course....

The nightclub activity was [also] restructured.... No longer referred to as a nightclub, the new performance task is entitled "The Diamond Jubilee of Confederation...." More aligned with significant content in the history of twentieth century Canada, the year 1927 was selected since it was the 60ᵗʰ anniversary of Confederation.... The students are asked to organize an exposition of Canadian achievement with the following instructions:

> The Liberal government of Mackenzie King has decided to celebrate the success of Canada as a newly recognized country on the international scene. This celebration will take the form of an exposition, the purpose of which will be both to educate and to entertain. You have been selected to be a member of the organizing committee. Your task is two-fold: to prepare a visual display and a brochure highlighting the accomplishments of Canada; and to organize different forms of entertainment.

Instead of simply researching different unrelated topics, the students examine specific themes:

- The development of Western Canada as an important region of Canada in terms of political, economic, and cultural change.
- The cultural accomplishments of Canadians in film, music, art, sports, and other areas of endeavour—in particular those which reflect Canada's new sense of national identity and nationhood....

...The nightclub activity evolved into a more effective performance task better connected to the entire course and to appropriate assessment requirements....

Both the visual displays and the brochures were organized according to the themes. Teachers, parents, and senior students formed the audience, circulating and asking students questions concerning their displays. "Explicit scoring systems," in the form of rubrics, were used to assess the students' visual displays, brochures, and performances. Students provided much of the leadership as different committees were established to prepare the various activities and to organize the entire day....

The "Diamond Jubilee" Project gave my students an excellent opportunity to "experience"

history. The local libraries and archives provided substantial information about the Jubilee. In *The Daily Intelligencer*, our local Belleville, Ontario, newspaper, students found several articles about the Jubilee....

For their own Diamond Jubilee the students recited some of [the original] prayers and re-enacted a commemorative ceremony for the war dead.... One student commented, "It helps you learn better. It's pretty neat. You find out what it was like to live in the 1920s." For one day history came alive for these students. They were able to re-enact an event of local and national scope....

– from Joseph Stafford, "The Importance of Educational Research in the Teaching of History," *Canadian Social Studies* Vol. 40, 1, 2006.

CONNECTING ASSESSMENT DESIGN AND CURRICULUM TARGETS

As Joseph Stafford discovered, one has to examine the quality and appropriateness of the assessment tasks that students must do to demonstrate their learning once the curriculum targets have been identified. While the "1920s Nightclub" was a fun activity for his students, he wasn't sure what evidence of essential learning it provided. In Stage 2 of the backward planning process, teachers must ask themselves, "What student products and performances will prove beyond a doubt that students have acquired the essential understandings and skills identified in Stage 1?" Following is what Joseph's revised task would look like, in the form of Template 3.

<table>
<tr><td colspan="3" align="center">**Template 3: Unit Culminating Assessment Task Plan**</td></tr>
<tr><td colspan="2">**Unit:** Canada Comes of Age</td><td>**Assessment Task Title:** The Diamond Jubilee of Confederation</td></tr>
</table>

Description of Task: The Liberal government of Mackenzie King has decided to celebrate the success of Canada as a newly recognized country on the international scene. This celebration will be an exposition. You are a member of the organizing committee. You will prepare a visual display and a brochure highlighting Canada's accomplishments. You will also plan the entertainment for the event.

Enduring Understandings:
• Western Canada emerged as a force for political, economic, and cultural change
• Canada asserted itself on the world stage through film, music, sports, and culture
• Canada's government played an active role in defending and promoting Canadian cultural and political independence
• The changing role and status of women in Canada resulted in significant political, economic, and social change
• Canada's military contributions to the Great War was a defining moment in establishing its presence on the world stage

Curriculum Outcomes/Content Standards:
• identify contributions to Canada's...
• explain why the federal government...
• explain how participation in international events...
• analyze economic development...
• etc.

Essential Skills:
• students will be able to research primary and secondary sources
• students will be able to organize and communicate their understanding
• students will express orally, visually, and in writing

Student Products and Processes

Assessment Strategy: Visual display	**Assessment Strategy:** Brochure	**Assessment Strategy:** Conference with teacher
Assessment Tool: rubric and checklist	**Assessment Tool:** rubric and checklist	**Assessment Tool:** rubric

Assessment Criteria:
• understanding of content
• organization
• audience impact
	Assessment Criteria:
	• understanding of content
	• organization
	• audience impact
		Assessment Criteria:
		• reflection on learning
		  – goals set
		  – goals met
		  – goals for improvement

Resources/Technology Integration: access to computer lab; local museum

Accommodations/Modifications: task will be scaffolded or extended according to student needs

Cross-Curricular Integration: English, Communications Technology

---

TOOLS 4.1–4.5

Program Planning Templates

This set of modifiable tools can be found on the DVD.

Let's consider two further examples to illustrate the logic that must connect assessment design and curriculum targets.

Example 1

The first example concerns assessment validity or, in other words, the extent to which a given assessment task provides evidence of the learning target it is designed to assess. Consider the following outcomes for a physical education unit dealing with establishing a personal fitness regimen:

■ Improve fitness levels by participating in vigorous physical activities for sustained periods of time, including appropriate warm-up and cool-down procedures

■ Implement and revise as required plans of action to achieve personal fitness goals

The phys. ed. planning team had decided to have students produce a fitness poster in order to assess students' progress toward these outcomes. Note that both of the outcomes involve the demonstration of skills and therefore imply the need for a performance assessment. The fitness poster will provide no such evidence of learning. It may reflect student understanding of the importance of fitness, and it may provide evidence of students' ability to draw or to use desktop publishing software. But these are very different learning targets than those stated in the two learning outcomes, which point to the need for a performance-based assessment task.

Example 2

The second example, while also concerning validity, illustrates how easy it is to believe that we are assessing a given learning target when, in fact, we are not. In the excellent book *A Handbook on Rich Learning Tasks*, Gary Flewelling, with William Higginson, urges teachers to question traditional mathematics questions in favour of rich assessments that demand creative thinking. Every mathematics curriculum that I have reviewed in the past decade has championed problem solving as an essential learning target. Consider the following statements from the Western and Northern Canadian Protocol's *The Common Curriculum Framework, Grades 10–12 Mathematics*, 2008.

> *Problem solving is one of the key processes and foundations within the field of mathematics. Learning through problem solving should be the focus of mathematics at all grade levels. Students develop a true understanding of mathematical concepts and procedures when they solve problems in meaningful contexts. Problem solving is to be employed throughout all of mathematics and should be embedded throughout all the topics.*

Now consider the following two examples and determine which of these tasks will provide evidence of students' problem-solving and reasoning skills:

Example 1: Buying Running Shoes
Chris is saving his allowance to buy a pair of shoes that cost $68.25. If Chris earns $3.25 per week, how many weeks will Chris need to save?

Example 2: Buying Running Shoes
Chris wants to buy new shoes that cost $68.25. Chris plans on saving money from his allowance to buy them. He gets an allowance of $3.25 per week.

1. Do you think Chris's plan for getting the shoes is a good one? Justify your answer.
2. Suggest a better plan. Explain why you think your plan is better.

While questions similar to Running Shoe Example 1 are found in every mathematics textbook, they elicit very little evidence of either problem solving or reasoning. Instead, they merely provide evidence that students can follow simple procedures and make simple computations. In contrast, the second example demands that the student demonstrate problem-solving skills. At the same time, it "opens a bigger and clearer window on the learner because it gives the learner a greater opportunity to demonstrate the use of a much larger skill set" (Flewelling & Higginson, 2000, pp. 58–9).

In Running Shoe Example 2, students are not required to merely fill in the blanks to a routine that has already been provided. Instead, they have to think creatively and use procedures correctly.

USING RUBRICS TO ASSESS CURRICULUM TARGETS

If problem solving is an essential skill in all mathematics courses, how does one assess the learning targets for Running Shoe Example 2? Let's begin by looking at Running Shoe Example 1. In my work, I continue to encounter large numbers of mathematics teachers who insist that all learning in mathematics is quantifiable because "calculations and solutions are either right or wrong." Among these teachers, some may focus only on whether students arrive at the correct answer to Example 1 and award a score of zero or one accordingly. Others may ask that students show their work, and will award one or more points for correct calculations, as well as one point for the correct answer.

I would suggest that even simple questions like that in Example 1 may be better assessed using a rubric. In fact, Flewelling and Higginson provide a rubric for this question:

EXAMPLE 1: Buying Running Shoes

Chris is saving his allowance to buy a pair of shoes that cost $68.25. If Chris earns $3.25 per week, how many weeks will Chris need to save?

Level 4: • identifies assumptions, correctly solves problem based on these assumptions, checks answer

Level 3: • correctly solves problem (21 weeks of saving needed), checks answer

Level 2: • needs some assistance to identify appropriate operation (solution may include an arithmetic error), needs encouragement to check answer

Level 1: • needs assistance to understand and solve problem

SOURCE: Adapted from Gary Flewelling with William Higginson, *A Handbook on Rich Learning Tasks*, 2000

Notice how the rubric describes what we might expect to see reflected in students' solutions to the question. Furthermore, a well-written rubric such as this one is especially helpful for students who struggle with the question, since it describes what they need to do differently to improve their work.

Turning to Example 2, the rubric is, of necessity, more complex, since the learning target is more complex:

EXAMPLE 2: **Buying Running Shoes** *(enriched version)*

Chris wants to buy running shoes that cost $68.25. Chris plans on saving money from his allowance to buy them. He gets an allowance of $3.25 per week.

1. Do you think Chris's plan for getting the shoes is a good one? Justify your answer.
2. Suggest a better plan. Explain why you think your plan is better.

Level 4: • gives convincing, mathematical and non-mathematical, justification for their answer to #1
 • describes a plausible (and original) alternative plan, clearly demonstrating its superiority to Chris's plan

Level 3: • gives an adequate justification, both mathematically and non-mathematically, for their answer to #1
 • describes an appropriate alternative plan, satisfactorily explaining its superiority to Chris's plan

Level 2: • provides some justification for their answer to #1
 • describes a slightly altered plan, needs encouragement to demonstrate its superiority to Chris's plan

Level 1: • provides little justification for their answer to #1
 • needs assistance to devise an alternative plan

SOURCE: ADAPTED FROM GARY FLEWELLING WITH WILLIAM HIGGINSON, *A HANDBOOK ON RICH LEARNING TASKS*, 2000

As we shall see in Chapter 8: Assessment Tools and Technology, a generic problem-solving rubric may be used for all kinds of mathematics problems. I have long heeded the words of Rick Stiggins, who wrote many years ago: *Most students can hit the target if they can see it clearly and if it stays still.*

If we provide a different rubric for each assessment task, then the target is definitely not staying still. Furthermore, we would quickly become overwhelmed under a sea of rubrics! Generic rubrics can be used to assess numerous tasks that address similar learning targets. When necessary, a generic rubric, like the one following, can be customized to suit a specific assessment task with the addition of task-specific examples.

				Problem-Solving Rubric			

Name: _____   **Date:** _____

Criteria	Level 1	Level 2	Level 3	Level 4
Think: Understand the Problem	• shows **limited** understanding of the problem (e.g., is unable to identify sufficient information or to restate problem)	• shows **some** understanding of the problem (e.g., is able to identify some of the relevant information but may have difficulty restating problem)	• shows **complete** understanding of the problem (e.g., is able to identify relevant information and to restate problem)	• Shows **thorough** understanding of the problem (e.g., is able to differentiate between relevant and irrelevant information and is able to rephrase problem)
Plan: Make a Plan	• shows **little or no evidence** of a plan (e.g., has difficulty producing an alternative to Chris's plan)	• shows **some** evidence of a plan (e.g., produces a slight variation on Chris's plan)	• shows evidence of an **appropriate** plan (e.g., produces a reasonable and better alternative to Chris's plan)	• shows evidence of a **thorough** plan (e.g., produces an original and superior alternative to Chris's plan)

TOOL 5.16

Generic Rubric for Mathematical Thinking, Inquiry, and Problem Solving

A generic, modifiable tool similar to the one above can be found on the DVD.

Each of these examples has emphasized the importance of matching assessment tasks and tools precisely with curriculum targets. In this way, you can increase the likelihood that the evidence of student learning you collect reflects student achievement of the essential learning of the unit. With curriculum targets and assessment tasks in place, you and your team are ready to move to Stage 3.

STAGE 3: PLANNING INSTRUCTION

For teachers armed with a clear sense of what is critical for students to learn, and one or more authentic assessment tasks to provide evidence of the learning, the third and final stage is relatively simple. Stage 3 involves mapping out the instructional sequence that will prepare students for the assessments. This sequence will include in-class lessons, out-of-class experiences, and a number of assessments *for* learning that will gradually build toward the end-of-unit, or culminating, assessments.

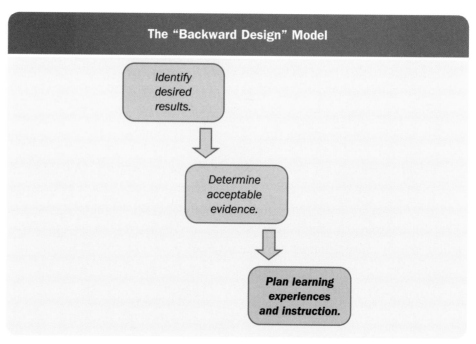

SOURCE: Grant Wiggins & Jay McTighe, *Understanding by Design*, 1998

A metaphor from my experience as a co-director of high-school musicals may be helpful here. My colleague and friend Jenny Peace and I co-directed several productions during the years we spent teaching at the same school. At the first rehearsal, we would show the cast a video excerpt of a professional production of whatever show we were staging that year. Although I didn't realize it at the time, this was "beginning with the end in mind." We provided the young actors with a clear vision of the achievement target—in this case, a polished performance. That way, everyone—cast, crew, and directors—had a clear sense of the destination. Stretching the metaphor somewhat, the opening night may be considered the "culminating assessment," since it was a final opportunity for the actors to demonstrate whether they had mastered the intended outcomes. Continuing to "plan backward," the rehearsal schedule was our "instructional sequence," or Stage 3.

All decisions that we made about rehearsals stemmed from our vision of the opening night performance: when to work with the whole cast, a small group, or an individual actor; when to work on memorizing lines, voice projection, or blocking; when to introduce the set or the pit orchestra—all these decisions were made "with the end in mind." They had to be, because the date of the opening night was not negotiable! Omitting the final scene because it wasn't ready was not an option—compare that with not getting to that "Weather Dynamics" unit after spending too much time on "Chemical Reactions." On the other hand, we didn't rehearse scenes that were not in the play—the equivalent of persisting in teaching that favourite lesson despite the fact that it has been removed from the new curriculum!

THE LOGIC BEHIND BACKWARD DESIGN

Wiggins and McTighe use the term *design logic* when describing their approach to backward design. Once learning targets and their corresponding assessment tasks are in place, then identifying the instructional sequence is a logical process. Teacher and students all benefit from a clear understanding of how each lesson in a unit connects to the essential learning and how the assessments will provide evidence of the learning.

Let's consider a Grade 10 Canadian History unit, "Canada and World War I," to see how a planning team used design logic to complete Stage 3 of their work. The following template illustrates their Stage 1 and Stage 2 work; namely identifying the enduring understandings and essential skills, the corresponding culminating or end-of-unit assessment, and the smaller, enabling assessments that build students' skills and understanding.

Template 2: Unit Curriculum and Assessment Plan

Unit Title and Focus: Canada and World War I

Enduring Understandings:	Essential Skills:	Title/Description of Culminating Task
• Know the causes, course, and outcomes of WWI • Understand why Canada became involved in WWI • Understand what life was like for Canadians at home and in the battlefield during the war • Understand how WWI changed Canada	• Formulate questions to guide research • Use appropriate methods of historical research • Communicate understanding in a format that is appropriate for the audience and purpose	You are a committee that has been asked to advise Veterans Affairs officials about what is an appropriate approach to Remembrance Day for the youth of Canada. You have been asked to consider how the legacy of WWI veterans, who are almost all deceased, should be preserved. You must explain why and how WWI should be commemorated on Remembrance Day.

Enabling and/or Other Assessment Tasks

| Learning Skills and Behaviours:
Teamwork
Initiative | **Title:** WWI—What we know; what we need to know
Diagnostic
Write/Say
Group word/image wall and INTU questions | Curriculum Outcomes/Content Standards:
✓ Describe Canada's and Canadian's contribution to the war effort overseas during WWI |

TOOLS 4.1–4.5

Program Planning Templates

This set of modifiable tools can be found on the DVD.

ELEMENTS OF THE INSTRUCTIONAL SEQUENCE

The instructional sequence—Stage 3—must include three elements:

- initial (diagnostic) assessment at the beginning of the unit to determine students' knowledge and skills *before* instruction begins
- lessons and other learning opportunities designed to develop the concepts and skills embedded in the essential learnings of the unit
- assessments *for* learning (formative assessments) that provide the teacher and students with ongoing evidence of learning and serve as opportunities to provide feedback to enable students to improve their learning prior to the assessments *of* learning at or near the end of the unit. Note: these may have been identified during Stage 2 work. See Template 2, above.

Initial (Diagnostic) Assessment

In Chapter 5 we will explore how teachers use the information from initial, or diagnostic, assessments to differentiate instruction for groups of students with differing learning needs. For now, it's enough to say that Stage 3 unit planning must include a variety of initial (diagnostic) assessment strategies and tools to determine what students know and are able to do before instruction begins. There is no quicker way to disengage students than to launch into a new unit of study that is not matched to their current levels of knowledge and skill. If the entry point of the unit is too far beyond students' current level, they will disengage out of frustration; if the entry point is below their current level, they will disengage out of boredom. Of course, the reality in most classrooms is that some students are beyond, some are at, and some are far behind the point at which the teacher had planned to begin instruction—thus the need for a differentiated approach.

Lev Vygotsky captured this reality succinctly when he coined the term the "zone of proximal development, or ZPD" (1978, pp. 79–91). I have reframed Vygotsky's thinking into four questions for teachers:

- What do students currently know and what can students currently do?
- Where do I want them to get to?
- How big is the gap?
- How do I ensure the gap is just right to challenge students in a way that maximizes learning?

▲ There is no quicker way to disengage students than to launch into a new unit of study that is not matched to their current levels of knowledge and skill.

The "gap" is the zone of proximal development. In sports, coaches stress the need for athletes to train "within the zone" to optimize their gains in fitness. Similarly, Vygotsky maintained that teachers maximize learning by ensuring that the gap between students' current levels and where we want them to be is such that students are challenged but not frustrated. Having spent much of my teaching career working in special education settings, I can say categorically that very few students want schoolwork to be easy. What they do demand is work that engages them. Most students love to be challenged. Watch adolescents—especially boys—playing video games. Are they satisfied with success at the lowest challenge level? Quite the contrary! The fun is winning in the face of extremely challenging competition. Yes, I can hear the skeptics: "Of course they want to be challenged when they're having fun, but school is about learning, and learning can't always be fun." Granted, but it can usually be made *engaging*. I contend that when students say they want learning to be fun, they are in fact demanding that learning be engaging. The fun may occur as a by-product. Our goal should not be to make all learning fun; our goal should be to maximize engagement. And one of the best ways to do that is to ensure that work is within each student's ZPD.

Lessons and Other Learning Opportunities

TOOLS 4.1–4.5

Program Planning Templates

This set of modifiable tools can be found on the DVD.

Stage 3 planning also includes identifying the sequence of lessons and other activities that will occur during the unit. By constantly referring to the learning targets and culminating assessments that were identified in Stages 1 and 2, teachers can ensure that all work is connected logically to these elements. Refer to the partially completed Stage 3 template below to see how this was accomplished for the Grade 10 Canadian History unit, "Canada and World War I."

Template 4: Unit Instructional Plan/Lesson Sequence

Unit Title and Focus: Canada and World War I

Introduction to Culminating Task: Class is organized into culminating task groups. Culminating task is introduced. Teacher provides a package of images, words, place names, dates, etc. to each group. Groups sort what is relevant to WWI and what isn't. Groups post their selections on a "word wall" in the class. Class discussion and correction of misconceptions. Word wall to be added to during unit. Groups begin to brainstorm INTU questions for Culminating Task. Exemplars of Homework Summary answers distributed. Homework calendar provided for completion and collection of homework. Homework assigned: read and make notes from textbook as per calendar.

Lesson 2: Video: Canada's Role in World War I. Class watches and adds information to "word wall." Groups discuss homework and create ques-

---

I should emphasize that while such instructional planning is essential, changes will necessarily be made to the instructional sequence as the unit unfolds in response to student needs. Similarly, while this sequence represents a master plan, differentiation will occur in response to the needs that have been identified through the diagnostic assessments at the start of the unit.

Assessment *for* Learning

The third element in Stage 3 planning involves identifying the assessments *for* learning that will occur at various points throughout the unit to build students' skills and understanding toward the culminating assessments *of* learning. As noted earlier, these "formative assessments" may have been discussed during Stage 2 work, since they should have grown naturally out of the planning for the culminating assessment (see Template 2 on page 44). But in Stage 3, they need to be strategically placed throughout the instructional sequence.

These assessments will be smaller in scope than those at the end of the unit, and they will assess a subset of the learning targets. In designing these assessments, teachers must view them as "practices" rather than "games"—meaning that teachers should expect student work on these assessments to include errors. Also, the feedback provided by the teacher and/or other students in response to such errors will improve learning and proficiency prior to the assessments *of* learning. As Chapter 6: Assessment *for* Learning will show, students should not be penalized in the form of numerical marks on these practice assessments. The purpose of these assessments is *not* to generate scores but to indicate to the teacher and student how well their learning is progressing at key points in the unit. Student errors on such assessments serve primarily to indicate to the teacher where the need for further coaching exists.

Summary

In this chapter we have considered a three-stage model for unit planning, using Grant Wiggins and Jay McTighe's work on backward design. All the templates appearing in this chapter are available in the Tools section of the DVD. As well, you'll find sample units of study to illustrate how teachers have utilized both the planning method and the templates. The DVD also has a video clip of a planning team following the three-stage process to develop a unit.

Video Clip 2

Planning a Unit Through Backward Design (15:16)

End-of-Chapter Activity

With some colleagues or your course team, watch the DVD clip of a planning session and examine the planning templates. Discuss your understanding of the backward design model and how the templates might be used in your own planning. You might then try planning a unit together.

Alternatively, examine a unit you are currently teaching and review it, with reference to your learning from this chapter. Consider:

1. Do the enduring understandings and essential skills truly reflect what students must know and be able to do by the end of the unit?
2. Does the culminating assessment(s) provide evidence that students have acquired these essential learnings?
3. Does the instructional sequence build logically toward the culminating assessment(s)?

CHAPTER FOUR

ASSESSMENT *OF* LEARNING

> ### BIG IDEA 1
> Assessment serves different purposes at different times; it may be used to find out what students already know and can do; it may be used to help students improve their learning; or it may be used to let students, and their parents, know how much they have learned within a prescribed period of time.

> ### BIG IDEA 3
> Assessment must be balanced, including oral and performance as well as written tasks, and be flexible in order to improve learning for all students.

ASSESSMENT *OF* LEARNING: REVIEWING THE CONCEPT

Assessment of learning includes all summative assessment; it is done when a teacher needs to determine a student's achievement in relation to an established standard.

Video Clip 3

Summative Assessment: Demonstrating Essential Learning (20:10)

Let's review the concept of "assessment *of* learning." These are the assessments that, generally, will comprise the report grade. They are the summative assessment tasks that are used to assess how much students have learned during a unit, term, or course. As Big Idea 1 suggests, teachers need to ensure that their assessment *of* learning tasks adequately sample the essential learning of the preceding instructional period. Big Idea 3 reminds us that the set of assessments on which a grade is based must include opportunities for students to demonstrate learning through demonstration and speaking as well as through writing.

First of all, some of you may be wondering why a chapter on assessment *of* learning precedes the chapter on assessment *for* learning. After all, we would expect to have students complete the assessments *for* learning (or practices) before the assessments *of* learning (the game). The reason for dealing with the "game" first is to be found in the logic of backward design. Remember that in Chapter 3, we explored the three stages of planning:

Stage 1: Identifying essential learning—identify targeted understandings and skills

Stage 2: Assessing essential learning—determine appropriate assessment of those understandings

Stage 3: Planning instruction—plan learning experiences and instruction that make such understanding possible

The assessments *of* learning will provide evidence of the extent to which students have achieved the targeted understanding. Those assessments need to be identified first, and then the smaller, enabling "practice" assessments can be planned as building blocks toward them. The needs of individuals and groups of students will also influence the teacher's decisions about formative assessments.

OBSTACLES TO A BALANCED ASSESSMENT PLAN

At the beginning of workshops, when I ask high school teachers and administrators to identify which of the eight Big Ideas are least evident in their classrooms and schools, it's inevitably Big Idea 3: *assessment must be balanced (including oral and performance as well as written tasks) and flexible.* When I probe further and ask why there is so little evidence of oral and performance assessment in their schools, the typical responses are:

- *Universities usually use written assessments, so we have to prepare students for those.*
- *I don't believe that my assessments of students' oral work and performances are as reliable as assessments of their written work.*
- *I can't assess all my students at once if I use oral or performance tasks.*
- *Parents expect assessment to be of written work.*

This chapter addresses these frequently asked questions:

- *What does balanced assessment mean?*
- *How much evidence of learning is required in order to have confidence in a report card grade?*
- *Shouldn't our assessment practices be more closely aligned with those used in post-secondary institutions in order to prepare our senior students for their academic futures?*
- *If I can't enforce strict deadlines, how will I manage my marking load?*
- *In the case of a late or missed assignment, should a student be required to provide a justifiable reason before being given a second chance to complete the assignment or an alternate?*

▲ A balanced approach to assessment is necessary for improving the learning of all students.

Let's begin by examining each of these concerns. Then we will consider how to achieve an appropriate balance of oral, written, and performance assessment in our plan for assessment *of* learning.

UNIVERSITY EXPECTATIONS

■ *Universities usually use written assessments, so we have to prepare students for those.*

True, most universities do still rely heavily on written assessments and examinations to provide evidence of student learning. And while I would argue that university faculties need to examine the question of balance as much as, if not more than, high school teachers do, poor practice in post-secondary education must not be used as a rationale for poor practice in secondary education.

Furthermore, we know that fewer than half of the students in high schools across Canada and the United States go on to university. For example, only between one-quarter and one-third of Ontario graduates go to university. I do, however, strongly endorse the practice of adjusting the balance of oral, written, and performance tasks in high school courses according to the intended post-secondary destination. University-track courses should tip the balance toward written assessments, whereas workplace courses should place more emphasis on oral and performance tasks. But, in all courses, there must be an appropriate balance of the three modes as reflected in a carefully constructed assessment plan.

Perhaps most importantly, high schools must prepare students for life *beyond* university, college, or apprenticeships. This aim is reflected in most school district mission statements. Since the challenges of daily life require us to perform and to communicate both orally and in writing (do, say, and write), classroom assessment must be balanced accordingly.

RELIABILITY AND VALIDITY

■ *I don't believe that my assessments of students' oral work and performances are as reliable as assessments of their written work.*

> "We have to engage students by teaching them science that's relevant to their lives and gives them opportunities to discuss issues among themselves."
>
> – LAURA BLACKMORE, SCIENCE TEACHER

Reliability is a measure of the confidence we have in the conclusions that we draw from an assessment. It is an important criterion in assessment design. Validity, another important criterion, is a measure of the extent to which the inferences we make from assessment data actually represent what students know or can do with respect to a given learning target. For example, think of assessing the knowledge and skills associated with driving a car. Driving programs assess students' basic knowledge of the rules of the road by means of a multiple-choice written test. The reliability of this test is maximized through its design—the various forms of the test all provide evidence of the same set of learning targets—as well as by controlling the conditions under which the test is written. For example, examinees write the test alone and do not have access to the driving manual. But, while the multiple-choice test allows for valid inferences to be made about an individual's knowledge of the rules of the road, it does not permit valid inferences to be made about the skills associated with driving. To test these skills, the examinee must take the in-car test. The in-car test is a "performance task," and it relies upon the observations of the examiner to assess the quality of the performance. While such an assessment *may* be less reliable than the multiple-choice written test, it is an essential part of the accreditation process to certify new drivers.

The point here is that both the multiple-choice written test and the in-car performance test are essential elements of the assessment plan. Each allows for valid inferences to be made about the respective performance targets: knowledge and skills. And while the reliability of the in-car test may be less than that of the written test, this in no way is reason to dispense with it.

Assessment plans in high school courses must reflect a similar commitment to assessing the various learning targets in valid ways. Whether in music, science, technology, mathematics, English, or German, assessments must be designed to appropriately sample skills targets as well as knowledge-and-understanding targets. It is quite reasonable to expect that an assessment plan for any one of these subjects will contain some assessments that are more reliable and less valid, while others may be high in validity but less reliable. As with the driving-test example, written tests may be high in reliability as a result of being well designed and administered under controlled conditions; however, for some students, these tests may not provide valid data about learning. For example, the inferences we might draw about a student's learning in science from the results of that student's written test may be invalid if the student suffers from test anxiety or if the student is not fluent in English and cannot understand much of the language on the test. In such a case, we may be able to make more valid inferences about the student's learning in science by observing him or her conduct a lab. Realize, though, that students usually work with partners during labs, and this can potentially reduce the reliability of such assessment opportunities. Achieving reliability and validity in our assessments requires astute planning.

▲ In some cases, we may be able to make more valid inferences about a student's learning in science by observing him or her conduct a lab.

Rubric: Inquiry Investigation

A modifiable version of the tool below can be found on the DVD.

SAMPLING PERFORMANCE

■ *I can't assess all my students at once if I use oral or performance tasks.*

It is true that oral and performance assessments present logistical challenges that may not exist with written assessments. One solution is to have a plan in place to sample student performance. Let's check in with Leanne to see how she manages this.

CASE STUDY 1 — Leanne's Approach to Sampling

Leanne teaches science. Her assessment plan in each of her courses includes an appropriate balance of "write, do, and say" assessment tasks. She believes strongly in the need to observe students "doing" science—conducting scientific inquiries and labs. When assessing their skills, she uses a generic rubric for scientific inquiry and observes from three to five groups during any given lab or inquiry.

Leanne uses a combination of check marks and anecdotal notes on the rubric to record her observations of individual students. She routinely shares some of these observations orally with individual students as she moves from group to group. Leanne records her observations into her electronic grade book, using her laptop, or with a PDA as she walks about the room. She has set up her sampling plan to ensure that she has three observations of inquiry/lab skills for each student before she has to report to parents. (See "Triangulation of Data" on page 57.)

Rubric: Inquiry Investigation				
Criteria	**Level 1 (Limited)**	**Level 2 (Fair)**	**Level 3 (Proficient)**	**Level 4 (Excellent)**
Initiating (Questioning and Hypothesizing)	• asks few questions about the task; questions are vague and unfocused	• asks simple questions that focus the investigation somewhat	• asks questions that clarify the task and focus the investigation	• asks relevant, clear questions about the task
	• demonstrates limited understanding of concepts related to the task	• demonstrates some understanding of concepts related to the task	• demonstrates general understanding of concepts related to the task	• demonstrates a thorough understanding of concepts related to the task
	• unable to generate hypothesis	• generates a questionable hypothesis	• generates a valid hypothesis	• generates an insightful hypothesis
Planning	• develops disorganized or unworkable procedures	• develops a partial set of simple procedures not all of which are appropriate	• develops an appropriate, complete set of procedures that may lack efficiency or clarity	• develops procedures that are appropriately efficient and complete
	• identifies and controls few variables	• identifies and controls some major variables	• identifies and controls most major variables	• identifies and controls all major variables

SOURCE: Nelson Science and Technology 7, Pure Substances and Mixtures Teacher's Resource, 2000

Technically speaking, it *is* possible to conduct oral or performance tasks "all at once" and, as with written work, review these tasks outside of class, at a time and place of the teacher's choosing. Communication Technology teachers frequently do this by capturing performance or oral tasks using audio or video recordings.

Some school districts have "unbanned" student-brought technology such as cellphones, cameras, PDAs, and MP3 players in regular classrooms. By allowing students to use the devices they routinely carry around, oral responses, interviews, performance tasks, short presentations, and other tasks can be readily captured in audio or video format. Students can then play back these recordings for self-assessment and improvement (in conjunction with effective feedback tools). Or students can submit the recordings for teacher feedback and assessment through upload, e-mail, wireless transfer, or memory stick. Either form of review and feedback can take place in or out of the class, as decided by the teacher.

PARENTS' EXPECTATIONS

■ *Parents expect assessment to be of written work.*

Many parents expect their children to be assessed in the same way as they were assessed during their own high school years. As I have stated elsewhere, given the rapid and significant ways in which the world is changing, it stands to reason that how we teach and assess student learning must change. I frequently speak to parent groups about these changes. By using analogies and many references to the "real world," I have no trouble getting most parents to understand why an appropriate balance of oral, written, and performance assessment is essential in gathering a valid and reliable picture of their children's learning. I use some examples, such as the two-pronged assessment for driver certification mentioned earlier in this chapter, or whether they would put their trust in a dentist who knows all about the causes of tooth decay but failed the practical exam in dental school. These examples usually put to rest any questions about the need for an appropriate balance of "write, do, and say" in any assessment plan!

SUFFICIENT EVIDENCE FOR GRADING

In workshops, when I ask teachers to identify their burning questions about classroom assessment, one of the most common responses is: *How much evidence do I need for grading purposes?*

We first need to examine the school or district's report card format. Does it use a single summary grade for each subject, as in: "Mathematics: 78%"? Or does it provide a grade for each of the major learning targets (strands, standards, enduring understandings) within each subject, as in: "Number Sense: B"; "Linear Relations: A"; "Analytic Geometry: B"? Since this second option is far more sound from a grading perspective (see Ken O'Connor, *How to Grade for Learning*, 2002), let's proceed with it. However, even if your district uses a single summary grade for each subject, you can still gather achievement data by strand and then combine these grades on the report card.

To establish how much evidence is required to support a grade for a given learning target, four guidelines should inform our planning. The report card grade for each learning target should be based on the following elements:

- a sample of critical evidence of learning
- polished work that reflects acknowledgment of teacher or peer feedback and corresponding revision
- triangulated data: a minimum of three pieces of evidence
- an appropriate balance of written, oral, and performance evidence

ELEMENT 1: A SAMPLE OF CRITICAL EVIDENCE OF LEARNING

Cast your mind back to the first Big Idea, from Chapter 1:

> *Assessment serves different purposes at different times; it may be used to find out what students already know and can do; it may be used to help students improve their learning; or it may be used to let students, and their parents, know how much they have learned within a prescribed period of time.*

Assessment *of* learning is concerned only with the third of these purposes: let students and parents know how much students have learned within a prescribed period of time. The sample of critical evidence for grading and reporting purposes should be a relatively small subset of all the work that students are required to do to achieve a learning target. That said, the critical sample must adequately represent the essential learning related to that target. To illustrate, consider the following critical sample for one strand of a mathematics course. Notice what evidence will be considered for reporting purposes, compared with all the work that students produce.

Evidence Gathered for Grade 9 Mathematics Strand: Number Sense	Considered for Report Card Grade?
Diagnostic to determine conceptual understanding of operations (addition, multiplication, exponents)	No
Oral checkup 1 (exponent operations)	No
Homework set 1 (exponent operations and contextual problems)	No
Contextual problem set (completed throughout unit with feedback and reworking)	Yes
Quiz 1, take-home (operations and rules)	No
"Rulefinder" investigation (whole-class activity)	No
Oral checkup 2 (exponent rules)	No
Peer interviews (rules and derivation)	No
Quiz 2 (rules)	Yes
Homework set 2 (exponent rules and derivation)	No
Test (rules and real-world situation)	Yes
Student–teacher conference: rules derivation	Yes
Journal entries (throughout strand, related to tasks above)	No

A criterion-referenced system identifies the critical evidence required to demonstrate that a student has learned the essential concepts and skills for a given subject and grade. This means that *all essential* evidence must be submitted before the teacher can make this determination. Again, consider the driver's test. Informing the examiner that you never did quite master driving in reverse and therefore wish to have it excluded from your test won't get you very far! Being able to drive in reverse is an essential driving task and must be demonstrated as a prerequisite of certification. Criterion-referenced assessment planning requires that teachers agree upon the essential evidence needed to certify students as competent and knowledgeable in a given subject—and then requires that students complete all these essential tasks.

If we are to change the culture of learning and assessment from one that encourages mediocrity to one that demands high-quality work from all students, then we must insist that all essential work is completed to a high standard. This message must be delivered with the caveat that instruction and/or assessment will be differentiated to create conditions for all students to meet with success (Cooper & O'Connor, 2009).

ELEMENT 2: POLISHED WORK THAT REFLECTS EARLIER FEEDBACK AND CORRESPONDING REVISION

Many of the arguments I hear from high school teachers when they take issue with current assessment reforms are framed in terms of preparing students for the harsh reality of the real world. I hasten to point out that in the real world adults have opportunities to draft, receive feedback, and then revise work before it "counts." For example, an architect's blueprints are usually revised many times before the design is approved. Yet in high school courses, first drafts, early tries, or practice work and quizzes are frequently scored, and marks on the corresponding polished work are compromised by the low scores on these "practices."

If we look back at Big Idea 1, the second purpose of assessment is "to help students improve their learning." Teachers' responses to these assessments *for* learning should be in the form of descriptive feedback that informs students about what they did well, where problems exist, and what needs to be done to improve the work. (You can explore this further in Chapter 5: Initial/Diagnostic Assessment and Differentiated Instruction.) The teacher's role is that of coach, not judge. Students must then be held accountable for implementing this feedback as they revise their work. Only the polished work needs to be given a mark. This mark informs the student about the quality of the final product, as judged against a known standard.

▲ The teacher's role is coach, not judge.

ELEMENT 3: TRIANGULATED DATA

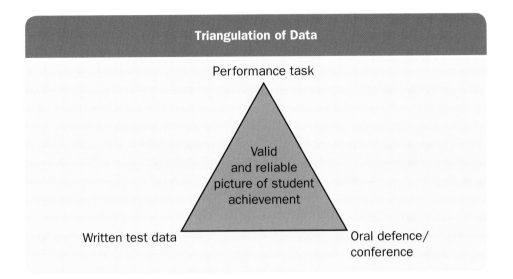

Triangulation of Data

Performance task

Valid and reliable picture of student achievement

Written test data

Oral defence/ conference

Triangulation of data is an important assessment concept maintaining that teachers, whenever possible, should base a grade on at least three pieces of evidence. Triangulation is important in maximizing the reliability of our assessments. If a report card grade for the writing strand in an English course is based on only one piece of writing, it is quite possible that the grade may be unreliable. For example, if the grade is poor, perhaps the student was experiencing a crisis at home. If the grade is surprisingly high, perhaps the student plagiarized the work. Can the reliability problem be solved by basing the grade for writing on two pieces of evidence? Not necessarily, because the two pieces of work may indicate contradictory evidence of the student's proficiency—one piece is excellent and the other poor. By basing the grade on at least three pieces of evidence, the teacher is able to apply a modal interpretation of the evidence. In other words, the grade assigned reflects the student's most consistent achievement.

Gr. 12 Physics—Forces and Motion: Dynamics	
Amusement Park Ride Design Project	Level 3
Forces in Sport Research Presentation	Level 3
Unit Test	31/50 (Level 2-)
Most Consistent Level	**Level 3-**

Video Clip 3

Summative Assessment: Demonstrating Essential Learning (20:10)

When determining grades, it's necessary to consider both triangulation and the importance of including only polished work. None of the three work samples in the triangle should be practice or formative work. The only exception to this rule may occur during the first term, when teachers may be required to determine report card grades before they have had enough time to gather three polished pieces. If this occurs, a teacher may have no choice but to dip into the formative sample of work for the third piece. In this case, the formative piece of work should be given considerably less weight than the two polished pieces. (You can read more about weighting in Chapter 9: Grading and Reporting.)

ELEMENT 4: AN APPROPRIATE BALANCE OF WRITTEN, ORAL, AND PERFORMANCE EVIDENCE

The two reasons for ensuring a balanced approach to assessment both deal with validity. The first is the need to ensure that you are assessing the student's learning of the intended targets, not a communication deficit. The second reason is curriculum-assessment alignment. Sean provides a good example of the first reason.

CASE STUDY 2   Sean

Some years ago, I was teaching a learning strategies course to a group of students with a variety of special needs. Knowing that they entered my classroom on that first day full of fear and anxiety about revealing their various shortcomings, I began by announcing that we were going on a time-travelling journey, ten years into the future. Using skills I had learned as a drama teacher, I conducted a guided visualization in which I had the students see themselves as young adults:

Where do you live? A house? An apartment? In the city? The country?
Are you married? Do you have children? What are their names?
It's Monday morning. You're off to work. How do you get to work? Bus? Drive?
Where do you work? In an office? A factory? Who's your boss? and so on.

My goal was to have these at-risk students imagine a productive future in which they were happy and gainfully employed. I brought the "journey" to an end by guiding students back to the classroom and then said:

Now I want you to write down everything you saw and heard during your journey. Write as quickly as you can and don't worry about neatness or spelling.

All the students except Sean busily set about the task. Sean remained still, making no effort to take out writing materials and record his experiences. I quietly went over to his desk and said, "Sean, if you're not comfortable writing down what you saw and heard, how about you just tell me?

"B...b...b...but, s...s...sir...I...c...cc...can't," Sean replied.

Over the next few days I discovered that Sean not only had a debilitating stammer but also had very serious difficulties with writing. As a result Sean refused to do most of the tasks I assigned the class, and certainly did not participate in any of the class discussions. About a week later, in response to some serious behavioural problems that occurred whenever I asked students to work with a partner or in small groups, I decided to focus a lesson on co-operative group skills. I assigned the following task and then planned to generate a list of positive and negative behaviours that the students themselves were able to identify as a result of working on the task:

> *Working in groups of four, your task is to use the materials provided to design and create the tallest possible free-standing structure. You will have ten minutes to complete the task, and I want you to work co-operatively.*

Each group received the same set of materials: a newspaper, a 30 cm strip of masking tape, and 10 plastic drinking straws.

As the groups worked away at the task, Lillian, the teacher's aide, said quietly to me, "Damian, can you believe Sean? He's running the show!" We both watched in muted amazement as Sean

confidently came up with a design for his group's structure and then, though stammering to some degree, delegated tasks to each group member. After ten minutes, Sean and his group won—by default. Theirs was the only structure still standing!

Some weeks later, we were focusing on comprehension and prediction as essential reading skills. I was using a wonderful little anthology of short detective mysteries. I would read a story aloud to the class as they followed along in their own books. At the height of the rising action, I would stop—much to the chagrin of the class!—and say, "Now I want you to write your own ending to the story. Tomorrow, I'll read the actual ending and you can check out your predictions."

Given Sean's writing deficits, he and I had agreed that he would come to my desk while the others were writing their endings and he'd tell me his ending while I scribed. Sean's ability to accurately predict the sometimes ingenious twists that occurred in each mystery was uncanny!

This case study reflects how a balanced assessment plan, one that includes oral and performance tasks, ensures that a student like Sean is able to communicate his learning of the intended targets. It also reflects the importance of teachers' willingness to gather assessment evidence through performance and oral tasks as alternatives to written tasks, especially when working with students who have special needs.

 Video Clip 8

Teaching and Assessing Students with Special Needs (11:55)

▲ When planning assessments, be sure to maximize student engagement through a variety of performance tasks.

MATCHING TASKS AND CURRICULUM TARGETS

A second reason for the importance of a balanced assessment plan is the need to ensure an appropriate match to a variety of curriculum targets. In their book *Understanding by Design*, Grant Wiggins and Jay McTighe stress the need to align assessment tasks with curriculum targets. It is interesting to note that the more important the curriculum target, the greater the likelihood that oral and/or performance tasks are necessary to gather evidence of the learning associated with that target.

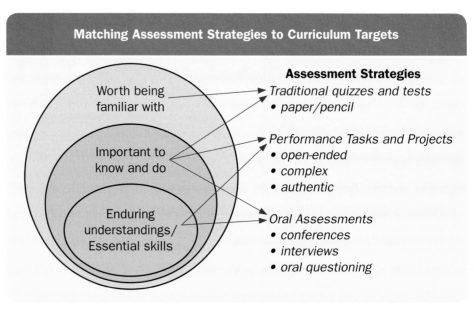

SOURCE: Adapted from Grant Wiggins & Jay McTighe, *Understanding by Design*, 1998

To facilitate the learning of the key messages from my workshops, I implore teachers to constantly check for an appropriate balance of "write, do, and say" when developing their assessment plans. It is with good reason that our default assessment option is to have students write—whether it is a test, an examination, or a position paper. As students, we all experienced a steady routine of written assessments through our high school and university experiences. And as we saw earlier, the logistics of assigning written work are much easier than those associated with oral and performance tasks.

As we can see in the above figure, the decision to use a performance task, an oral task, a written task, or a combination must be made by examining the nature of the learning target. Frequently, the verbs appearing in a curriculum statement will give a hint about the appropriate assessment mode. Consider each of the following learning targets and decide on the assessment mode: write, do, say, or a combination.

By the end of this course, students will:

1. *develop and use appropriate questions to define a topic, problem, or issue and to focus a geographic inquiry;*
2. *gather geographic information from primary sources (e.g., field research, surveys, interviews) and secondary sources (e.g., reference books, mainstream and alternative media, CD-ROMs, the Internet) to research a geographic issue;*
3. *evaluate the credibility of sources (e.g., authority, impartiality, expertise) and the reliability and usefulness of information (e.g., accuracy and relevance, absence of bias or prejudice, arguments substantiated by evidence);*
4. *identify various career opportunities in the field of geography, and the educational requirements associated with them.*

    – Ontario Ministry of Education, *The Ontario Curriculum Grades 9 and 10: Canadian and World Studies, 2005*, p. 34

While outcomes 1, 3, and 4 suggest a written response, outcome 2 requires a combination of skills, including "doing" field research. Such research may involve formulating survey questions and interviewing members of the public. The data from this research may then be graphed in any one of a number of ways. The research process is therefore a "rich performance task" that will likely involve a combination of "write, do, and say" elements. Of course, even an outcome such as #4, which seems to suggest a traditional written assessment, may be designed as an engaging oral and performance task, such as a job fair.

RICH PERFORMANCE TASKS

There has been much debate among assessment experts about the meaning of the terms *performance assessment*, *authentic assessment*, and *rich performance task*. While the debate can sometimes be an exercise in semantics, here's an attempt to clarify these terms. Consider these definitions:

> *Performance assessment — a variety of tasks and situations in which students are given opportunities to demonstrate their understanding and to thoughtfully apply knowledge, skills, and habits of mind in a variety of contexts. These assessments often occur over time and result in a tangible product or observable performance…. They sometimes involve students working with others* (Marzano, Pickering, & McTighe, 1993).

> *Performance assessment is assessment based on observation and judgement. Students engage in an activity that requires them to apply a performance skill or create a product and we judge its quality* (Stiggins, Arter, Chappuis, & Chappuis, 2004).

Common to both definitions is a focus on students *demonstrating* their skills and the assessor *observing* the demonstration. Performance assessment has always played a significant role in subject areas such as music and physical education, in which the focus is on the demonstration of skills. Its introduction into traditionally academic areas, such as the humanities, mathematics, and English, has focused on the creation of products, as reflected in both definitions.

For example, here is the scenario for a performance task developed by Andrea Orr, Jake Bricknell, and Leah Penny from St. Joseph's High School in Barrie, Ontario. The task is presented to students as part of an integrated Grade 11 Science/Mathematics Course Culminating Task (CCT) designed to give evidence of these essential skills:

- problem solving using science
- using technical terms in a report
- co-operating with others to achieve a goal
- communicating effectively for a specific purpose

> *A crime scene was discovered early this morning at St. Joseph's High School. Your Crime Scene Investigation (CSI) team has been called in to investigate a murder. Initial reports indicate that the victim died trying to protect a secret recipe for chocolate cake. Apparently Mr. McCann's birthday is fast approaching, and the teachers were all trying to develop the perfect cake recipe. The detectives first on the scene have narrowed the suspect list down to ten individuals. All of these teachers were present at the school last night and all of them have been working tirelessly to develop the perfect cake recipe for Mr. McCann's birthday. You will process the crime scene and collect evidence from it. You will also collect evidence from the list of ten suspects that the detectives have submitted to you. You must analyze the evidence to determine the guilty party, prepare a report, and present it to your team leader.*

In this example, while the one obvious product is the solving of the crime, we might also consider the written evidence, the report, and the presentation of the report to the team leader to be "products."

AUTHENTIC TASKS

Video Clip 4

An Authentic Performance Task: The G7 Summit (14:23)

This discussion of performance tasks leads us to the concept of an "authentic task." Perhaps you're thinking that any work that students produce in school may actually be considered a "product." You might be wondering, "Doesn't that mean that all my assessments are 'performance assessments?' No, it does not.

Fundamental to performance assessment in traditional academic areas is the need for relevance. Grant Wiggins urges teachers to design tasks that resemble "what big people do."

▲ Authentic tasks are performance assessments that mimic real-world tasks.

> *Assessment is authentic when we anchor testing in the kind of work real people do, rather than merely eliciting easy-to-score responses to simple questions.... We thereby learn whether students can intelligently use what they have learned in situations that increasingly approximate adult situations, and whether they can innovate in new situations* (Wiggins, 1998).

The more that school tasks resemble work in the real world, the more engaged students will be; the more engaged students are, the more likely they will be to produce quality work. "Authentic tasks" are, therefore, performance assessments that mimic real-world tasks. As such, they often involve assigning students adult roles and may require turning the classroom into a courtroom, an office, a conference room, or even a crime scene. The "crime scene" task is an authentic performance task. Its effectiveness is increased significantly when students take their roles seriously, both in collaborating with a group to solve the crime, as well as when presenting their report to their team leader. The element of competition between groups as they try to be the first to solve the crime leads to improvement in all the skills related to this task.

TIPS FOR DESIGNING RICH PERFORMANCE TASKS

- Rich performance tasks must provide evidence of essential learning.
- To be "rich," a performance task must demand innovation and creativity on the part of the student.
- A rich performance task should present students with an engaging challenge that requires persistence to complete.
- A rich performance task should engage students in problem solving and decision making.
- Tasks must be appropriate to all students.
- If a performance task involves co-operative groups, there must be provision for individual accountability.
- When assessing a performance task, the criteria must reflect the essential learning, and these criteria must be communicated to students before they begin work.

See "Evaluating the Quality of a Performance Task" on page 71 and Tool 1.3 on the DVD. Use this self-assessment tool to assess your own performance tasks.

MOTIVATING STUDENTS TO COMPLETE ASSESSMENTS *OF* LEARNING

Of all the issues related to assessment and grading that I am asked to address as a consultant, there is one that wins hands down in terms of frequency, namely: *"What should we do about late and missed assignments?"*

While some educators view late and missed work as inevitable problems, I frequently meet teachers for whom these are not issues at all! So clearly we must all find out what strategies are used by these teachers and seek to implement them across schools and districts. I am often asked to visit school districts to tell teachers and administrators how best to deal with students when they submit work late, or not at all. My response is to explain that no significant change will occur if we continue to respond in a reactive way. Policies that merely tell teachers what to do when students do not behave according to our expectations are mere band-aids.

School policies that permit the use of penalties for late work and zeroes for missing work and other behavioural infractions, such as academic dishonesty, stem from a belief in the power of threat and punishment. But as Guskey and Bailey point out, "no studies support the use of low grades or marks as punishments. Instead of prompting greater effort, low grades more often cause students to withdraw from learning." Some teachers will argue that the threat of late penalties and zeroes does motivate students to complete all work and on time. But a quick survey of work completion in any middle or high school will indicate the fallacy of this argument (Cooper & O'Connor, 2009).

Instead, we need to take a proactive approach that is consistent with a criterion-referenced model of grading. As we saw earlier, the message has to be communicated to students that *all* essential work must be completed to a high standard. What does this proactive approach look like in terms of classroom practice and school policy? Here is a set of guidelines that includes my own suggestions as well as strategies gleaned from teachers who have largely conquered the "late/missed assignment problem":

Guidelines for Ensuring that Critical Tasks Are Completed

- Identify for students and parents the tasks that are *essential* as proof of learning.
- Operate on the understanding that *all* these tasks must be completed to meet the requirements of the subject or course.
- Timelines for completion of these tasks must be communicated to students and parents to facilitate student and teacher workload.
- Conduct frequent "process" checks.
- Provide plenty of in-class time to work on essential tasks.
- Identify strategies for addressing non-completion of essential tasks; for example:
  - completion contract
  - supervised learning centre
  - method for tracking missed tasks

▲ Provide plenty of in-class time for students to work on essential tasks.

Let's examine each guideline in terms of its implementation:

• *Identify for students and parents the tasks that are* **essential** *as proof of learning*

For as long as I've been an educator, high school teachers have relied upon a course mark breakdown sheet to communicate to students and parents how report card grades are determined. Consider the following outline.

Demonstration of Learning: Grade 10 Science		
Formative and Summative Evaluations	70%	You will be expected to demonstrate your understanding of the key learnings of the course as well as skills in thinking, communication, and application. Demonstration of understanding will be through quizzes, tests, oral questions and answers, journals, investigations, and reports.
Inquiry Performance Task	10%	You are expected to complete a culminating project on a topic or issue that integrates the key learnings of one strand of the course.
Final Examination	20%	The final exam will consist of a variety of types of questions (short-answer, multiple-choice, extended response) that will represent a sampling of the key learnings of the course.

I suggest that this type of vague communication needs to be replaced by specific and detailed descriptions of the essential assessment *of* learning tasks. If possible, these should include due dates for each task. Teachers may choose to send home a hard copy, as well as post these lists on their school or personal website. Consider the following partial example from a Grade 10 Science course.

Grade 10 Science: Critical Tasks and Due Dates		
Light Webquest	Students will compile a series of questions for classmates, based on websites exploring the properties and applications of light and light technologies.	February 13
"Could Be Good, Could Be Bad?" Energy Impact Assignment	A method of energy generation involving a chemical reaction (e.g., natural gas, biofuel, gasoline, etc.) will be analyzed and evaluated for environmental impact. A related reaction that addresses an environmental challenge will also be outlined.	February 25
Matter Matters "Quizzignment"	Matching, prediction, and short-answer questions on a variety of simple chemical reactions (take-home).	February 28
Earth Systems Interaction Mindmap	A detailed, connected map of various earth systems will be created using computer software or art media. The map must show at least 6 systems, sub-points for each system, with connections to all other systems.	March 7

- *Operate on the understanding that* **all** *these must be completed to meet the requirements of the subject or course*

On the first day of classes in my last year of teaching, a young man came to my desk and said, "You just need to know that I'm only here to get a 50 [percent]."

"We don't do 50s in my class," I replied.

I went on to say, "In this class, we're all about excellence. I won't be asking you to do dozens of assignments, but I will expect you to do some tasks, and they're meant to be engaging and challenging. I expect that you'll do every one of these tasks, and that you'll make them the best they can be. If a task isn't the best it can be, I'll keep sending it back to you to work on it until it is. I'll give you lots of feedback to help you make it better."

"Any questions?" I asked when I was done.

- *Timelines for completion of these tasks must be communicated to students and parents to facilitate student and teacher workload*

If we are going to identify a set of critical tasks that must all be completed in order to certify students as proficient in the essential knowledge and skills in a given course, then many of our students will require process timelines to help them manage their time. The amount of support that we provide to students may vary from course to course, depending on the post-secondary destination. As well, within a given course, some students will require more reminders than others to stay on top of the workload. But if our goal is to have all students be successful, as our goal *must* be in a criterion-referenced system, then adjusting the degree of support to suit individual needs is just part of what we do.

Research Project Timeline and Checklist

Work to Be Completed	Status	Comments
Formulate research question	√	Approved by Mr. C.
Develop plan to conduct research	√	Approved by Mr. C.
Locate sources: print, Internet, public	√	Still have to conduct survey
Record and organize data		
Write first draft		
Revise and produce 2nd draft		
Prepare presentation slides and handout		
Deliver presentation		
Debriefing conference		

INTU ARTICLE

Integrating Assessment with Instruction through Student-Directed Research Projects can be found on page 246.

• *Conduct frequent "process" checks*

Once we have assigned an engaging task and given a process timeline to students—and in some cases to parents—we need to make frequent checks to determine that all students are managing their time effectively. If you study the timeline on the preceding page, you will see that at Checkpoint 1, it is necessary to verify that all students have identified an INTU ("I need to understand"; see Chapter 3) inquiry question. This may be accomplished in a number of ways, as follows.

- All students must submit their INTU questions for the teacher to check.
- While students are working, the teacher conducts a visual check to verify that every student has an INTU question.
- The teacher visually checks a representative sample of students.

The practice of checking a representative sample of students is essential from the standpoint of manageability. At Checkpoint 1, the teacher *must* check on those students who are least likely to have identified their INTU question. When teachers conduct what may appear to the class as random checks as a routine part of their classroom practice, students are kept on their toes. At Checkpoint 2, the teacher checks in with another sample of students. This sample may include those students from Checkpoint 1 who did not have their INTU question ready. Once again, the message to students is that you are a step ahead of them. And when someone blurts out, "You're always picking on me," simply reply, "No, I'm just providing you with support so that you don't fall behind."

• *Provide plenty of in-class time to work on essential tasks*

Perhaps the simplest and most effective strategy for avoiding students' incompletion of major tasks is to have them do a major portion of the work during class time. This seems a simple solution, but it's one that, in my experience, is rarely used. The usual reason is: "There's too much curriculum to cover as it is without giving students class time to do their assignments." I'm afraid that when I hear this, I suggest that "backward planning" is the only sensible way to deal with curriculum overload. (See Chapter 3: Planning with the End in Mind.)

If we consider for a moment the range of problems that might be solved by devoting a significant portion of class time to having students work on essential assessment tasks, I believe that all teachers would be willing, at the very least, to give it a shot. Consider the following advantages.

- The teacher is able to monitor all students' progress on assigned tasks.
- The teacher is able to intervene early with students who are habitually late in submitting work.
- The potential for plagiarism is significantly reduced when the teacher is monitoring the work.
- The dilemma of missing tasks is avoided.
- The opportunities for formative assessment—informal feedback while work is in progress—are dramatically increased.
- The opportunities to involve students in self- and peer assessment are dramatically increased, thereby increasing student understanding of what is expected, as well as reducing the teacher's marking load.

• *Identify strategies for addressing non-completion of essential tasks*

Despite having all these strategies in place, there may be some students, like Marsha, who continue to have difficulty completing one or more of the essential "assessment *of* learning" tasks.

Marsha is a student who seems mature beyond her years. She has a sister and brother at the junior school whom she must pick up immediately after school each day. Marsha is quick to answer, debates in class, and brings an insightful perspective to daily classroom discussions. Although her daily work reflects outstanding performance, Marsha has great difficulty completing major assessment tasks that demand persistence over time. When major tasks are submitted, they are inevitably late. The four major assessment tasks you have marked are all Level 4/Excellent, but she still owes you three major tasks for this term.

▲ Devoting plenty of class time to having students work on essential tasks provides more opportunities for formative assessment—informal feedback while work is in progress.

Both pressure and support—from the teacher and parents—need to be employed with students like Marsha. For example:

- Marsha and her parents must sign a "Completion Contract" that identifies the missing work and a timeline for completing it.
- Marsha is then assigned to a supervised study room that operates before and after school, as well as during lunch and spare periods. Marsha and her parents must agree on the times of day when Marsha will attend supervised study. Once Marsha completes the missing work, she earns back her free time.
- The subject teacher, supervising teacher, and parents communicate regularly about Marsha's progress on the missing tasks.

Summary

This chapter explored assessment *of* learning—summative assessment designed primarily to determine what and how well students have learned by the end of a significant period of instruction. The chapter outlined the need for balanced assessment—the inclusion of oral and performance tasks as well as written tasks—and the need for performance tasks that are rich and authentic. We ended the chapter by acknowledging and addressing the fact that, however rich the tasks may be, some students simply need extra motivation to complete them. Note that some of the issues in this chapter relate closely to grading, a topic that is covered more thoroughly in Chapter 9: Grading and Reporting.

End-of-Chapter Activity

Try the following reflective activities with colleagues.

- Conduct an audit of one course or all courses in your department to determine the extent to which your assessment plans are balanced appropriately according to "write, do, and say." Set an achievable goal to address imbalances revealed through the audit.

- Seek out teachers in your department or school who have expertise in designing the kinds of tasks—e.g., authentic performance tasks—that are lacking.

- Use the self-assessment tool Evaluating the Quality of a Performance Task (see below) to assess your own performance tasks.

- In a department meeting, review and consider the possible application of this chapter's Guidelines for Ensuring that Critical Tasks Are Completed (see page 65).

Evaluating the Quality of a Performance Task		
Quality Criterion	**Evaluation of Task* (✓) or (✗)**	**Maintain / Modify / Change**
Task provides evidence of essential learning		
Task demands innovation and creativity on the part of the student		
Task presents students with an engaging challenge that requires persistence to complete		
Task engages students in problem solving and decision making		
Task is appropriate for all students		
If task involves co-operative groups, there is provision for individual accountability		
Assessment criteria for task reflect the essential learning		
Assessment criteria are communicated in student-friendly language before students begin work		

* Meets individual criterion or is substandard

TOOL 1.3

Evaluating the Quality of a Performance Task

A modifiable version of this tool can be found on the DVD.

1. Assessment serves different purposes at different times; it may be used to find out what students already know and can do; it may be used to help students improve their learning; or it may be used to let students, and their parents, know how much they have learned within a prescribed period of time.

3. Assessment must be balanced, including oral and performance as well as written tasks, and be flexible in order to improve learning for all students.

4. Assessment and instruction are inseparable because effective assessment informs learning.

5. For assessment to be helpful to students, it must inform them in words, not numerical scores or letter grades, what they have done well, what they have done poorly, and what they need to do next in order to improve.

6. Assessment is a collaborative process that is most effective when it involves self-, peer, and teacher assessment and when it helps students to be reflective learners who take ownership of their own learning.

8. Grading and reporting student achievement is a responsive, human process that requires teachers to exercise their professional judgment.

Section 3

Assessment That Promotes Learning

The chapters in this section focus on assessment as an integral part of improving student learning. Assessment needs to benefit all students and help them think about how to improve their work.

Chapter 5: Initial/Diagnostic Assessment and Differentiated Instruction is about gathering initial assessment data to inform teachers about what students know and can do—and how to use this data to plan differentiated instruction.

Chapter 6: Assessment *for* Learning explains how assessment is not separate from teaching and learning; rather, it is part of both. The chapter offers strategies and guidelines for self-, peer, and teacher assessment, including sample rubrics and checklists (all available on the DVD).

Chapter 7: Teaching and Assessing Students with Special Needs offers strategies and case studies to assist in planning, managing, grading, and reporting for a differentiated classroom.

CHAPTER FIVE

INITIAL/DIAGNOSTIC ASSESSMENT AND DIFFERENTIATED INSTRUCTION

> **BIG IDEA 1**
>
> Assessment serves different purposes at different times; it may be used to find out what students already know and can do; it may be used to help students improve their learning; or it may be used to let students, and their parents, know how much they have learned within a prescribed period of time.

> **BIG IDEA 4**
>
> Assessment and instruction are inseparable because effective assessment informs learning.

WHY DIFFERENTIATE?

Initial/diagnostic assessment is assessment to determine appropriate starting points for instruction.

The function of schooling has changed dramatically during the past two decades, yet the three frequently asked questions on the next page reflect the difficulties that many teachers are experiencing as they try to adapt to the change. As we saw in Chapter 2, the new mission of schools is to educate all students to high levels of proficiency. Until the late 1980s, schools—and high schools in particular—were expected to sift and sort students into groups of high, average, and low achievers in preparation for one of several post-secondary destinations: university, college, or the workplace. Beginning in the 1990s, school districts across Canada and the United States began to adopt grade-by-grade curriculum standards, reflecting the new mission of secondary education: to ensure that *all* students, regardless of their post-secondary plans, leave school with the knowledge and skills deemed essential to lead a productive life.

In Chapter 2, we also examined how this new mission has necessitated the move away from norm-referenced assessment and grading practices in favour of criterion-referenced approaches. Remember, a norm-referenced grading model is designed to spread achievement scores across the full range of possible values, and achievement is measured by comparing one student's work with the work of other students. By contrast, a criterion-referenced grading model is used when the goal is to certify proficiency on a known set of learning targets (content standards) to a known level of performance (performance standards). While it is inevitable that some students may require more time than others, and some may require more support than their peers, the goal is to have all students achieve proficiency. The reference point for determining proficiency is a known standard—what we sometimes call, to use a high-jump analogy, "the bar."

This chapter addresses these frequently asked questions:

- If I know the student has earned the prerequisite credit to the course, why should I do diagnostic assessment?
- If I differentiate my assessment practices for some students, does it give them an unfair advantage?
- I taught the unit of study to the students. Many failed the test and some even asked for a retest. Don't the students have to take responsibility for their own learning?

▲ The reference point for determining proficiency is a known standard—what we sometimes call "the bar."

There are many teachers who struggle with this new mission. They cling to the "sift and sort" approach, as reflected in the three questions in the margin, above. However, as I work with high school teachers and administrators across Canada and the United States, I can say that the vast majority are desperately trying to learn *how* to teach and assess in ways that *will* enable all students to "clear the bar." And because teaching and learning is a complex process that involves the interplay of curriculum, assessment, and instruction, I stress the importance of looking at how diagnostic assessment and differentiated instruction are connected. In workshops, I introduce this concept by saying, "You can't do D.I. until you've done D.A!" In other words, diagnostic or initial assessment must precede differentiated instruction. Teachers must become proficient in using the data they gather about students' knowledge and skills at the beginning of a term, a unit, or even a lesson in order to make decisions about *how* to differentiate instruction for groups of students in the class.

HOW DO I DIFFERENTIATE?

Some teachers I meet cringe at the term *differentiated instruction*, so I quickly switch to speaking about *responsive teaching* instead. It is what all good teachers do intuitively and instinctively. But the challenge of content-laden curriculum in many high school subjects often dissuades excellent teachers from doing what they know is best for their students. As one teacher announced recently in a workshop, "Even without differentiating instruction for any of my students, there's still way too much content to cover." As we saw in Chapter 3, backward planning is essential if we are to solve the curriculum-overload problem. But crucial to efficient planning is an understanding that differentiated instruction is *not* individualized instruction. It does *not* require teachers to plan thirty or more separate units of study or the equivalent number of daily lessons. Efficient unit and lesson planning begins with one basic plan for the class. Generally, this means having the same broad learning outcomes, or the same lesson goal, for all students (Stage 1 of planning).

Similarly, remembering the planning model from Chapter 3, Stage 2 involves identifying how to assess the intended learning. Once again, begin with the same assessment tasks for all students. Next, develop a general plan for how new material will be taught—the instructional sequence (Stage 3 of planning). With an overall unit or lesson plan in place, consider the different groups of students in the class and ask three questions:

- How might the learning targets or lesson goal need to change for some students?
- Is it necessary to *adapt* or *modify* the assessment tasks for some students? (See Chapter 7: Teaching and Assessing Students with Special Needs.)
- How might the instructional sequence need to change for some students?

It is relatively common practice for teachers to use one or more assessments at the start of a semester or term to determine students' current levels of skill and understanding. What I rarely find, however, is a strategic and systematic follow-up plan for *using* the data gathered from such assessments to tailor instruction for different groups in a given class. It is more common for teachers to examine the data and, if a significant number of students exhibit learning gaps, to conduct an extensive review of background knowledge or skills for the whole class. The result of this "one-size-fits-all" approach is that students not requiring such a review are bored, while others who need a more extensive review are still not ready to engage with the curriculum.

"Differentiating instruction does include:

- *Using a variety of groupings to meet student needs*
- *Providing alternative instruction/assessment activities*
- *Challenging students at an appropriate level, in light of their readiness, interests, and learning profiles*

Differentiating instruction does not include:

- *Doing something different for every student in the class*
- *Disorderly and undisciplined student activity*
- *Using groups that never change, or isolating struggling students within the class*
- *Never engaging in whole-class activities with all students participating in the same endeavour"*

LEADING MATH SUCCESS: MATHEMATICAL LITERACY GRADES 7–12, ONTARIO MINISTRY OF EDUCATION, 2004

"To differentiate instruction is to recognize students' varying background knowledge, readiness, language, preferences in learning and interests, and to react responsively."

TRACEY HALL, NICOLE STRANGMAN, AND ANNE MEYER, 2003

▲ Responsive teaching: it's what good teachers do intuitively and instinctively.

GATHERING INITIAL ASSESSMENT DATA: NADINE'S GRADE 9 ENGLISH CLASS

So what does an effective plan look like for using diagnostic assessment data to differentiate instruction? Let's consider Nadine's approach in her Grade 9 English class. This chapter will follow Nadine's methods, step by step. We will focus only on the Reading and Literature strand, although Nadine follows a similar approach for the Writing and Oral Communication strands ("strands" refer to those in the Ontario Curriculum).

Important Note: The strategies Nadine employs are applicable in all subject areas in which reading is a major component.

The support staff in the district where Nadine teaches has produced a guide to help classroom teachers assess their students' reading skills. The following diagram from this guide highlights three types of assessment:

- a class-wide, start-of-semester assessment of all students' reading skills
- a more thorough assessment of students who, as a result of this initial screening, appear to be reading below grade level
- a process for assessing the reading level of course texts or other materials to determine their grade-appropriateness

Flow Chart: Screening and Diagnostic Assessment of Reading

Screening and Diagnostic Assessment of Reading

Groups of Students	Individual Reading Problems	Appropriateness of Texts
Questions about My Group/Class I've got a **new group of students**, and I want to get an idea of which students are at-risk with respect to their reading skills and which are expert readers, so that I can plan to differentiate my instruction appropriately. • What is my first step? • How do I begin?	**Questions about Individual Students** I've got **two or three individual students** who are struggling with the reading demands of my course. (I may have found this out through my own group screening, from information from other teachers/professionals, or from parents.) I want to differentiate instruction appropriately. Where do I go next?	**Questions about Texts/Materials** I want to know if the reading level of a textbook is appropriate for my class. OR I want to help students pick appropriate books/materials for their independent reading. • How do I do that?
Group Screening A balance of: • teacher observations of the group • preliminary interviews with students • standardized group testing	**Individual Diagnostic Assessment** A compilation of information on an individual student from a variety of sources: • individual student records • other teachers (past and present) • parents • student • informal testing/data collection	**Evaluation of Texts/Materials** • Cloze procedure
	Individual Program Adaptation or Modification • and/or Referral to School Team and/or School Resource Team for further problem solving, which may include the use of further standardized assessments	**Other Options** • pre-teach vocabulary • choose a different text • provide ongoing vocabulary support • use reciprocal reading strategies (see page 80)

SOURCE: Adapted from "Guidelines for Assessing the Reading Skills of your Students," Halton DSB, 1998

BROAD LEARNING OUTCOMES

Nadine's provincial curriculum identifies four broad learning outcomes for the Reading strand of all Grade 9 and 10 English classes. Nadine knows that her initial, or diagnostic, assessment process (which is the first column in the above diagram) must provide information about her students' current skill levels with respect to these four outcomes. For students whose current skills appear to be lagging in one or more of these, she will need to conduct further, more intensive assessment (see the second column in the diagram) to determine which specific reading outcomes they are struggling with. The broad outcomes identified by the curriculum are as follows.

By the end of this course, students will:

1. **Read for Meaning:** read and demonstrate an understanding of a variety of literary, informational, and graphic texts, using a range of strategies to construct meaning

2. **Understand Form and Style:** recognize a variety of text forms, text features, and stylistic elements and demonstrate understanding of how they help communicate meaning

3. **Read with Fluency:** use knowledge of words and cueing systems to read fluently

4. **Reflect on Skills and Strategies:** reflect on and identify their strengths as readers, areas for improvement, and the strategies they found most helpful before, during, and after reading

– Adapted from *The Ontario Curriculum, Grades 9 and 10, English,* 2007

STANDARDIZED TESTS

While Nadine recognizes the importance of a balanced approach to assess the reading skills of each of her classes, she knows that a standardized reading test can yield some useful data. Consequently, she has chosen to use the Gates-MacGinitie test as an initial screen to identify students who may be reading below grade level.

Nadine uses the percentile scores from the test as an indicator of which students may have difficulty with the reading demands of her course. A percentile is a norm-referenced score out of 100. A student scoring at the 45th percentile has performed better than 45 percent of the sample on which the test was normed. According to the statistical information accompanying the Gates-MacGinitie test, students scoring between the 25th and 75th percentile are performing in the "average" range. Given a mean score of 50, students are deemed to be at risk of reading difficulty if they score one standard deviation or more below the mean—in the case of this test, these are students who are scoring below the 16th percentile.

It is important to remember that percentiles are *not* the same as percent scores. Hence, 50 percent is not a passing score and anything below 50 a failing score. In fact, a student scoring at the 32nd percentile is well within the average range of performance on the test.

A BALANCED APPROACH TO INITIAL ASSESSMENT

Nadine is well aware that scores on the Gates-MacGinitie test, taken alone, are not conclusive. A student scoring below the 16th percentile is not necessarily at risk. He may not have been trying to do his best; he may not be sufficiently fluent

Gates-MacGinitie tests are standardized reading tests to help teachers determine students' levels of reading achievement.

When you are considering this chapter in terms of your students with special needs, you might want to also refer to Chapter 7: Teaching and Assessing Students with Special Needs. In that chapter, I point out that subjecting these students to a battery of early diagnostic tests, especially written tests, can quickly damage their self-esteem. I recommend triangulating the data—gathering samples of evidence involving students writing, doing, and saying—and holding individual conferences with students. See page 130.

In Mathematics, Science, and Social Sciences, I strongly encourage teachers to conduct a quick assessment of students' awareness of the standard features of a text. For example, use the "Introduction to Nelson Mathematics 10" (Zimmer et al, 2001) on pages 8–14 to familiarize students with the organization of that text. Then instruct students to work with a partner to locate each feature and explain how it functions in a specific chapter. The teacher observes which students have difficulty and prepares to differentiate instruction accordingly.

The data that Nadine and her colleagues in the English department gather about students' reading skills is shared with other departments to inform teachers across the school about students who may have difficulty reading course text materials.

in English; he may not have heard the test instructions clearly … or he *may*, in fact, have some legitimate reading difficulties. Nadine knows that she needs to gather several other kinds of data about her students' reading skills, behaviours, and attitudes before drawing conclusions on which to base instructional decisions. She therefore creates anecdotal records, based on what she sees and hears while students are interacting with a wide variety of texts.

For example, she notes the texts that students select themselves during a visit to the resource centre; she observes and listens as students, working in small groups, take turns reading aloud from a short-story anthology; she watches carefully and asks questions to check for comprehension while students are conducting online research about local libraries and bookstores—part of her clandestine plot to encourage her students to read more fiction! She also sets up a schedule to work closely with a few students at a time, using the reciprocal teaching model (Palinscar & Brown, 1984).

RECIPROCAL TEACHING

This is a highly effective approach that involves the teacher facilitating small-group, oral reading of a text. At strategic points, Nadine asks students to use one of three strategies to help her assess their comprehension. The strategies are:

1. summarizing the passage just read
2. predicting what will happen next
3. posing questions they have, based on their reading so far

Struggling students benefit from listening to their peers and are supported in this non-threatening social interaction with the text.

▲ Small-group oral reading supports students because it provides a non-threatening social interaction with texts.

SURVEYS AND INTERVIEWS

Nadine also has each of her classes complete a survey of their reading attitudes and habits. She discusses each student's responses on the survey during brief, one-on-one interviews conducted during the first two weeks of the semester. She uses material such as the following CASI (Comprehension Attitude Strategies Interests) Reading Assessment.

TOOL 5.10

Reading Attitude Survey

A modifiable version of this tool can be found on the DVD.

Reading Attitude Survey

Name: _____ Grade: _____

Term: _____ Date: _____

Circle the number of books to show your opinion of each statement. Remember, there are no "right" answers!

- I do not agree.
- I agree a little.
- I agree.
- I strongly agree.

1. I enjoy listening to someone read aloud.
2. I like to talk about ideas and information after I have read something.
3. I enjoy reading at home.
4. I think nonfiction is easier to read than fiction.
5. Other people think I am a good reader.
6. I read for enjoyment.
7. I feel good about how quickly I read.
8. I only read to do schoolwork.
9. Reading is being able to say all the words correctly.
10. Reading is important for subjects like science, writing, social studies, art, or math.
11. After I have read a book, I like to read more books by the same author.
12. Reading is boring.
13. I read to find out about new things.
14. I choose books to read that other people have recommended.

Comments:
_____
_____
_____
_____
_____

SOURCE: Adapted from *CASI Reading Assessment Teacher's Guide*, 2003, p. 33

TOOL 5.11

Reading Interview

A modifiable version of
this tool can be found on
the DVD.

Reading Interview	
Name: _____ Age: _____	
Grade: _____ Term: _____ Date: _____	

1. Do you think you are a good reader? How do you know?	
2. a) When you are reading and you come to a word you do not know, what do you do? (Prompt if necessary. *Do you ever do anything else?*) Which of these strategies do you use most often?	
b) How do you know when you don't understand what you are reading? What are some things you can do about it?	
3. Think of someone who is a good reader. What do you think makes that person a good reader? What do you think that a person does when the text does not make sense?	
4. Do you read in any other language(s) at home or at school? Which one(s)?	
5. What kinds of reading do you do using technology (e.g., websites, e-mail, CD-ROMs, messaging)?	
6. a) If you knew that someone was having difficulty reading a story, how could you help?	
b) If you knew that someone was having difficulty reading an information article, how could you help?	
7. How do you decide what to read? What do you like to read? Why?	
8. As a reader, what would you like to do better?	

SOURCE: Adapted from CASI *Reading Assessment Teacher's Guide*, 2003, p. 32

Similar types of early assessment take place in other subject areas in Nadine's school. For example the Phys. Ed. teachers conduct observational assessment of fitness, hand–eye coordination, mobility, and balance during a variety of physical activities. In Science, teachers might assess students' knowledge of basic concepts regarding, for example, matter or organisms, as well as their skills, such as their safe behaviour in the lab.

USING INITIAL ASSESSMENT DATA TO DIFFERENTIATE INSTRUCTION

Nadine integrates all of these assessments—the Gates-MacGinitie test; observational assessment done while students interact with a variety of texts; reciprocal reading groups; reading surveys and interviews—into her routine for the first two weeks of class. As a result of data gathered during this process, she has identified five students who will likely struggle with the reading requirements of her course. For these students, she initiates the more intensive reading assessment process outlined in the second column of the diagram on page 78. She also collaborates with the Special Education Department and communicates with parents to ensure that the needs of these students will be met in her class.

Based on the data she's gathered, Nadine has determined that four of the students—Elissa, Chan, Brent, and Anita—are experiencing similar kinds of difficulties: namely, they are all struggling with three of the broad learning outcomes:

1. **Read for Meaning:** read and demonstrate an understanding of a variety of literary, informational, and graphic texts, using a range of strategies to construct meaning
2. **Understand Form and Style:** recognize a variety of text forms, text features, and stylistic elements and demonstrate understanding of how they help communicate meaning
3. **Read with Fluency:** use knowledge of words and cueing systems to read fluently

The fifth student, Dan, exhibits proficient reading skills whenever he's working at a computer. His problems appear to be more attitudinal and behavioural, as evidenced by his reluctance to read any of the required texts. Nadine has decided to adopt a gentle approach with Dan, characterized by flexibility and choice. She knows he can read but is putting up barriers as part of a "tough guy" persona. In her experience, students like Dan often come around when given opportunities to read—and speak and write about—materials of their own choosing. She'll worry about the couple of compulsory course texts—*Twelfth Night*, for example—later in the semester.

▲ Surveys and one-on-one interviews are held early in a semester to help teachers gather assessment data for planning differentiated instruction.

"At this time, we are studying William Shakespeare's Twelfth Night. *I was able to find an online version of the script. Rather than bury my students' noses in their books, we read the script aloud from the interactive whiteboard. It offered more interactivity in the reading process. Secondly, I was able to find streaming songs that are found in the play. My students were able to hear the songs performed as they were intended, rather than being butchered by me! Finally, I was lucky enough to find a complete performance of the play performed by an award-winning student group. This allowed my students to see the play performed by individuals their own age. As a class, we would read a scene, and then access that scene on video. This sped up the teaching process by roughly two weeks, and I know that my students have a much stronger grasp of the material."*

SCOTT JOHNSON, ENGLISH TEACHER

And I would add that they probably emerged from the experience eager for more Shakespeare, rather than turned off the bard for life!

We need to "differentiate" our concept of the effective reader. Too often in our schools, we use "read" to refer only to the reading of printed texts. We then describe students, especially boys, as non-readers because they don't choose to read books. In fact, many reading surveys include an implicit bias that a reader is, by definition, a reader of books. As a result, many students identify themselves as "non-readers" when they may be proficient "digital readers."

ASSESSING THE READING LEVEL OF A CLASS TEXT

Many teachers that I meet express frustration about students' inability to read compulsory class texts, as reflected in comments such as "Didn't these kids learn *anything* in elementary school?" The diversity that characterizes today's classrooms demands a more proactive approach. By *expecting* some students in the class to struggle with the reading demands of core texts and *planning* for this eventuality, teachers can better meet these students' needs and reduce their own levels of frustration. One strategy for dealing with this problem is to routinely assess the match between students' current reading skills and your course text. A cloze placement test is an efficient method for accomplishing this task.

THE CLOZE PROCEDURE

The cloze procedure is a simple way to assess students' reading comprehension. It requires students to predict the specific words that have been deleted from a text and thereby to indicate their ability to read and comprehend that text. On the basis of the cloze assessment, teachers often find that three groups of students emerge: those able to read the text independently, those who will require some support from the teacher and/or their peers, and those who will likely have significant difficulty with the text and may require alternative resources to support their learning.

Following is an excerpt about constructing and administering cloze passages, from *Understanding Reading Problems: Assessment and Instruction* (7th edition) by Jean Wallace Gillet, Charles Temple, and Alan Crawford.

Constructing a Cloze Passage

1. Choose a text selection of about 275 to 300 words that students have not read.
2. Leave the first sentence intact (or the first two sentences, if the first sentence is very short.) Randomly select one of the first five words in the next sentence and delete every fifth word thereafter, replacing it with a blank. Make each blank the same size. If a word to be deleted is a proper noun, skip it and delete the next word.
3. Continue in this fashion until you have 50 blanks. Finish the sentence in which the 50th deletion occurs and include one more intact sentence. Make a separate answer sheet or have students write answers directly on the passage.

Administering a Cloze Passage

1. Show students how to complete a cloze passage, using example short sentences or short paragraphs. Encourage them to use what they already know as well as language in the passage to try to figure

out the *exact word* that belongs in each blank. Some classes or groups may need extended practice before doing the "real thing."

2. Explain that no one will get every word correct, and that getting about half of the words right is a good score. If they don't know this in advance, students can get very anxious and some might give up in frustration.

3. Allow as much time as needed to complete the passage individually without rushing. This is not a timed exercise.

Scoring and Interpreting a Cloze

1. Count as correct every *exact* word from the text, even if it is misspelled. Don't count synonyms, even if they make sense. Doing so will affect the score criteria, which were developed using exact replacements only. Also, students will argue endlessly about what is "close enough."

2. Multiply the total number of correct replacements by 2 to determine each student's score on the 50-item passage.

3. Create 3 lists:

   ■ Students whose score was above 60 percent correct. The material is at or close to their independent reading level. They can probably use this material without guidance or support.

   ■ Students whose score was between 40 and 60 percent correct. The material probably represents their instructional reading level. They can read it most effectively if they are given support and guidance such as visual organizers, study guides, or directed discussion.

   ■ Students whose score was below 40 percent correct. The material is likely at their frustration level and is too difficult for them to read. More suitable material should be found for them. If they are required to read that material, they will need extensive support and guidance such as listening to the material read aloud and direct experience with the topic.

   – from *Understanding Reading Problems: Assessment and Instruction,* 7th ed. by Jean Wallace Gillet, Charles Temple, and Alan Crawford, 2007

Using the Cloze Diagnostically

If you want to use the cloze procedure diagnostically—to find out what students know and can do, or to help them use context clues—delete key words rather than every fifth word. If this is done before asking students to read a particular text, the cloze can show what vocabulary or concepts you may need to focus on. If the cloze is used after reading, it can show what vocabulary and concepts students have learned. Oral cloze passages can also be used to help teachers observe students' listening and comprehension skills. With this method, the teacher reads the passage aloud, leaving out key words, which the student fills in orally as the passage is being read.

Nadine plans to use a short-story anthology during the first unit of her Grade 9 English course. She has created a cloze assessment based on one of the stories to determine her students' readiness to handle the reading demands of this text. But Nadine has also told her colleagues in other departments about the power of using cloze passages to assess student readiness to handle text. Geoff teaches Career Education and has designed the following cloze to assess his students' readiness to handle the core text in one of his courses.

> Monitoring of performance can add to employees' stress. At call centres, computers can _____ the number of calls, the _____ spent on each call, and the speed at which the _____ is processed. In many workplaces, _____ used to chat with customers. But now they have _____ time for human interaction. One stressed cashier _____, "If I'm _____ friendly, the computer will show that I'm not _____ customers through fast enough, and I could _____ my job."

"There is no contradiction between effective standards-based instruction and differentiation. Curriculum tells us *what* to teach: Differentiation tells us *how*. Thus, if we elect to teach a standards-based curriculum, differentiation simply suggests ways *in which* we can make that curriculum work best for varied learners. In other words, differentiation can show us how to teach the same standards to a range of learners by employing a variety of teaching and learning modes."

CAROL ANN TOMLINSON, 2000

COMMUNICATING WITH STUDENTS AND PARENTS ABOUT ACHIEVEMENT IN THE DIFFERENTIATED CLASSROOM

From an assessment perspective, Nadine fully understands the crucial distinction between content standards and performance standards. Her goal for the end of the course is to have Elissa, Chan, Brent, and Anita reading grade-appropriate texts (content standards) at Level 3/Proficient (performance standard), according to the following generic reading rubric used by her English department. She understands that to improve these students' current skill levels, she will have to use below-grade-level texts. This is a crucial teaching principle. When students have weak skills, they must be presented with simple content if they are to succeed in improving those skills. High school teachers must be willing to substitute less complex content material for students like Elissa, Chan, Brent, and Anita.

USING RUBRICS IN THE DIFFERENTIATED CLASSROOM

A frequent question that I face during workshops is "How do I modify my rubrics to assess the work of my weaker students?" My short answer is "You don't!" After the surprised chatter quiets down, I go on to explain what Nadine already knows: a rubric is the equivalent of a metre stick. It's a measurement instrument. As such, you must not change its length or it becomes meaningless! In the criterion-referenced classroom, a "B" must mean the same for all students. Hence, the generic rubric (below) must remain unchanged for all students. In fact, this same rubric may be used at all grade levels. What changes for certain students, or for different grade levels, is the *level of difficulty* of the reading material on which students' skills are assessed.

Generic Reading Rubric				
Categories/Criteria	Level 1 (Limited)	Level 2 (Fair)	Level 3 (Proficient)	Level 4 (Excellent)
Reasoning				
• demonstrates an understanding of the text by selecting and describing relevant information and ideas	• demonstrates a limited understanding of the text by selecting and describing a few ideas that may not always be relevant	• demonstrates some understanding of the text by selecting and describing some simple but relevant ideas and information	• demonstrates a general understanding of the text by selecting and describing most relevant ideas and information	• demonstrates a thorough understanding of the text by skillfully selecting and describing almost all relevant ideas and information
• infers meaning	• demonstrates a limited ability to make and support simple inferences	• demonstrates some ability to make and support simple inferences	• demonstrates a general ability to make and support inferences of some complexity	• demonstrates a strong ability to make and support complex inferences
• interprets and analyzes information from the text	• demonstrates a limited ability to interpret and analyze ideas and includes little or no supporting detail	• demonstrates some ability to interpret and analyze simple ideas with some supporting detail	• demonstrates a general ability to interpret and analyze ideas of some complexity with supporting detail	• demonstrates a strong ability to interpret and analyze complex ideas with extensive supporting detail
Communication				
• demonstrates an ability to explain, support, and apply what has been read	• demonstrates a limited ability to explain, support, and apply ideas and information	• demonstrates some ability to explain, support, and apply ideas and information	• demonstrates a general ability to apply ideas and information	• demonstrates a strong ability to apply ideas and information
• demonstrates an ability to make connections among text, personal experiences, and life situations	• makes a few simple connections among text, personal experiences, and life situations	• makes some straightforward connections among text, personal experiences, and life situations	• makes connections of some complexity among text, personal experiences, and life situations	• makes complex and logical connections among text, personal experiences, and life situations
Organization of Ideas				
• identifies and describes the features and organization of different forms of text (e.g., fiction, non-fiction, poetry, scripts)	• identifies and describes a limited number of features and organization of the text	• identifies and describes some features and organization of the text	• identifies and describes most features and organization of the text	• identifies and describes all/almost all features and organization of the text
• uses knowledge of the organization, form, and features of different forms of text to help understanding	• uses a limited knowledge of organization, form, and features to help understand text	• uses some knowledge of organization, form, and features to help understand text	• uses a general knowledge of organization, form, and features to help understand text	• uses an extensive knowledge of organization, form, and features to help understand text
Application of Language Conventions				
• identifies and uses the convention of written text (e.g., skills, word/ sentence order and patterns, punctuation, grammar) to assist in reading	• demonstrates a limited understanding of the required conventions	• demonstrates some understanding of the required conventions	• demonstrates a general understanding of required conventions	• demonstrates a thorough understanding of the required conventions

SOURCE: Adapted from *CASI Reading Assessment Teacher's Guide*, 2003, pp. 36–37

In Nadine's class, for example, Elissa, Chan, Brent, and Anita will be reading below-grade-level texts, at least for the duration of the first term. So while Nadine will use the same generic reading rubric for all students, the achievement levels she records for these four students will be with reference to simpler texts. This type of differentiation must be fully understood by students and parents alike. For example, Nadine may communicate to Elissa's parents, either orally or on the report card, "Elissa is currently performing at Level 1 in Reasoning and Communication when reading Grade 5-equivalent texts." As soon as Elissa performs at Level 3 on these texts, Nadine will introduce more challenging reading material, always ensuring that the student is working at a challenging, but not frustrating, level of difficulty.

From a grading and reporting standpoint, it is essential that these students and their parents clearly understand that their current achievement status, as reflected in rubric levels or grades, has been accomplished only through the use of below-grade-level subject content. The goal by semester's or term's end will be for these students to demonstrate understanding of at-grade-level material, though possibly at a lower performance level.

DIFFERENTIATING ASSESSMENT TASKS

This leads us to the question of differentiating assessment tasks. Recall my emphasis on beginning with the same learning outcomes and the same instructional plan for *all* students and then differentiating these components according to the needs of groups of students. The same principle applies to the design of assessment tasks: design a common assessment for *all* students and differentiate the task according to the needs of specific groups of students. What does such differentiation look like in Nadine's class?

There are five ways in which a given assessment task may be differentiated:

1. Adjust the scope of the task.
2. Adjust the complexity of the task and the level of support provided to students.
3. Adjust the constraints placed on the task.
4. Adjust the assessment criteria for the task.
5. Provide an alternative medium for the student to demonstrate the required learning.

Note: Teachers may find it necessary to differentiate a given assessment task in several of these ways for some students.

"Equality in education does not require that all students have exactly the same experiences. Rather, education in a democracy promises that everyone will have an equal opportunity to actualize their potential, to learn as much as they can."

ELLEN FIEDLER, RICHARD LANGE, AND SUSAN WINEBRENNER. 2002

We will use a sample of assessment tasks from the three English courses that Nadine teaches to examine each of these options:

1. **Adjust the scope of the task.**

Task: Grade 10 Final Written Examination—Students are to write a three-paragraph essay about the themes of the course.

Differentiation: Students who have significant writing difficulties complete the examination on computers and, instead of writing on the themes of the course, are provided with a more familiar, less abstract topic.

2. **Adjust the complexity of the task and the level of support provided to students.**

Task: Grade 9 Poetry Assignment—Students are to prepare a report that examines the poetic merit of the lyrics of contemporary music. They must scan the lyrics of five songs from five different artists, using the Internet, CD sleeves, or any other medium. For each set of lyrics, they must comment on

- the type of poetry
- the poetic techniques used
- the effectiveness and impact of the lyrics on the listener

Differentiation: Nadine provides Elissa, Chan, Brent, and Anita with a graphic organizer to prompt them at each stage of the task. She also works with them in a small group to help them locate and scan the lyrics into their reports. These interventions reduce the open-ended nature of the original task.

3. **Adjust the constraints placed on the task.**

Task: Grade 10 Final Written Examination—Students are to write a three-paragraph essay about the themes of the course.

Differentiation: The 1 ½-hour time limit for the examination is waived for students who have significant writing difficulties. They may work on the task until they complete it.

4. **Adjust the assessment criteria for the task.**

Task: Grade 9 Oral Presentation to Peers—The rubric for this task includes among the assessment criteria Audience Engagement and Handling of Questions from Audience.

Differentiation: Nadine has four students in her class who are learning English as a second language. To reduce the anxiety level for these students, she has each of them present their material to her alone. She focuses on Ideas and Speaking Skills since these are the most important criteria for these students to master at first. She doesn't assess them on either Audience Engagement or Handling of Questions from Audience until the students gain confidence.

5. **Provide an alternative medium for the student to demonstrate the required learning.**

Task: Grade 12 Independent Reading Task—Students read two novels by their chosen novelist and write a compare/contrast paper. The paper must include commentary on themes, style, characters, etc.

Differentiation: For a student with learning disabilities, who has significant reading difficulties, Nadine allows books on tape to be used along with the printed texts.

◀ Design a common assessment for all students and differentiate the task according to the needs of specific groups of students.

PRESERVING THE PURPOSE OF THE ASSESSMENT

While all of these changes are made to support students in their learning, Nadine is careful to ensure that she does not undermine the integrity of any of the tasks with respect to the learning targets they are designed to assess. This is a common mistake made by teachers less experienced in differentiation than Nadine. When differentiating an assessment task for a group of students, the teacher must carefully examine the curriculum outcomes to ensure that any changes made to the task preserve the assessment purpose of the task. For example, the Grade 10 Final Written Examination that has students write a three-paragraph essay about the themes of the course is designed to assess students' ability to organize an argument and supporting evidence in *written* form. Allowing students with writing difficulties to produce a collage of images related to the themes will *not* provide evidence of this learning target!

Summary

This chapter has focused on diagnostic assessment—gathering initial assessment data that lets teachers know what students know and can do—and how it is used to plan for differentiated instruction. Key points are:

- create a systematic plan for using the data to tailor instruction
- use the same learning outcomes and instructional plan for all students and then differentiate the components according to students' needs
- assess the match between your course text and students' current reading skills
- understand the distinction between content standards and performance standards; be ready to substitute less complex content material
- differentiate assessment tasks according to the needs of specific groups of students
- communicate with students and parents about how students' needs are being met

End-of-Chapter Activity

With some colleagues, try one or more of the following reflective activities:

- Select one unit from a course you already teach. Follow the approach described in this chapter to differentiate the content for an individual student or for a group of students with similar needs.
- Review your current approach to diagnostic assessment and the use you make of the data gathered at the start of a term or semester. Examine the strategies suggested in this chapter and explore changes you may wish to make to improve instruction.
- Since reading is crucial to learning in all subjects, apply one or more of the strategies suggested regarding the assessment of reading in one or more of your courses.

CHAPTER SIX

ASSESSMENT *FOR* LEARNING

BIG IDEA 1
Assessment serves different purposes at different times; it may be used to find out what students already know and can do; it may be used to help students improve their learning; or it may be used to let students, and their parents, know how much they have learned within a prescribed period of time.

BIG IDEA 5
For assessment to be helpful to students, it must inform them in words, not numerical scores or letter grades, what they have done well, what they have done poorly, and what they need to do next in order to improve.

BIG IDEA 6
Assessment is a collaborative process that is most effective when it involves self-, peer-, and teacher assessment and when it helps students to be reflective learners who take ownership of their own learning.

HOW DOES ASSESSMENT *OF* LEARNING DIFFER FROM ASSESSMENT *FOR* LEARNING?

This chapter answers these frequently asked questions:

- *How do I get my students to take assessment for learning seriously if they know it doesn't count?*
- *How do I find the time within a reporting cycle to include assessments that don't count?*
- *What kind of feedback is most helpful for improving student learning?*
- *How do I get students to use the feedback I give them?*

"Assessment *for* learning" is seen by some as the latest educational bandwagon. And, given the flavour-of-the-year syndrome that sees educational innovations come and go, it's no wonder that many teachers become cynical when they're told to embrace a new approach to assessment. So what is "assessment *for* learning" and why should we pay attention to it?

> *Assessment for learning is any assessment for which the first priority in its design and practice is to serve the purpose of promoting students' learning. It thus differs from assessment designed primarily to serve the purposes of accountability, or of ranking, or of certifying competence"* (Black, Harrison, Lee, Marshall, & Wiliam, 2004, p. 2).

"Assessment *of* learning" on the other hand, is defined as:

> *…those tasks that are designed to determine how much learning has occurred after a significant period of instruction. The data from such assessments is often used to determine report card grades* (Cooper, 2007).

▲ Assessment *for* learning is about providing feedback that informs students how to improve.

Assessment *for* learning is not about grading and reporting; it's about teaching and learning. And that is why it is so important. As Dylan Wiliam, an expert in the practice of assessment *for* learning, has said, "changing teachers' minute-to-minute and day-by-day formative assessment practices is the most powerful way to increase student achievement..." (Leahy, Lyon, Thompson, & Wiliam, 2005).

This chapter will explore the changes that teachers can make to their practice to bring about this improvement in student achievement. You may already be using the strategies described; in fact, many of them have come from teachers I've had the privilege to work with. Or you may see ways you could adapt some of the strategies to better suit your own students.

Just a note about "assessment *as* learning." This term appears much less frequently in the research. It is, however, frequently cited in Canadian resources.

> *Assessment as learning is a metacognitive process in which students take ownership for improving their own learning. It involves students setting learning goals as well as monitoring, reflecting upon, and adjusting their own learning, often in response to feedback from the teacher and their peers* (Earl, 2003, p. 2).

Before examining what assessment *for* learning looks like in the classroom, let's take a moment to briefly review the impetus for this movement. In a now famous meta-analysis (the findings were published in *Inside the Black Box*, 1998), Paul Black and Dylan Wiliam reviewed more than 250 studies from several countries to determine what assessment practices led to the greatest gains in student achievement.

In a follow-up publication, *Beyond the Black Box,* the following practices were identified as having the greatest impact:

- providing effective feedback to students
- actively involving students in their own learning
- adjusting teaching to take into account the results of assessment
- recognizing the profound influence assessment has on motivation and self-esteem
- recognizing the need for students to be able to assess themselves and understand how to improve (Assessment Reform Group, 1999)

It was also noted that for these practices to be effective, two principles need to be maintained:

1. The practices are not add-ons that involve huge amounts of additional work for teachers; rather, they need to be fully integrated into teaching and learning.
2. The practices need to be implemented in a culture that believes all students can be successful learners.

WHAT DOES ASSESSMENT *FOR* LEARNING LOOK LIKE IN THE CLASSROOM?

Many experts in the field have identified key strategies that correspond to each of the above research conclusions. In my own work, I have seen the greatest gains in teacher efficacy and student response by focusing on six strategies:

1. Communicating learning goals to students
2. Communicating to students the performance standards for assigned work
3. Having students routinely self- and peer-assess their work
4. Ensuring that oral questioning techniques include all students and promote increased understanding
5. Providing individual feedback that informs students how to improve
6. Working one-on-one or with small groups of students to support them in using feedback to improve their work

We will examine each of these in some detail, in the form of questions about our practice. Some of the strategies are simple to implement and can lead to almost immediate improvements in students' time-on-task and engagement. Others are complex and may require teacher training, support from colleagues, and some time to perfect. Keep this advice in mind: think big but start small.

"The aim of assessment is primarily to educate and improve student performance, not merely to audit it.... Once assessment is designed to be educative, it is no longer separate from instruction; it is a major, essential, and integrated part of teaching and learning."

Grant Wiggins, 1998

DO I ROUTINELY SHARE LEARNING GOALS WITH MY STUDENTS SO THEY KNOW WHERE WE ARE HEADING?

This one is easy! Identify and write the learning goal for each lesson on the board (blackboard, whiteboard, or interactive whiteboard). The goal must be brief, relevant, and derived from the mandated curriculum, but worded in student-friendly language. Here are some examples:

- By the end of class, you will understand how perspective is used to create the illusion of depth.
- By the end of class, you will be able to use titration to determine the concentration of an acid or base in a solution.
- By the end of class, you will know the safety rules that must be followed in this machine shop.

Notice that learning goals are *not* activities. They state what students are expected to know or understand, be able to do, or be aware of by the end of the lesson. Teachers can ensure that learning goals are appropriately worded by using one of the following stems:

- By the end of today's lesson, you will be able to…
- By the end of today's lesson, you will know that…
- By the end of today's lesson, you will understand that…
- By the end of today's lesson, you will be aware of…

Learning goals assist teachers and students in a number of ways:

- They assist teachers in managing instructional time by ensuring that essential curriculum targets are taught and learned.
- They assist students by clarifying the purpose for what they will be doing during the lesson.
- They provide the teacher with a focus for instruction as well as an indication of what to assess.
- They assist both the teacher and students as a reminder of what has to be accomplished during a lesson.

Recently, while visiting a secondary school in the United Kingdom that had been working on an assessment *for* learning initiative for almost three years, I asked a group of teachers what changes in their practice had made the most significant difference in their teaching and in student learning. Several of them said that identifying a learning goal for every lesson had made the greatest difference.

▲ A clear learning goal focuses teachers and students on essential learning.

DO I ROUTINELY COMMUNICATE TO STUDENTS THE STANDARDS THEY ARE AIMING FOR BEFORE THEY BEGIN WORK ON A TASK?

In the early 1990s, Grant Wiggins developed a "Student Assessment Bill of Rights." The second of these rights was students' entitlement to "clear, apt, published, and consistently applied teacher criteria in grading work and published models of excellent work that exemplify standards" (Wiggins, 1993, p. 28).

Before students undertake a piece of work that will be assessed, they need to know two things: the criteria to be assessed and the indicators that will be used to assess the quality of student performance, for each criterion. In students' words, they need to know "what are you looking for, and what do I have to do to get a Level 4/Excellent?"

Gone are the days when students achieved high marks by guessing what the teacher was looking for. Criterion-referenced assessments must include clearly articulated statements about quality that are communicated to students *before* they begin work on a task. These statements take several forms, including rubrics, checklists, and anchors. These will be discussed in more detail in Chapter 8: Assessment Tools and Technology, but the following is an overview.

Rubrics

To put it briefly, well-designed rubrics are powerful tools because they can serve as both instructional and assessment tools.

TOOL 5.18

Rubric: Inquiry Investigation

A modifiable version of this tool can be found on the DVD.

Rubric: Inquiry Investigation (partial)

Criteria	Level 1 (Limited)	Level 2 (Fair)	Level 3 (Proficient)	Level 4 (Excellent)
Initiating (Questioning and Hypothesizing)	• asks few questions about the task; questions are vague and unfocused	• asks simple questions that focus the investigation somewhat	• asks questions that clarify the task and focus the investigation	• asks relevant, clear questions about the task
	• demonstrates limited understanding of concepts related to the task	• demonstrates some understanding of concepts related to the task	• demonstrates general understanding of concepts related to the task	• demonstrates a thorough understanding of concepts related to the task
	• unable to generate hypothesis	• generates a questionable hypothesis	• generates a valid hypothesis	• generates an insightful hypothesis
Planning	• develops disorganized or unworkable procedures	• develops a partial set of simple procedures, not all of which are appropriate	• develops an appropriate, complete set of procedures that may lack efficiency or clarity	• develops procedures that are appropriately efficient and complete
	• identifies and controls few variables	• identifies and controls some major variables	• identifies and controls most major variables	• identifies and controls all major variables
Conducting and Recording	• follows few of the prescribed procedures	• follows some of the prescribed procedures	• follows most of the prescribed procedures	• follows all of the prescribed procedures
	• recordings are disorganized and contain major errors or omissions	• recordings are somewhat organized and contain several major errors or omissions	• recordings are organized and contain few errors or omissions	• recordings are organized efficiently and effectively with practically no errors
	• demonstrates required skills and strategies in a limited way	• demonstrates required skills and strategies with some competence	• competently demonstrates required skills and strategies	• demonstrates required skills and strategies with a high degree of competence

SOURCE: *Nelson Science and Technology 7, Pure Substances and Mixtures Teacher's Resource*, 2000

In the above rubric (note that it is a portion only), Level 4 identifies the desired achievement in science inquiry skills. This rubric may be used for diagnostic assessment at the beginning of a semester to determine students' current skill levels so that the teacher can differentiate instruction. It may be used during the semester as an assessment *for* learning tool; this involves informing students about the progress they have made, as well as letting them see what they need to do further to improve their performance. The same rubric may also be used as a summative or assessment *of* learning tool to determine students' skills at the end of a semester.

Checklists

Checklists are most helpful, like the one below, if they are developed from a rubric.

TOOL 5.19

Inquiry Investigation Skills: Self-Assessment Checklist

A modifiable version of this tool can be found on the DVD.

Inquiry Investigation Skills: Self-Assessment Checklist

Name: _____ Class: _____

Place a √ or an X to indicate "yes" or "no" for each question.

Date					
Initiating (Questioning and Hypothesizing)					
Do I understand the task?					
Do I have a testable hypothesis?					
Planning					
Have I developed a clear set of procedures to follow?					
Do I know what variables I need to control?					
Conducting and Recording					
Have I followed the procedures that I set out in my plan?					
Do I know how to perform all the procedures safely?					
Do I know how to use all of the tools, equipment, and materials?					
Have I made enough observations to produce good data?					
Have I recorded the relevant data in an organized way?					

SOURCE: *Nelson Science and Technology 7, Pure Substances and Mixtures Teacher's Resource*, 2000

The preceding checklist was developed by taking the Level 4 indicators—representing exemplary performance—from the science inquiry rubric and turning them into questions that students can use for self- or peer assessment. Checklists are easier than rubrics for students to use reliably, because student assessors simply have to determine whether a given skill was demonstrated; they don't have to decide at what level the skill was demonstrated. By basing the checklist on the Level 4 indicators, we can ensure that students focus on the desired level of performance.

Anchors

Anchors are samples of student work that are "anchored" to the performance levels on a rubric. The term *exemplar* refers to an anchor that reflects work at the highest level on a rubric. Anchors are powerful tools because they show students what the desired product or performance actually looks like. But there are some caveats for using them:

1. Ensure that there are at least two anchors to accompany each performance level.
2. Be open to the possibility of some students achieving at a level beyond the highest-level exemplars.

The first point is critical. With only one anchor per level, students will try to mimic it. And teachers may perceive that only the work that exactly matches the anchor is representative of work at that level. Having two or more anchors per level, and ensuring that they are as different as possible, shows both students and teachers a full range of possible performance for the levels. Secondly, exemplars must not represent a performance ceiling. Students should be encouraged to redefine excellence at the highest levels of achievement.

Developing Performance Standards: Collaborating with Students

Many assessment experts recommend that teachers develop performance standards collaboratively with students (Davies, 2000). I agree that many students will be more committed to achieving targets that they have helped to develop. For example, in Chapter 10, I describe having students observe my "bad" oral presentation, which I followed with a "good" presentation. As a class, we then developed a list of indicators that characterized a quality presentation. This is an excellent strategy for getting students themselves to identify what "quality" looks like.

However, I discourage teachers from spending valuable class time developing complete rubrics with their students. Rubric design is a difficult task and must be done by referring to provincial or state performance standards. Also, as I explain in Chapter 8, careful attention must be given to ensuring that the increments from one level to the next are equivalent across all indicators. We simply can't expect teachers to address all the intricacies of rubrics if they're developing them with students.

In summary, by all means collaborate with students to identify assessment criteria for a product or performance. But for rubrics—develop them with your colleagues, and refer to provincial, state, or local performance standards to ensure alignment.

▲ Rubrics can serve as both instructional and assessment tools. They communicate to students the standards to aim for.

DO I ROUTINELY HAVE STUDENTS SELF- AND PEER-ASSESS THEIR WORK IN WAYS THAT IMPROVE THEIR LEARNING?

Self- and peer assessment are not add-ons or only-for-fun activities that belong only in primary and junior classrooms. Engaging students directly in the assessment process is an essential element of assessment *for* learning. Only by assessing their own work and the work of their peers are students able to internalize the standards for quality work. As long as students are dependent on the teacher to tell them whether their work meets a known standard, they have not learned the most important lesson in assessment: to be able to objectively monitor the quality of their own work and to make adjustments to improve the quality of that work. If students are coming up to me in the classroom and asking, "Mr. Cooper, how did I do?" or "Mr. Cooper, what did I get?" and they really have no idea what I'm going to say, then I have not been successful in my assessment efforts.

Video Clip 6

Peer Assessment (7:57)

My goal as a classroom assessor sounds like this:

Mr. Cooper: So, Ben, how do you think you did on your report?

Ben: Well, Mr. Cooper, according to the rubric, I think my report is a Level 3 overall.

Mr. Cooper: What's your evidence, Ben? Are you sure it's not Level 4?

Ben: No. I did really well on presenting my argument and supporting it with details. But I think my conclusion was weak.

Mr. Cooper: Let's take a look at your conclusion. *[Ben and Mr. Cooper review the conclusion together while referencing the rubric.]* Okay, Ben. What do you need to do to improve this?

Ben: Instead of just sort of repeating my introduction, I need to say what next steps need to be taken—based on my findings—to get more hybrid cars on the road.

Ben has internalized the standards for a quality report and is now able to objectively assess the strongest features of his work, and also identify a weakness. Most significantly, he already has a plan for what he needs to do to improve his work.

Self-Assessment in Mathematics Class: Traffic Lights

In the above scenario, Ben is conducting self-assessment in a one-on-one context with his teacher. But self-assessment can also occur as a whole-class strategy. Pete uses "traffic lights" in all his math classes to constantly monitor students' understanding of new concepts and procedures. As students enter the classroom, they each pick up a "traffic light."

On the day I visited his classroom, Pete used "traffic lights" at the start of a lesson on equivalent fractions, decimals, and percentages to assess his students' prior knowledge. He began the lesson by posing a question to the whole class: *Okay, everyone. Do you know what the word* equivalent *means? Show me your traffic lights.*

Students held up their traffic lights with either the red or green side toward Pete. He scanned the room to get a quick sense of who did and did not know the meaning of *equivalent*. He asked Sarah, who was displaying the green light, to explain the meaning in her own words. Without saying a word, Sarah rotated her sign to the red side. From the pattern of red and green signs, Pete could adjust his planned approach for the whole class, or begin to differentiate instruction for some of his students. At critical points during the lesson, Pete asked students to show their traffic lights so he could see who was understanding the learning and who was struggling.

There are several benefits to this form of self-assessment: students who fear embarrassment find traffic lights to be a risk-free way of letting the teacher know that they don't understand; Pete finds that scanning the room for red and green traffic lights is an easy way to get a quick measure of who "gets it" and who doesn't; Pete has found that traffic lights are an efficient and effective strategy for

"If the results don't get back in time for teachers to adjust instruction, then it's not formative assessment."

W. JAMES POPHAM, 2006

conducting frequent formative assessment checks that enable him to differentiate instruction "on the fly." This is precisely the kind of strategy Dylan Wiliam has in mind when he says that the most effective assessment occurs "minute-to-minute and day-by-day."

Peer Assessment in Music Class: The Fishbowl

I meet many high school teachers who are reluctant to engage students in peer assessment. The most common reasons they give are: "They don't know what to look for"; "They don't take it seriously"; and "They'll just misbehave." These reasons all highlight the need to follow a few simple guidelines:

1. Model for students what effective peer assessment looks and sounds like.
2. Provide opportunities for students to practise the skills of peer assessment.
3. Provide students with simple-to-use, high-quality assessment tools.
4. Focus students' peer assessments only on what has been taught.
5. Make peer assessment part of your weekly routine so that students are able to hone their skills.

During a high school visit, I observed a music class that reflected the teacher's commitment to all of these guidelines. The class was coming to the end of a month-long unit about jazz music. They had learned some of the history of jazz, as well as related musical theory. On the day of my visit, students were sitting in groups of three at electronic keyboards. The teacher, Estelle, introduced a short jazz composition that had three parts to be played simultaneously: a chord progression, a melody, and a riff.

Students practised playing the three parts in unison for about fifteen minutes. Estelle then asked each group to play the piece in turn while the rest of the class listened, ready to provide feedback by using a checklist. Here is some of the feedback delivered to one of the groups:

> *Rachel:* Holly went too fast.
> *Sam:* You all need to listen more to each other.
> *Teacher:* Now, who hasn't given any feedback yet? Tam, tell Emma's group how they did, and remember to be specific.
> *Tam:* Emma's fill was really good. Everyone was in good time.
> *Teacher:* Are you sure about that, Tam? [*Tam hesitates.*] Michael, what did you think about Emma's group?
> *Michael:* They all started out together, then Freddy seemed to get lost, but then they finished together.
> *Teacher:* Good feedback, Michael. Emma's group, do you agree with what Michael said?

Modelling Effective Behaviours/Skills: The Fishbowl

1. *Ask for volunteers to demonstrate the skills to be assessed, e.g., two students to role-play a job interview.*
2. *Ask for two volunteers to be peer assessors of the interview.*
3. *Seat the two students doing the interview in the middle of the room, and the peer assessors in a suitable location for observing and listening.*
4. *Arrange the rest of the class in a circle around the four students in the "fishbowl."*
5. *Have the two students conduct the interview, then ask the peer assessors to provide constructive feedback while referring to a checklist or rubric.*
6. *Following the peer assessment, construct a "Looks like … Sounds like …" T-Chart to identify the indicators of effective peer assessment. Build the chart by asking students in the outer circle what they saw and heard.*
7. *In subsequent class periods, have increasing numbers of students move from the outer observation circle into the "fishbowl" to participate, either as task performers or as peer assessors.*

▲ Peer assessment helps students improve performance.

Afterwards, I had the opportunity to discuss with Estelle some of the approaches she had taken to get the students to this level of peer assessment. Let's use the guidelines to organize what she told me:

1. *Model for students what effective peer assessment looks and sounds like.*
   Estelle explained how she had used the "Fishbowl" strategy to model effective peer assessment for the class.

2. *Provide opportunities for students to practise the skills of peer assessment.*
   The Fishbowl strategy allows for both modelling and practice of peer assessment. Estelle was able to gradually have more of her students move from observing what effective peer assessment looks and sounds like to actually participating in it. Those students who spent the longest time observing rather than participating did so because they had shown they were not yet ready to act responsibly in the role of assessor.

3. *Provide students with simple-to-use, high-quality assessment tools.*
   Estelle uses a simple observational checklist for both self- and peer assessment. Here is a sample describing Level 4 (Excellent) performance. Students are encouraged to set their own performance goals.

Level 4

I can:

- ☐ perform from simple notations
- ☐ maintain my own part with awareness of others
- ☐ improvise melodies and rhythms
- ☐ compose using musical shapes
- ☐ describe, compare, and discuss different kinds of music using musical vocabulary
- ☐ suggest improvements to my own work and others' work

---

4. *Focus students' peer assessments only on what has been taught.*

   Estelle has learned the importance of having students focus on a small set of skills when assessing their peers. These skills are highlighted on the assessment tool that students use during the lesson.

5. *Make peer assessment part of your weekly routine so that students are able to hone their skills.*

   Estelle's students expect to participate in peer assessment regularly; she has made it one of the routines in her class. Only by practising these skills frequently are they able to refine them enough so that their feedback is as helpful as the teacher's.

Let's now explore a peer assessment strategy in a senior academic class. While this particular example took place in an English class, the strategy can be used in all subjects requiring students to write longer expository prose such as term papers, essays, or exam question responses.

Peer Assessment in English Class: The Snowball

Steve was preparing his Grade 12 class for their end-of-semester English Literature examination. It had been some weeks since they had been required to write an extended response to a test or exam question, so a review of their prior knowledge was in order. Time for the "Snowball." Here is a summary of Steve's lesson:

1. Steve conducts a "Snowball" activity to activate students' prior knowledge about writing an effective response to an essay question. He says:

   Take out a blank piece of paper. Think back to the last time you had to answer an essay question. You have six seconds to write down one thing that every good essay response contains. [Steve counts down.] *Six, five…one. Stop writing. Scrunch your piece of paper into a snowball and toss it across the room to another student.* [Steve waits for the chaos to subside.] *Now find one of the snowballs, open up the paper, read what it says, and you have six seconds to write a second thing that every good essay response contains. Six, five…one. Stop writing, scrunch up your paper, and throw it to another student.* [Steve repeats this process twice more.] *Now I want everyone to look at the piece of paper they have in front of them and start calling out the points that are written on it. One at a time, so I can write them on my chart paper.*

   In this way, Steve and his students have reviewed their prior knowledge about the required elements of a good essay response.

2. Steve then consolidates this information on the board.

3. Steve presents a sample question on the board—a question similar to those that will appear on the exam. Then he presents his written response to the question. Next, he invites his students to assess the quality of his response, using the scoring guide, below. Students identify the elements and he underlines them on the board, using the appropriate colours. Then he asks the students to assign a letter grade to his response, based on what has been underlined.

4. Then it's the students' turn. Steve presents a different sample question on the board and tells the students that they have 15 minutes to answer it. As they write, he distributes coloured markers in preparation for the students to peer-assess the responses.

5. After 15 minutes, he tells the students to stop writing, exchange responses with a partner, and use the scoring guide and the coloured markers to assess each other's work.

6. For the last step, Steve tells students to return the marked responses and to discuss the accuracy of the letter grades with their partner. It's important to note that these grades are *not* included in the teacher's grade determination. They are simply practice grades to help students understand more clearly the criteria for an effective response.

Essay Response: Peer Assessment Scoring Guide

- Underline in <u>blue</u> the best sentence. Explain your choice.
- Underline in <u>red</u> the worst sentence. Explain your choice.
- Underline in <u>green</u> a good choice of quotation.   **D**
- Underline in <u>purple</u> a good explanation of the effect of a quotation.   **C**
- Underline in <u>orange</u> a good link back to the question.   **B**
- Underline in <u>pink</u> 3 words you think I'd get excited about.   **A**
- Underline in <u>brown</u> anything you think is correct but that I didn't teach you.   **A+**

Circle the appropriate letter grade.

Teachers can employ this process at different times throughout the term to help consolidate students' understanding of what quality work looks like. And, again, while this example is from an English class, the strategy is appropriate for any academic subject.

Self- and Peer-Assessment Guidelines

We all know that, even for qualified teachers, assessment is challenging, so we can understand that students need a good deal of training if they are to become effective participants in the assessment process. Students need to see effective assessment modelled, they need support as they develop assessment skills, and they need opportunities to hone their skills. The following guidelines help to ensure that these three elements are present.

- **Self- and peer assessment require modelling and training**. The Fishbowl and Snowball activities model what effective practice looks like. In the Fishbowl activity, the teacher relied on just three students to assess three peers while the rest of the class observed what peer assessment looked and sounded like. In the Snowball activity, the teacher guided the class in assessing his essay response by referring to an explicit set of scoring criteria. In both cases, students then attempted to replicate the skills that were modelled while the teacher coached them toward mastery.

- **To be effective, self- and peer assessment require high-quality but simple-to-use tools**. The Snowball activity relied on a simple but specific scoring guide to increase the reliability of students' assessments. Generally, checklists are much simpler tools for students to use than rubrics. A checklist simply requires the student to answer the question "Did I or my peer do what was expected or not?" A rubric requires students to determine whether the desired skill or attribute is evident, and also at what level it is evident; for example, "Was it Level 2 or Level 3?" (See Chapter 8 for more on assessment tools.)

- **Focus assessment on what was taught**. This principle applies to self-, peer, and teacher assessment. Students become overwhelmed and frustrated when they receive marked work that suggests they are doing everything incorrectly! Whether conducting the assessment yourself or having students peer-assess, focus the assessment on only one or two elements at a time. Also, those elements should be the very same ones that have been the focus of instruction. For example, if a French teacher has been teaching students how to correctly use the passé composé in their narratives, then only that skill should be the focus of students' peer assessments.

- **Begin with short sessions**. This principle follows from the need for focus, described above. Self- and peer assessment sessions should initially be very brief—just a few minutes—when students are inexperienced. This will reduce off-task behaviour. As students' assessment skills become more sophisticated, sessions may increase in duration. And, of course, you will need to differentiate the assessment process, based on students' skills and their behaviours. Peer-assessment sessions provide excellent opportunities for teachers to work one-on-one or in small groups with struggling students.

▲ Make peer assessment part of your weekly routine so that students are able to hone their skills.

- **Self- and peer assessment need to be part of your routine**. In this type of classroom, students expect to assess their own or their peers' work, and they understand that the practice can significantly improve the quality of their polished work. We can dramatically improve the quality of work we are to mark by routinely following this simple procedure: On a Work Due Day, say to students, "Okay, you know the routine: take out your assignment and checklist. Work through your assignment step by step, using the checklist to ensure that you have all of the required elements. When you've finished, if your assignment is complete, sign your initials. If it's incomplete, get busy fixing it. If it is complete, have your neighbour check it. If he or she considers it complete, he or she will initial it. If your peer's work is incomplete, explain what's missing, with reference to the checklist. Again, if your partner indicates 'Incomplete,' get busy. René, repeat what I just said, please."

- **Self- and peer assessment must be assessment *for* learning *only*.** At this point I replace my teacher hat with my parent hat and insist that no part of my son's or daughter's grades should be determined by other students. Self- and peer assessment must focus on informing students what they need to do to improve their work; scoring and grading is the teacher's responsibility.

DOES MY QUESTIONING TECHNIQUE INCLUDE ALL STUDENTS AND PROMOTE INCREASED UNDERSTANDING?

Oral questioning is a strategy found in every teacher's instructional toolkit and in classrooms from kindergarten to college and university. In my work, I spend hours sitting in classes, listening and observing as teachers and students engage in the Socratic method. There are several problems that repeatedly catch my attention:

1. Too few students participate.
2. Questions and responses are simplistic and fact-based.
3. The teacher is the focus of attention and is looked to for affirmation.

Let's consider each of these problems and some approaches to take in correcting them.

Problem 1: Lack of Student Participation

Teachers often begin a lesson with a question like this: "Think back to what we did yesterday. What was the most important concept we learned about energy?" At this point, several hands shoot up and the teacher asks for a response from one of this group, whom I call the "'Pick me!' kids." When I ask about the assessment purpose behind this practice, teachers say that they are checking on students' understanding from the previous day's lesson. My response is to ask, "Which students do you need to hear from? The 'Pick me!' kids, or the students who are thinking, 'I hope she doesn't pick me,' or 'She never picks me,' or 'I'll just tune out until she makes us work'?"

The problem with this situation is that very few students are thinking about what was learned yesterday, and the teacher is not gathering useful data about who learned what. The solution is quite simple: the teacher begins the class with the same question: "What was the most important concept we learned about energy yesterday?" but then adds, "No hands! Everyone quickly write down an answer—don't worry about neatness and spelling—and turn to the person beside you to compare your answers. Then form groups of five and compare your answers. In five minutes, I want to hear a spokesperson from each group tell the class what your group concluded about yesterday's lesson. Off you go." The teacher then moves around the class, ensuring that every student is thinking and writing down an answer. Consider the benefits of this slight change in practice:

- All students are held accountable for thinking about their learning.
- Reluctant students, as well as those who may be afraid to offer responses in front of the whole class, can check out their thinking in a safe environment.
- The teacher is able to quickly sample evidence of the learning that occurred during a previous lesson; this may identify a need to review or reteach parts of the lesson for the whole class or for some groups.

Problem 2: Simplistic Questions and Responses

Teachers should consider their purpose carefully when undertaking oral questioning with students. For example, is the purpose:

- to engage students' interest in new material before beginning instruction?
- to assess students' prior knowledge before introducing new material?
- to review what has already been learned before moving ahead with new learning?
- to assess students' critical-thinking skills in response to specific material?
- to consolidate learning at the end of a theme or unit?

Assessment for *Learning*

For each of these purposes, the teacher can adopt a more traditional approach, or what I like to call "The Quiz Show." With this approach, students try to guess what the teacher is looking for. Alternatively, teachers can opt for an assessment-for-learning approach, in which the teacher's role is to facilitate discussion. Let's examine these two approaches as they may play out in the classroom.

The Quiz Show Model: An Example

Teacher: What were the different sources of power we learned about yesterday? Anna?

Anna: Um, I think they were…uh…one was fossil fuel and um…

Teacher: Eric, how about you? What other sources of power are there?

Eric: Nuclear, I guess wind…

Teacher: Yes, so we have fossil fuel, nuclear, wind, hydroelectric, solar, and geothermal. Does anyone have questions from yesterday? No? Okay. For today….

The Assessment for Learning Model: An Example

Teacher: Everyone take one minute to discuss with a partner why yesterday's examination of alternative sources of energy is important to you as a young adult today. [*after one minute*] Could I have a volunteer to share with the class what you and your partner discussed?

Anna: Kim and I said that we all have to be willing to explore other kinds of energy because fossil fuel is going to run out.

Teacher: Thanks, Kim. Is there another group that discussed a different reason?

Eric: We talked about fossil fuels causing climate change and stuff.

Teacher: Thanks, Eric. Are there other groups with reasons different from those identified by Anna and Eric?

The teacher hears from several other groups and then asks each spokesperson to come to the board and write, in point form, their reasons for the importance of yesterday's focus on alternative energy sources. Having encouraged students to make this personal connection between yesterday's topic and their own futures, the teacher goes on to have students identify and discuss the pros and cons of each energy source. This course of questioning begins with facts that the students learned about each energy source, but then moves to students evaluating the advantages and disadvantages of each one. For example:

Francine: Nick and I think that wind power is the way to go because it's the cleanest.

Teacher: Could I see a show of hands for those who agree with Francine and Nick? Elise, I notice you didn't raise your hand. What alternative energy source do you favour and why?

Elise: We said nuclear because we already have lots of reactors.

Such questioning demands critical thinking and encourages students to take a stand on an issue and defend their positions. Far from just guessing what facts the teacher wants to hear, students develop their own positions and understand that they need to support those positions with evidence.

Problem 3: Student Dependence on Teacher

In the Quiz Show model, the teacher's questions are largely about facts that the teacher knows and the students are expected to recount. The skills focus is the ability to memorize. In the assessment *for* learning approach, students are required to discuss their previous learning with a partner. The teacher then asks a series of open-ended questions designed to identify a variety of student perspectives. Each student response is met by further and deeper questions from the teacher. In this way, teachers shift the focus for validation of student responses from themselves to the students. The skills focus is critical thinking and active listening.

Dylan Wiliam uses wonderful metaphors for these two approaches to questioning. In a keynote address ("Using Assessment to Improve Learning," Summer Leadership Conference, Penticton, BC, 2008), he suggested that the first method is like a game of ping-pong. He urges teachers to, instead, adopt a method of questioning that is like a basketball team passing the ball around as they make their way closer to the basket.

How can teachers improve their oral questioning techniques? The first step is to identify the need for improvement. Indicators of poor oral questioning include:

- students' lack of interest and engagement, shown by a lack of participation
- students' body language that says, "Who cares about this?"
- teachers doing most of the talking
- student tardiness and absenteeism

The best teachers of effective oral questioning are your peers. In almost every school I visit, I encounter teachers who are highly skilled in this area. I implore principals to identify these teachers and provide opportunities for them to work collaboratively with their peers. This might involve collaborative lesson planning, observation of the lesson, and debriefing, first by one teacher and then by the other. This provides the opportunity for teachers to receive feedback and coaching from their peers. Such work is truly reflective of a professional learning community (DuFour & Eaker, 1998) in which teachers are constantly examining their practice and exploring ways to improve it.

DO I ROUTINELY PROVIDE INDIVIDUAL FEEDBACK THAT INFORMS STUDENTS HOW TO IMPROVE?

"Feedback from classroom assessments should give students a clear picture of their progress on learning goals and how they might improve.

Feedback on classroom assessments should encourage students to improve."

ROBERT MARZANO, 2006

Video Clip 7

Assessment without Marks (12:24)

Current assessment research is unequivocal in its identification of descriptive feedback as being essential to improving student learning. Dylan Wiliam lists "providing feedback that moves learners forward" as the third of his "five keys to formative assessment" (2007).

Whether feedback is delivered orally or in writing, it must meet several criteria:

■ Feedback must cause thinking, so don't provide students with the "answer." The goal of all assessment is, ultimately, to enable students to be able to assess their own work independently and to make adjustments. To promote such independence, all feedback must cause students to think about what they need to do to improve their work or their learning.

■ Feedback must not be evaluative; feedback is part of the assessment *for* learning process. As such, it is not concerned with judgment; instead, it must be descriptive. The evaluation will occur once the feedback has been acted upon and students submit polished work for assessment *of* learning purposes.

■ Feedback must direct students toward improvement; hence, after identifying what a student has done well and where there are problems, a key question is, "What do you need to do to correct or improve this?"

■ Feedback must make reference to specific quality indicators; a rubric or checklist, coupled with an exemplar, when appropriate, will communicate to the student what quality work looks like. Feedback should include reference to these tools to ensure that the feedback is specific and directs the student toward improvement.

■ Feedback must include an expectation that it will be implemented. All too often we take the time to provide students with lengthy feedback, especially on their written work, but then fail to demand that students act on the feedback to improve their work. This sends two messages to students: the feedback is unimportant, and quality is optional. Instead, students need to become firmly convinced that quality is non-negotiable and that you will keep turning work back to them until it is excellent. Teachers can promote excellence by employing a feedback log (see the following example). This is a chart that includes the date of the feedback and the specific feedback given.

The student fills in the date and where the teacher will find evidence of implementation of the feedback.

Feedback Log		
Teacher Feedback	**Student Use of Feedback**	**Teacher or Student Comments**
p. 5 You are using subordinate clauses as full sentences.	p. 5 I think I fixed the errors. Please check again.	Let's go over this during our conference on Tuesday.

DO I ROUTINELY WORK ONE-ON-ONE OR WITH SMALL GROUPS OF STUDENTS TO SUPPORT THEM IN USING FEEDBACK TO IMPROVE THEIR WORK?

When I talk to teachers about the importance of meeting with individuals or small groups of students either to provide oral feedback or to discuss written feedback, there are usually plenty of nodding heads. But then the hands go up: "How do I make time to meet with students to deliver feedback?" and "What is the rest of the class supposed to be doing while I'm conferencing with individual students?" These questions highlight the need for teachers to match effective assessment strategies with the requisite instructional and classroom management skills. Consider Krista's Mathematics class in the following case study.

"The most powerful single modification that enhances achievement is feedback. The simplest prescription for improving education must be dollops of feedback."

J.A. HATTIE, 1992

One-on-One Conferencing During Homework Take-Up

Krista is teaching a math course for students whose post-secondary destination is the workplace. She knows that many students in her class have conceptual misunderstandings below the grade level and that the misunderstandings vary by student. She has decided to hold frequent one-on-one conferences to ensure that her students master the essential learning of the course. She has created a conferencing schedule that provides three meetings with each student per reporting period. She's found that the best time to do this is while students are taking up homework. Rather than standing at the board and asking students to share their solutions, she pairs students so they can solve problems together and identify difficult problems that neither of them was able to solve. Students may also visit other pairs to see if anyone in the class was able to solve the problems that have stumped them. Any problems that no one was able to solve are written on the board. Students know that they are expected to write their attempted solutions to these problems on the

board so that Krista and the class can examine them after she has held her conferences.

During Krista's one-on-one meetings, she discusses with students their progress in math—any specific difficulties they are having or any issues that have come to light through the assessment data she has been gathering about their learning. At the end of the class, Krista announces which students are scheduled for a one-on-one conference the next day and asks them to think about specific questions or issues they would like to discuss at the conference.

Conferences are typically only two minutes long; Krista knows the importance of meeting with each of her students regularly to monitor their learning. She records key anecdotal observations about each conference using a simple spreadsheet application.

Krista has found that frequent conferencing not only enables her to monitor students' learning effectively, but also helps her compile rich anecdotal data to share with parents and to help her prepare report card comments.

Anecdotal Observations from Conferences

Student	Essential Concepts					Essential Procedures					Notes
	Counting principles	Whole number place value	Decimal place value	Multiplication	Fractional counting and quantity	Skip count by 2, 3, 5, and 10	Counting on from 50+	Partition 3-digit numbers (standard)	Partition (non-standard)	Mult. to 12 x 12	
Evan	√	digit mis-concept				work on 3					assign skip-counting practice for home
Jamie	√	√	whole # thinking			√	√				time on class odometer
Katya	√	√	100ths only			12+ start					likes calculator; encourage use of repeat function for skip-counting practice
Liping	√	√	√	unsure		√	√	√			reseat with Evan, try mult. concept again

USING TESTS AS ASSESSMENTS FOR LEARNING

Consider the following two contrasting responses to the use of test data.

| CASE STUDY 2 | Whajyaget and Howdwedo |

Mr. Whajyaget's Class

Mr. Whajyaget's students wrote a science test last week and he marked their papers over the weekend. It's Monday, and as he returns the tests, students are busy comparing their marks:

> *Samir:* Ethan, what did you get? I bet I beat you!
> *Ethan:* So what else is new? You always do. 18 out of 30. You?
> *Samir:* Yes! I got 27.

Meanwhile, Mr. Whajyaget is cautioning the class, "Check my addition. You know I'm prone to errors when I'm feeling stressed." And, sure enough, several students discover that the total score on their tests is incorrect when they add the scores for each question. After a few minutes, Mr. Whajyaget says, "Okay everyone. Tests away. We're beginning a new unit today."

This is the "I've covered the curriculum; too bad if some of you didn't learn it" approach. With this method, quizzes and tests are simply devices to audit how well students have achieved the intended learning outcomes; they are not analyzed in order to identify next steps for differentiating instruction. The result of using tests in this way is to confirm the view that there are some bright students in the class, some average students, and some weak students. (See Chapter 2.)

Ms. Howdwedo's Class

Ms. Howdwedo has just returned a set of math quizzes to her students. Gradually the volume level increases as students pair up or form small groups and refer to their quiz papers in front of them. As an observer in the class, I'm curious and ask some of the students if I may see their quizzes. "Sure," they say. Much to my surprise, there are no scores to be found anywhere—not for individual questions nor for the quiz as a whole. The only hint of Ms. Howdwedo's marking are circles, in pencil, where students have made errors. Their task during this lesson, I discover, is to work with their peers to figure out where they went wrong and to correct their solutions.

Once her students have corrected all the errors they can, Ms. Howdwedo surveys the class to check which problems no one was able to solve. Clearly, the material relating to these questions requires some reteaching, or perhaps a different approach. In her marks program, Ms. Howdwedo has recorded each student's achieved score on this quiz; however, these scores are merely formative data to help her and her students target specific concepts and procedures they need to work on before next week's unit test—an assessment *of* learning. The scores from the unit test will be factored into students' grades.

At the end of class, I asked Ms. Howdwedo about her approach and, in particular, how she managed to get her students to work so hard to correct their errors when they knew their quiz score, in their words, "didn't count." She told me that the process definitely hadn't gone this smoothly from the start! Initially, students had been ready to mutiny when their quizzes were returned with no scores. She said that she had asked the class, "Do you want quizzes and tests just to tell you what you don't know, or should we turn them into opportunities to improve our learning?" By the time I visited the class, students were in tune with Ms. Howdwedo's approach, because they realized it allowed them to make mistakes and figure out what they had done wrong without fear of being penalized by lower marks.

In the preceding case study, Ms. Howdwedo had to work very hard to turn around the marks-driven culture of her classroom and get the agenda back to the business of learning. Students enter the early grades of school excited by the thought of learning. None of them enter Kindergarten or Grade 1 motivated by scores, percentage grades, or beating their classmates. But all too soon, and in too many cases, students learn that school is not really about learning—it's about racking up maximum points with minimum effort! However, assessment *for* learning holds the promise of refocusing the mission of schools on learning. From my perspective, assessment *for* learning is the most significant change to have occurred in education since I entered the profession more than thirty years ago. In the words of the Assessment Reform Group, "assessment which is explicitly designed to promote learning is the single most powerful tool we have for both raising standards and empowering lifelong learners" (1999).

Motivation without marks? In a secondary school culture that focuses on scores and percentage grades, motivating students to work hard for the intrinsic rewards of learning and improving skills is a significant challenge.

"Does this count?" is the pervasive adolescent query before students set to work on any task. The thinking behind such queries is, "If it doesn't count, either I won't do it or I won't put much effort into it." How are we to respond? Relevance, ownership, and patience are the keys.

AUTHENTIC TASKS

Today's teenagers demand relevance for the work they are expected to do. Grant Wiggins (1998) urges us to strive for authenticity in the tasks that we set for students. Students can sense when their tasks are mere busywork, as opposed to meaningful, purposeful opportunities to demonstrate their learning. When teachers design tasks that replicate real-life challenges, they increase the relevance of those tasks for students. Consider the book report—a timeworn task that many English teachers favour yet few students find either relevant or engaging. But by simply reframing this task as a "book review," the task becomes authentic. In the real world, book reviews are actually written and published. Let's listen in as Sandra introduces this task to her students.

Good morning, everyone. I think you're all close to finishing the novel you chose to read, so I want to introduce the first assessment task related to your reading. You're going to write a book review, suitable for publication in a newspaper or magazine. Now, instead of just providing you with a rubric telling you what to include, I want you to figure out the criteria for yourselves. So your task for today is to work independently to find an online published

▶ Video Clip 4

An Authentic Performance Task: The G7 Summit (14:23)

"Two elements are fundamental: authentic tasks and built-in performer-friendly feedback.... Assessment is authentic when we anchor testing in the kind of work real people do, rather than merely eliciting easy-to-score responses to simple questions.... We thereby learn whether students can intelligently use what they have learned in situations that increasingly approximate adult situations, and whether they can innovate in new situations."

GRANT WIGGINS, 1998

book review. Then you're going to print it out, and meet in groups of four to discuss and compare the reviews. Then I want you to agree on four to six criteria that could be used to assess the quality of a book review. Jaden, could you please summarize what I just said for the class?

There are a number of ways to take traditional yet inauthentic tasks such as the book report and, with some slight revisions, turn them into authentic tasks. Consider these examples:

- Turn collage-making into making a poster that has a clear purpose and audience.
- Turn a science project on the environment into a Global Environmental Summit of world leaders.
- Turn a French oral test into a Paris Sidewalk Café.
- Turn a geometry test into developing a blueprint for a garden shed.

When teachers modify inauthentic assessment tasks to become real-life challenges, students see what they are asked to do as more relevant and worth working hard at. When they work hard at a task they learn more, and when they learn more, they achieve better results. Furthermore, in my own experience, when students are engaged in tasks they perceive to be meaningful, they are much less likely to misbehave or to be truant.

▲ Make assessment tasks authentic and meaningful to students.

Assessment for *Learning*

PATIENCE AND PERSEVERANCE

As we saw in the example of Ms. Howdwedo's "no-marks" test strategy, students' initial reactions were negative. They had come to expect marks for individual test questions, with a summary score at the end. But by explaining her intent to the class and persevering with the strategy, she urged students to realize that her approach actually helped them improve their learning and achieve much better results on the marked tests.

In my English classes, I would encounter students who would say, "If I don't get a mark for my rough draft, I'm not doing it!"

"That's your choice," I would respond. "But I do need to inform your parents that you've told me you're not going to take advantage of the free, in-class coaching that I offer my students. And, in my experience, students who don't come to practise rarely play well in the game, if they get to play at all."

In most cases, those students would eventually approach me—after seeing their peers conferring with me about how to improve their first drafts—and ask whether they could reconsider.

THE IMPORTANCE OF SELF- AND PEER ASSESSMENT

The assessment *for* learning research has unequivocally established that self- and peer assessment is a requirement of an effective learning environment (Black, Harrison, Lee, Marshall, & Wiliam, 2004). We have explored what effective feedback looks like in the classroom, and how it requires the teacher's guidance and students' active involvement. To focus further on roles in assessment, let's examine several reasons why students need to collaborate in the assessment of their learning.

1. The teacher does not have the time to be the only assessor. With secondary school class sizes often exceeding 30 students, teachers cannot possibly provide sufficient attention to each student when conducting assessment *for* learning. Students must acquire the skills to become objective assessors of their own learning so that, gradually, they become able to monitor and adjust their work to achieve the desired performance standard.
2. In order to work independently and effectively after secondary school, whether in the workplace or at college or university, students must have developed the skills of self-assessment. Unfortunately, our over-reliance on teacher assessment in secondary schools can cause students to be too dependent on adult feedback to inform them about the quality of their work.

3. When students are required to self- and peer-assess their work as a routine part of their learning, they are able to internalize the standards for quality work. For example, if a teacher requires students to first self-assess and then peer-assess each major piece of written work before submitting it for marking, the quality of the work will improve. To facilitate this process, I recommend the use of a generic writing checklist such as the following.

If students themselves, or a peer, discover errors or omissions when applying the checklist to their work, then they must be required to improve the piece before submitting it to the teacher. As an English teacher, it took me many years to discover a simple truth: *There was often an inverse relationship between the time it had taken a student to produce a piece of work and the time it took me to mark it.*

<table>
<tr><td colspan="2">Editing/Proofreading</td></tr>
<tr><td>Name: _____</td><td>Term: _____</td></tr>
</table>

Record the date each time you use this checklist.
Make a check mark under the date when you are able to reply "Yes" to the question.

Date

Style

Have I...

- made each paragraph focus on one main idea?
- arranged the sentences in each paragraph logically?
- used a variety of sentence types and lengths?
- varied the rhythm of my sentences?
- avoided sentence fragments and run-on sentences?
- used transitional words and phrases to link sentences and paragraphs?
- maintained a consistent tone appropriate for my purpose and audience?
- used a level of language appropriate for my purpose and audience?
- used figures of speech appropriately and effectively?
- written clearly and concisely?
- acknowledged all outside sources properly?
- checked for redundancy?
- used the correct format for metric units?
- used a consistent style of numbering?

Grammer and Usage

Have I...

- used either first person or third person consistently?
- checked for agreement between subjects and verbs, and between pronouns and their antecedents?
- used a verb tense consistently?
- used active or passive voice appropriately?

SOURCE: *Nelson English, Literacy and Media 11, Teacher's Guide,* 2002

TOOL 5.6

Editing/Proofreading Checklist

A modifiable version of this tool can be found on the DVD.

My students knew that, regardless of the quality of the work they had produced, I would collect it all and mark it. On reflection, this was absurd! When I began to demand quality work from my students—and refused to accept work that did not meet the minimum criteria identified on the

"Damian: Your work was extremely well-received.... One secondary English department made 75% the minimum achievement in all of their classes and are utilizing any number of formative assessment practices to ensure this level of learning occurs."

JILL REID, COQUITLAM SCHOOL DISTRICT, BC

checklist or rubric—the quality improved dramatically. When teachers today ask me if I worried about getting calls from parents when I refused to accept students' work, I tell them that I welcomed such calls, as I welcomed the opportunity to talk to parents about my expectations for their children in trying their best.

4. Students have to rely on critical thinking skills when they are required to assess their own (or their peer's) work to answer, "What was done well, what problems exist, and what needs to be done to improve the work?" Consider the sophisticated thinking that is required to answer these questions. Also consider Bloom's cognitive taxonomy:

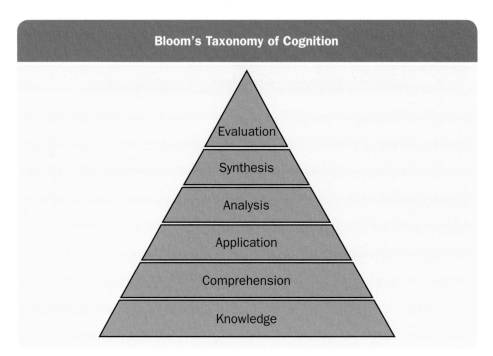

Bloom's Taxonomy of Cognition

Evaluation
Synthesis
Analysis
Application
Comprehension
Knowledge

"Evaluation" sits at the top of the pyramid, above "Synthesis" in terms of the level of cognition required. The more students are expected to think critically about their own work and their peers' work, the more sophisticated their understanding of the attributes of quality work becomes. But for this reason, do *not* require students to score their own or their peers' work. Scoring is the teacher's job. Instead, require students to assess work according to:

■ what is correct, good, or effective
■ what needs improvement
■ suggestions for how to make those improvements

Remember: Involve students whenever possible in assessment *for* learning, but assessment *of* learning is the job of the teacher and the teacher alone.

▲ When students are asked to think critically about their own work and their peers' work, their understanding of the attributes of quality work becomes more sophisticated.

MARKING PRACTICES: EFFECTIVENESS AND EFFICIENCY

Marking consumes hours of most secondary teachers' lives. Yet when I ask teachers, "Does the time you spend marking lead to enough improvement in student work to justify such a commitment?" they invariably say no. Marking strategies tend to be governed more by habit and routine than by purpose and effectiveness. I encourage teachers to examine their marking practices, as well as the results that are reflected in student work, with a view to improving both their effectiveness and their efficiency. Try applying the following questions to your own marking practices:

1. Do I mark in ways that demand my students to think critically about their work, or am I doing the thinking for them? For example, drawing attention to errors by circling them is good practice, but correcting errors for students absolves them of the need to think—and probably doubles your marking time!

2. Do I mark all work, for everything, all of the time, or do I focus on one or two criteria? There is no surer way to discourage students from improving their work than to indicate all the things they have done incorrectly. Teachers need to focus their assessment on one or two criteria at a time.

3. Do I identify errors throughout an entire paper, or do I identify them only on the first page and instruct students to work through the rest of the paper? In my experience of marking long assignments, students tended to make the same errors on the last page as those they made on the first page, yet many teachers painstakingly pore over every page, circling and correcting the same mistakes. This adds endless hours to a marking session and, once again, absolves students from having to think.

4. Do I always mark the same way, or do I mark differently depending on whether the task is an assessment *for* learning (the "practice") or an assessment *of* learning (the "game")? Assessments *for* learning do require analytic assessment; the teacher or a peer identifies specific elements requiring attention. Assessments *of* learning, on the other hand, may be assessed holistically and assigned an overall score.

5. Do I assign a score to assessments *for* learning or do I focus students' attention on feedback? Numerical scores and letter grades communicate to students that a piece of work is over. By using feedback, not scores, on practice work, students come to see such tasks as works in progress that require improvement.

▲ Mark in ways that demand students to think critically about their work; don't do the thinking for them.

Summary

This chapter focused on assessment *for* learning—assessment designed to promote learning, *not* to generate grades. Key points to remember about assessment *for* learning are:

- It is a collaborative process, involving teacher, self-, and peer assessment.
- It helps students take ownership of their learning and understand the standards to strive for.
- It provides students with descriptive feedback that informs them about what they have done well, what needs improving, and how to improve it.

End-of-Chapter Activity

Use the Tool: Implementing Assessment *for* Learning in My Classroom. Examine your current practice by answering the checklist questions on the form. Then use the space provided on the form or use your journal for writing planning notes about changes you can make to implement more of the assessment *for* learning strategies you have read about in this chapter.

Implementing Assessment for Learning in My Classroom

Use the chart below to examine your current practice. Your responses will likely affirm many of the strategies you are presently using, but you may also discover some areas where you may wish to try different approaches to better meet the needs of your students.

After you have finished checking off your responses, describe on this chart or in a journal what you plan to do to include this strategy in your repertoire.

R = Rarely   S = Sometimes   C = Consistently

Do I?	R ✓	S ✓	C ✓	Notes
1. Do I share learning goals with my students so they know where we are heading?				
2. Do I communicate to students the standards they are aiming for **before** they begin work on a task?				
3. Do I have students self- and peer assess their work in ways that improve their learning?				
4. Does my questioning technique include **all** students and promote increased understanding?				
5. Do I provide individual feedback to students that informs them how to improve?				
6. Do I provide opportunities for students to make use of this feedback to improve specific pieces of work?				

TOOL 1.4

Implementing Assessment for Learning in My Classroom

A modifiable version of this tool can be found on the DVD.

CHAPTER SEVEN

TEACHING AND ASSESSING STUDENTS WITH SPECIAL NEEDS

BIG IDEA 1
Assessment serves different purposes at different times; it may be used to find out what students already know and can do; it may be used to help students improve their learning; or it may be used to let students, and their parents, know how much they have learned within a prescribed period of time.

BIG IDEA 3
Assessment must be balanced, including oral and performance as well as written tasks, and be flexible in order to improve learning for all students.

BIG IDEA 8
Grading and reporting student achievement is a responsive, human process that requires teachers to exercise their professional judgment.

This chapter addresses these frequently asked questions:
- *How can I plan effective units when I have such a wide range of students in the same class?*
- *How do I modify my units, and especially my assessments, for students with special needs?*
- *How do I use rubric levels with students with special needs? Should they mean something different?*

IDENTIFYING SPECIAL NEEDS

First of all, which students are we concerned with in this chapter? While many students occasionally struggle with new learning, this chapter addresses the needs of those students who demonstrate pervasive deficits with respect to one or more of the academic and behavioural indicators listed in the following pages. These students are at risk in a "one-size-fits-all" classroom; they will not be successful unless the teacher makes specific adjustments to the curriculum, instruction, and/or assessments that have been planned for the majority of students in the class.

Policy documents categorize exceptionalities as Behavioural, Communicative, Intellectual, or Physical. While I have not endeavoured in this chapter to address the specific needs of students with physical disabilities, or students with specific intellectual disabilities such as Down syndrome, I have tried to address what every secondary teacher needs to know about adapting curriculum, assessment, and instruction to meet the needs of three groups of students who, in my experience, are integrated into the regular classroom in the largest numbers: students with learning disabilities; students demonstrating behavioural disorders; and students whose first language is neither English nor French.

▲ All teachers should know about their local or district integration policies and about adapting curriculum, assessment, and instruction to meet the needs of students with special needs.

STUDENTS WITH LEARNING DISABILITIES

Students with learning disabilities often struggle in the regular classroom, and their difficulties inevitably result in significant discrepancies between their assessed intellectual ability and their academic achievement. These students may struggle in one or more of the following areas: listening, reading, thinking, conceptualizing, speaking, writing, and mathematical computation. Students with learning disabilities often have difficulty following a lesson, contributing to class discussion and activities, and/or working independently on assigned tasks. While it is a common mistake to conclude that students with learning disabilities are "weak students," skilled teachers recognize that with appropriate adjustments to resources, instruction, or assessment tasks, these students can be very successful.

 Video Clip 8

Teaching and Assessing Students with Special Needs (11:55)

STUDENTS WITH BEHAVIOURAL EXCEPTIONALITIES

Students who have been identified with a behavioural exceptionality can cause even the most patient among us to consider a different career! Without adequate proactive planning, they can monopolize our time, distract other students, and, at the end of the day, still have to be dismissed from the classroom, having produced little or no evidence of learning. Students exhibiting a behavioural exceptionality may also have a learning disability. In such cases, the behaviour must be dealt with first since it will preclude progress in academic areas.

ENGLISH/FRENCH LANGUAGE LEARNERS

The numbers of students in classrooms whose first language differs from the language of instruction varies greatly according to geography, with large urban areas naturally recording the highest numbers. For these students, the classroom teacher must simultaneously address language learning as well as instruction in specific subject content. As students' language proficiency increases, they are expected to cope with the more complex concepts and skills associated with the subject area. It is crucial for teachers to recognize that oral language proficiency will develop more quickly than written language proficiency. Hence, they need to allow students to demonstrate their understanding by "saying" and "doing" before they are expected to write about their learning. (See Chapter 4: Assessment *of* Learning.)

STUDENTS' CHALLENGES

All three groups of students typically have difficulty doing one or more of the following:
Academic Tasks

- understanding course materials
- reading required grade-level texts
- remembering and recalling important grade-level subject matter
- demonstrating skills at grade level
- undertaking research independently
- solving open-ended problems and challenges
- communicating their learning orally and/or in writing
- applying their learning to new situations

Behaviours and Learning Skills

- following classroom routines
- listening attentively in order to learn
- adhering to classroom behavioural expectations
- getting started on assigned tasks
- organizing time and materials
- staying on task
- persevering when problems and challenges arise
- working independently on assigned tasks
- working with others
- completing work at home

Of course, what teachers see students demonstrating in the classroom is often a complex interplay of both academic and behavioural deficits. Students experiencing significant academic challenges often resort to inappropriate behaviours, either to mask their difficulties or out of frustration. This is why classroom teachers must work collaboratively with special education resource teachers, parents, educational assistants, and school administrators when seeking solutions to the challenges these students present. Teachers' proactive responses are always more effective than reactive responses. So, as a matter of course, upon receiving their class lists, teachers must immediately acquaint themselves with all the information available pertaining to those students who are identified as having an Individual Education Plan (IEP), Individual Program Plan (IPP), or any other special needs designation.

◀ Students experiencing significant academic challenges often resort to inappropriate behaviours, either to mask their difficulties or out of frustration.

CHALLENGES AND MYTHS IN MEETING DIVERSE NEEDS

You may have noticed that three of the eight Big Ideas of assessment appear at the start of this chapter.

- Big Idea 1 highlights the importance of diagnostic and formative assessment to identify the prior knowledge and skills of students with special needs. Such assessments enable teachers to plan instruction to optimize learning.

- Big Idea 3 reminds us that, when asked to demonstrate their learning, many students with special needs have more difficulty with writing than they do with speaking or doing.
- Big Idea 8 identifies the critical role of the teacher's professional judgment when making grading and reporting decisions about students with special needs.

In today's secondary schools, one might well argue that every teacher needs to be a special education teacher! We saw in Chapter 2 that the purpose of our schools has changed from sifting and sorting students into high, average, and low achievers to ensuring that *all students* acquire the essential knowledge and skills to be productive, responsible citizens of the information age. Similarly, it has become necessary that *all teachers* differentiate their classroom strategies to meet the diverse needs of their students.

The majority of high school teachers I meet want to know: *"How do I differentiate my teaching to meet the needs of the wide range of students I have in my classes?"* Based on my own work, it would appear that most teachers today, regardless of how recently they were certified, have received little training in their pre-service programs on how to differentiate instruction. For those wishing to explore differentiation in depth, I highly recommend the work of Carol Ann Tomlinson (see References, page 254).

STUDENTS' CAPABILITIES: ADDRESSING THE MYTHS

INTU ARTICLE

Integrating Assessment with Instruction through Student-Directed Research Projects can be found on page 246.

Before we explore the assessment and grading issues related to students with special needs, I'd like to dispel a number of myths that continue to thrive in secondary schools. In addition to the following, see my account of the "INTU projects" for convincing evidence that counters many of these myths. As a veteran teacher who has spent much of his career working with students with special needs, I consider my perspective to be well grounded in experience.

Myth 1: These students can handle only simple concepts and will only produce simple work.

Students with special needs will happily tackle complex learning and undertake challenging tasks as long as they perceive such work as relevant to their needs and find such work to be intrinsically engaging. This requires teachers to take the time to discover students' interests and passions and be willing to show flexibility in adapting resources and assessment tasks accordingly. Very often, a student's greatest obstacle to success is a lack of confidence. Hence, the teacher's first tasks at the beginning of a semester are to win the student's trust and to create a supportive environment in which the student's self-esteem can improve. "Success breeds success."

CASE STUDY 1   Vicky

Vicky entered my Grade 9 class showing little self-confidence and convinced she would never be a good writer. The written work she produced during the first two weeks of the semester certainly challenged me, the reader, both in terms of organization and logic. But by encouraging Vicky to write from her strengths—notably fictional narratives about her peer group—as well as spending a great deal of one-on-one time with her to address deficits, she made steady improvement over the first term. The first time Vicky received Level 4 on one of these narratives, she screamed with delight! From that moment on, she wouldn't stop revising, editing, and proofreading each piece of writing until it was rewarded with a Level 4.

Myth 2: These students require everything to be broken down into simple steps.

Not true! Some students will require more scaffolding and some less as they approach more complex, multi-step tasks lasting several days. But providing scaffolding to enable students to undertake complex challenges is very different from believing that they must be spoon-fed and can never progress beyond short, simple tasks. Scaffolding, by definition, is temporary; it is erected to support learning as students acquire new skills but should gradually be dismantled as students develop autonomy.

Myth 3: These students cannot engage in sophisticated thinking.

The truth is that all students need to become proficient in what Robert Sternberg calls "the other three R's: reasoning, resilience, and responsibility" (2008). We do a serious disservice to students with special needs when we limit their learning to simplistic content and workplace preparation. We may, however, find it necessary to expend more time and effort helping these students understand that complex issues involve multiple perspectives; that excellent work usually requires multiple drafts or attempts; and that worthwhile rewards are more often deferred than immediate. Such teaching requires patience and perseverance!

Adam's IEP identified both a behavioural exceptionality as well as a learning disability affecting his writing. After several explosive encounters and one violent incident, I made sure that when assigned any academic task, Adam worked alone and was protected from any potential distractions. During the month-long INTU inquiry projects (see page 246), despite having to do at least twice as much work as his classmates who were all paired with another student, Adam produced an exceptional piece of research about the pit bull terrier controversy in Ontario.

INTU ARTICLE

Integrating Assessment with Instruction through Student-Directed Research Projects can be found on page 246.

Myth 4: These students will not persevere with long-term tasks.

Just as students require scaffolding to undertake complex, multi-step tasks, they also require clear timelines to enable them to meet key deadlines. With a clear timeline posted in the classroom, as well as a copy in each student's daily planner, the teacher must conduct frequent process checks to ensure that students are managing their time efficiently. Furthermore, many students will need to complete most of their work in the classroom. Whatever their exceptionality, many students with special needs will have difficulty completing work outside of the classroom. Teachers can avoid frustration and conflict by acknowledging this reality and accepting that the bulk of the work will occur during class time.

▲ A teacher's first tasks are to win the students' trust and create a supportive environment.

Myth 5: These students cannot be expected to work with others.

They can and must be expected to work with others in productive ways. Granted, these students may require modelling and coaching before they are able to work cooperatively, but these are life skills—and school is one of the best places to learn them.

A strategy such as the "Fishbowl" (see page 101) is helpful because it provides special needs students with the opportunity to observe their peers demonstrating cooperative learning skills before having to demonstrate these skills themselves.

Myth 6: These students cannot be taught to assess their own work.

Once again, they can and must be taught self-assessment skills. But, as stated before, students with special needs may initially require more teacher and peer support. They may also need a modified self-assessment tool. For example, a checklist is a much easier tool to use than a rubric (see page 98). When coaching students in oral presentation skills, I required them to use the following checklist to assess both their own and their peers' work. By modelling how to make objective observations and providing frequent opportunities to self- and peer-assess, students became proficient in using this checklist.

TOOL 5.2

Formal Presentation Checklist

A modifiable version of this tool can be found on the DVD.

Formal Presentation

Name: _____   Term: _____

Record the date each time you use this checklist.
Make a check mark under the date when you are able to reply "Yes" to the question.

	Date										
Are the ideas in my speech creative and original?											
Is the information in my speech correct?											
Are my ideas sufficiently complex to suit my purpose and audience?											
Have I responded to questions with answers that are clear and appropriate?											
Is my opening engaging and does it clearly introduce the topic?											
Have I presented my ideas in a logical sequence?											
Is my conclusion clear and effective?											
Was my audience engaged most of the time?											
Did I choose a level of language that was appropriate for my purpose and audience?											
Was my speech fluent, expressive, and audible?											
Were my gestures and facial expressions appropriate?											
Were my visual elements effective?											
Did I use technology that suited my purpose and audience?											
Did I use language conventions correctly and effectively (i.e., grammar and usage)?											

Summary of Things I Need to Work on

_____

_____

_____

SOURCE: Adapted from *Between the Lines 11 Teacher's Guide*, 2002, p. A9

All students must become autonomous assessors of their own work before they leave high school. As long as students continue to be dependent on the teacher to know if their work meets a desired standard, they have not learned the most important lesson in assessment.

In summary, these six myths are pervasive and can seriously limit educational opportunities for students. Proving the myths wrong requires oodles of patience and flexibility on the part of teachers. But when these students succeed, the rewards are magical!

DETERMINING SPECIFIC NEEDS AND PLANNING PROGRAM

HOW DO I DETERMINE THE SPECIFIC NEEDS OF STUDENTS WITH SPECIAL NEEDS?

Teachers must first communicate with special education resource teachers to familiarize themselves with IEPs/IPPs that may already be in place for these students. But teachers must discover for themselves the strengths and needs that each of these students demonstrates in a given course. This is why I say, "*Spend the first two weeks of a new semester or term having students produce samples of all the different kinds of work they will be expected to do in your course.*" Use these samples to assess each student's current strengths and areas of need. (Note that this process is described in Chapter 5: Initial/Diagnostic Assessment and Differentiated Instruction.)

While we may be tempted to call this strategy "diagnostic assessment," I hesitate to use the term in this chapter. In the past, diagnostic assessment of students with learning/behavioural difficulties often involved subjecting students to a battery of tests during the first week of classes and then analyzing the data to identify those students who would be referred to the special education department. Given the importance of the affective domain—how students feel about themselves as learners—these batteries of diagnostic tests often further damage self-esteem, because they usually provide far more data about students' deficits than about their strengths.

As Big Idea 3 points out, many students know and understand much more than they are able to demonstrate on a written test. Despite time constraints, in order to arrive at a valid sample on which to base instructional decisions, teachers should strive to triangulate data pertaining to each major learning target. (See Chapter 4, page 60, to review learning targets.) That is, they should gather three samples of evidence by having students write, do, and say. (See Chapter 4, page 57, to review triangulation of data.) To gather sufficient data on which to base instructional interventions, the teacher needs to spend some one-on-one time with struggling students. Depending on the subject area, these sessions may include informal discussion, having a student read course material to the teacher, observing a student solve a problem, or asking a student about accomplishments in previous grades, to name a few strategies. Proactive classroom management is a prerequisite to the teacher making productive use of these individual conferences. (See How do I manage my class...? later in this chapter, page 137.)

When analyzing the data from these initial assessments, it is necessary to identify major areas of need demonstrated by groups of students. Then instruction may be planned, including mini-lessons and remedial work, for each group rather than for individuals. (See Chapter 5: Initial/Diagnostic Assessment and Differentiated Instruction.)

▲ The teacher needs to spend one-on-one time with students to gather sufficient data for planning instruction for all types of special needs, including those students working above grade level.

HOW DO I CONSIDER STUDENTS WITH SPECIAL NEEDS WHEN I PLAN MY PROGRAM?

You may wish to review the general principles of "backward design" in Chapter 3: Planning with the End in Mind in connection with this next section.

Managing the Curriculum for Exceptional Students

Lev Vygotsky identified the "zone of proximal development" as the gap between a student's current knowledge and skill and the knowledge and skill the student is expected to demonstrate as a result of instruction (1978, pp. 79–91). He maintained that teachers should optimize learning by ensuring this gap is challenging but not frustrating for the student. For students with special needs, teachers must ensure that they are working at the appropriate grade level. Simply saying, "This is a Grade 10 course so all students have to work at grade level" is to deny the reality of today's classroom. That is, no matter how the teacher may feel about the situation, most classes contain some students who are working at grade level, some who are working below grade level, and some who are working above grade level.

By examining the initial samples of student work, described previously, and by observing and listening to students during the first few weeks of the term or semester, a teacher can identify those students who appear to be struggling. Checking individual student records and talking to special education teachers may shed further light on these initial concerns. Once the teacher has determined that a student is having difficulty with grade-level curriculum material, a clearly defined protocol must be followed to ensure an appropriate match of student with course content. This protocol (see the following section) requires the teacher to ask three questions:

1. Can the student work at grade-level curriculum if I provide accommodations?
2. If, with accommodations in place, the student is still unsuccessful, at what grade level can the student achieve success?
3. (In extreme cases) If the student is unable, by virtue of his or her special needs, to work on prescribed curriculum outcomes at any grade level, what learning outcomes need to be put in place that are appropriate for this student?

Protocol for Matching Course Material to Students with Special Needs

The goal must always be to have all students independently working on and achieving at-grade-level learning targets. When a student is experiencing difficulty, the teacher's first intervention should involve trying one or more *accommodations* to course materials; if the student continues to be unsuccessful, it may be necessary to *modify* the program. *Substituted* learning targets will only be necessary for students with very significant exceptionalities.

1. **Accommodations:** changes made to the materials, instruction, and/or assessments while maintaining at-grade learning outcomes.

Accommodations to course materials may involve a simpler text, fewer problems to be solved, scaffolding to provide more direction, and so on. Accommodations to instruction may include a different learning location, support from a teaching assistant, access to a study buddy, and so on. Accommodations to assessment may include a more structured task, different assessment criteria, and so on.

Consult your local/ provincial/state policy documents for specific interpretations of the terms accommodations, modifications, *and* substitutions.

2. **Modifications:** changes made to the learning targets to enable a student to meet with success.

   Often, this requires the teacher to have the student work on learning targets from a lower grade level, although for gifted students, modification may involve targets at a higher grade level. From an assessment and grading standpoint, it is critical that students and parents are clear about the grade level at which the student is working.

3. **Substitutions:** learning targets are not from mandated provincial or state curriculum but are developed specifically for the student in question.

   Students with very significant learning needs—students who are mentally challenged, for example—may be fully integrated into the regular program but require an individualized program. In such cases, learning targets are developed to meet these needs and are substituted for the learning targets in the designated curriculum.

◀ Analyze diagnostic assessment data in order to group students according to common areas of difficulty.

Francine is teaching a unit focusing on Shakespeare's *A Midsummer Night's Dream* in her Grade 9 English course. Some of the overall learning targets for the course include:

- **Reading for Meaning:** read and demonstrate an understanding of a variety of informational, literary, and graphic texts, using a range of strategies to construct meaning.
- **Speaking to Communicate:** use speaking skills and strategies appropriately to communicate with different audiences for a variety of purposes.
- **Developing and Organizing Content:** generate, gather, and organize ideas and information to write for an intended purpose and audience.

The Ontario Curriculum Grades 9 and 10, English, 2007

While the generic nature and broad wording of these learning targets is appropriate to the wide range of abilities demonstrated by the students in her class, Francine realizes that the play will present a significant challenge to many of them. More specifically, Francine knows that four students will require particular attention as she plans this unit. Alex and Sophie have been formally identified as learning disabled; Lee and Keisha are recent immigrants and are designated English Language Learners (ELL).

Reading: Based on the initial reading assessment she conducted at the beginning of the semester, Francine has decided that Alex, Sophie, Lee, and Keisha will all read an abridged version* of the play. She plans to conduct regular oral reading sessions with all four students while the rest of the class completes assigned work. Francine will clearly communicate to these students and their parents the grade level at which they are able to read successfully. (The abridged version of the play is written at a Grade 5 reading level. A four-level rubric will be used to assess how well each student is able to read the text.)

Speaking: While Alex and Sophie will have no trouble demonstrating the oral language learning targets, Francine knows that Lee and Keisha will require a great deal of coaching and individualized instruction. While they will participate in paired and small group discussions with other students in the class, she will not assess their performance in these situations. Instead she will assess their growing proficiency in oral comprehension, vocabulary, grammar, and oral fluency in conferences with one or two of the students at a time.

Writing: Again, based on the samples of writing gathered at the beginning of the semester, Francine knows that she will have to adapt the writing component of the unit. Here is a list of the written tasks that the class will be required to produce:

1. A series of letters, written in role as one of the major characters. These letters will demonstrate students' understanding of the escalating conflicts and crises as the action develops.
2. A director's description of an alternative staging of the play using a time and place selected by the students.
3. A review of the film adaptation of the play, suitable for publication in a newspaper or magazine.
4. An alternative ending to the play, written either in modern or Elizabethan English.

Francine will modify each of these tasks to suit the current skills and understanding of Alex, Sophie, Lee, and Keisha. For example, she will

---

*Examples of abridged versions are Lois Burdett's Shakespeare Can Be Fun! series: A Midsummer Night's Dream for Kids and David McAleese's Shakespeare Shorts.

provide all four students with a scaffolded version of the letter writing and film review tasks:

Letter Writing in Role (with Prompts)

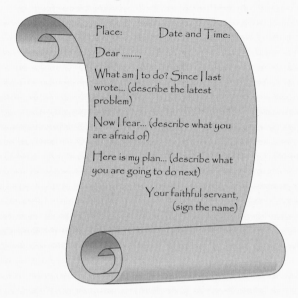

Place: Date and Time:

Dear ....,

What am I to do? Since I last wrote... (describe the latest problem)

Now I fear... (describe what you are afraid of)

Here is my plan... (describe what you are going to do next)

                    Your faithful servant,
                    (sign the name)

For Task 2 (director's description of staging) and Task 4 (alternative ending to the play), Francine will work with all four students in a series of small group sessions to support them in their work. (See Planning and Managing the Differentiated Classroom, page 137.) These sessions will involve the following:

- helping the students understand the task
- brainstorming ideas for each task
- developing a plan to guide their writing
- producing a first draft (etc.)

When assessing the writing produced by these students, Francine will use her experience and professional judgment in responding. Specifically:

1. She will assess each student's work according to how much improvement has occurred

compared with the beginning-of-semester samples. (self-referenced assessment)

2. As soon as is appropriate, she will introduce the rubrics she has designed for each task to assess whether each student is beginning to demonstrate the skills identified in the curriculum. Note: since the overall learning targets are not grade-specific, it is reasonable to expect her special needs students to demonstrate these skills. (criterion-referenced)

3. She will not employ at-grade-level anchors to assess the work of these four students since the pieces they produce are likely to fall far short of the standard for Grade 9 written work.

Francine's approach with Alex, Sophie, Lee, and Keisha is designed to create a supportive, nurturing learning environment in which they can improve their skills and understanding. Her goals for them are to develop independence, proficiency, and understanding that approximate grade-level standards.

From a grading and reporting standard, Francine will provide frequent and ongoing information to the students and their parents about three variables:

1. At what grade level is the student currently working? (curriculum)
2. How well is the student performing on this material? (assessment evidence)
3. How much support is the student receiving? (student independence)

Note that Grading and Reporting for Students with Special Needs, page 143, explores this further.

HOW DO I DIFFERENTIATE MY INSTRUCTION FOR STUDENTS WITH SPECIAL NEEDS?

In my workshops, I describe today's classroom as needing to resemble a three-ring circus! This metaphor reflects the diverse nature of most secondary schools. Teachers cannot hope to have all students learn by delivering a "one-size-fits-all" program. That said, differentiating instruction does *not* mean that teachers have to prepare countless different unit plans, lessons, and assessment tasks for students who have special needs (Tomlinson, 2001).

"Differentiation" means beginning with the same unit plan, lesson, or assessment task and then differentiating each of these according to the needs of groups of students in a given class.

Successful approaches to differentiation begin with students' strengths and extend to gradually address their areas of need. All subject areas include skills that students are expected to acquire as well as content they are expected to know and understand. Students with learning difficulties cannot handle challenging skills and difficult content at the same time. Teachers must clarify whether the focus for a given lesson is conceptual understanding or skill development and differentiate their approach accordingly (Gregg, 2007).

To explain:

- When the learning goal for a student involves developing or improving skills, you may need to simplify the content. For example, when the goal of instruction is to improve a student's reading comprehension through the use of context clues, it is necessary to use material that is well within the student's grasp. Inevitably, this will require selecting material that is below grade level for the course, e.g., a text from an earlier grade. When the content is familiar, the student is able to focus attention on improving the skill.

- When the learning goal is to have a student master essential course content such as a critical concept, allow the student to work in whatever mode is most comfortable. For example, allow the student to view a video and follow it with a discussion with you; or use concrete objects to illustrate the concept of mass when a student is unable to understand through a traditional "read the text and answer questions" approach. When the learning mode is changed to suit the student's strength, a challenging concept is understood more easily.

Let's now look at a method for differentiated lesson design. While the specifics of differentiating instruction can only occur once you've met your students and determined their particular needs, generic strategies can significantly reduce the amount of time you have to spend planning.

PLANNING AND MANAGING THE DIFFERENTIATED CLASSROOM

Step 1: Analyze diagnostic assessment data and ungraded early work samples in order to group students according to common areas of difficulty.

Step 2: Develop mini-lessons to address the specific knowledge and skill deficits exhibited by each group. These mini-lessons may begin with a teacher demonstration of a certain skill, or with a teacher-led examination of student work samples presented on an overhead projector or interactive whiteboard. Alternatively, conduct a teacher-facilitated discussion to clarify a troublesome concept.

Step 3: Orally check each student's level of skill or understanding following the mini-lesson. Draw the other students in the group into your oral questioning to consolidate their learning of the material.

Step 4: Present students with practice questions, tasks, or exercises in which they are encouraged to work collaboratively to consolidate their new or fragile learning. Monitor the success of individuals during this practice work and intervene as necessary. Some in the group will require further one-on-one support to grasp the material presented in the mini-lesson.

Step 5: Have students demonstrate their knowledge or skill independently. Again, monitor each student's readiness to work independently and adjust the amount of support provided to move each student toward autonomous work. Within the mini-lesson group, some students may be ready to rejoin the rest of the class quite soon, while others may need further input from you. As always, monitor and adjust the amount of support you provide each student to help them achieve independent mastery of the skill or concept.

HOW DO I MANAGE MY CLASS WHEN I NEED TO SPEND EXTRA TIME WITH STUDENTS WITH SPECIAL NEEDS?

Effective unit and lesson planning includes the provision of time to work with students who will require differentiated or individualized instruction. For you to be able to work productively with these students, norms of behaviour must be established with the class as a whole at the beginning of a semester and reinforced frequently until they become second nature.

Establishing and Monitoring Classroom Behavioural Norms

It's the first day of a new semester in my Grade 9 French class. Once I've taken care of introductions and essential housekeeping, I invite the class to brainstorm their understanding of the term "Norms for Our Classroom." I use students' ideas to introduce a discussion about my behavioural expectations for them. But I quickly add that they probably have expectations for me, too—returning work promptly; treating them all with respect, and so on. By the end of the period, we've collaborated in the development of the following class norms:

Norms for Our Classroom

1. We will all arrive promptly and begin work immediately.
2. We will treat each other with respect in our words and actions.
3. We will do our best each day to produce high-quality work.
4. We will listen attentively to each other in order to learn.
5. We will take responsibility for our actions and accept the consequences.

Each day, depending on the nature of the work we are doing, I review one or more of the norms with the class. For example, if students are going to be working in cooperative groups, we'll review Norm 4 and we'll also review the "Looks Like/Sounds Like" T-chart that we developed together the day before our first attempt at working with peers.

Active Listening T-Chart

Looks like...	Sounds like...
• eye contact	• one person speaks at a time
• face speaker	
• nod head when you agree	• ask questions to clarify

Every Friday, we hold our Week in Review to monitor how well we performed as a learning community with respect to our norms. I chair the first two meetings of the semester to model the procedure, but the students co-chair meetings for the rest of the semester. The agenda for the Week in Review is very simple:

- What did we do well this week?
- What did we do poorly this week?
- What needs to change next week?

One of the student co-chairs invites the class to make observations in response to these three questions. We have a few simple rules, such as this one: *No student will be identified by name.* For example, if students are commenting on Norm 2, they know that instead of saying, "Justin swore at Emma," the appropriate observation is "Some of us used inappropriate language on Tuesday."

The other student co-chair records observations on the board. Responses to the third question—*What needs to change next week?*—are captured on chart paper and posted as improvement goals for next week.

The combination of prominently displayed classroom norms, daily review of one or more of the norms as a precursor to the day's lesson, and weekly monitoring of our adherence to the norms encourages students to assume responsibility for the learning environment. They realize that the amount of learning that occurs, their level of engagement, and, yes, their enjoyment of the class is more a function of their own behaviours than it is of the teacher's.

When the rest of the class has learned how to manage themselves and their time effectively, teachers find it much easier to work effectively with students with special needs. At the beginning of a new term or semester, small-group and individual conferencing sessions with students with special needs should be brief; they may be lengthened as the rest of the class acquires the necessary attitudes and behaviours to work productively.

HOW DO I DIFFERENTIATE MY ASSESSMENTS FOR STUDENTS WITH SPECIAL NEEDS?

CASE STUDY 5   Introducing a Major Project

Recently, I sat in with a Geography class as the teacher (we'll call her Marisa) introduced an independent research project called "Travelinks," which students would be working on for approximately a week. Marisa distributed a six-page outline of the project and began walking students through the steps in the project. For 25 minutes, she read the outline and explained her expectations. Periodically she paused and asked the class if they had any questions. At each of these points, the same handful of students asked questions—questions that indicated they fully understood the project and couldn't wait to get started! The period ended as Marisa concluded her introduction to the project. Immediately after the class, we met to chat:

> *Marisa:* It gets so frustrating! I just know that half of my students either won't be *able* to do a good job on the project, or else won't be *bothered* to do a good job. It's always the same.
>
> *Damian:* Marisa, it seems to me that you've probably got three groups in your class: the students who can't wait to get started because they've already got great ideas for their projects; a second group that will be ready to get started once they've had the chance to clarify what's required or have had an opportunity to

toss around ideas with their peers; and a third group that haven't a clue where to begin and will require a good deal of support from you before they can even get started.

> *Marisa:* How do you know my class? You were only in there for half an hour!
>
> *Damian:* I'm describing what I call the three-ring circus that characterizes almost every class I visit.
>
> *Marisa:* Really? So what do you suggest?
>
> *Damian:* You need to plan ahead of time—*proactively*. In other words, plan with differentiation in mind instead of being frustrated—*reacting*—when many of your students are unable or unwilling to do the work you've assigned them.
>
> *Marisa:* So what does this kind of planning look like?
>
> *Damian:* When I described your class just now, you weren't surprised, were you? That means you've already gathered evidence—in terms of what students have written, said, and done—to be able to identify the needs of different students in your class. Are there students in your class who have been formally identified and have IEPs?
>
> *Marisa:* Yes, there are five students. Mostly learning disabled, as well as some ADD.

(continued)

Damian: Is it reasonable to assume that those students will be part of that third group that I described?

Marisa: Definitely!

Damian: So here are some suggestions for how to plan a differentiated approach when you introduce a project like "Travelinks":

- First: introduce the project at the beginning of the period so you'll have plenty of time to check that your students with special needs understand what to do—and to explain it further if they don't.
- Second: involve your students in reading and coming to an understanding of what you're looking for. Instead of you reading aloud to the whole class, group students heterogeneously, have them read the project outline in their groups, and then ask for a summary from each group of what you expect them to do. Better still, hand over responsibility for developing research questions to the students themselves, perhaps using the INTU model. (See page 246 for more about the INTU model.)
- Third: if you did decide to introduce the whole project to the class by reading it to them, pause after each section of the project and say, "Take two minutes to discuss this section of the project with a partner and identify any questions that are preventing you from understanding what I want you to do."
- Fourth: rather than asking if *anyone* has questions, check specifically (and unobtrusively) with the students who typically struggle with assigned work whether *they* understand what you're asking them to do.

Might I be correct in thinking that all of the questions that were asked last period came from your most capable students? (At this point, Marisa smiled and nodded!)

Marisa: And I guess I could use this approach whenever I introduce a project?

Damian: Exactly. The key to differentiation, without sacrificing your sanity, is to develop generic processes and templates, such as I've just described, and use them as a routine part of your practice. You don't want to be reinventing the wheel. Furthermore, share these generic approaches with colleagues so that you can support each other by sharing the workload.

IS IT FAIR TO OTHER STUDENTS IF I DIFFERENTIATE ASSESSMENT FOR STUDENTS WITH SPECIAL NEEDS?

In his book, *Fair Isn't Always Equal: Assessing & Grading in the Differentiated Classroom* (2006), Rick Wormeli invites teachers—and indeed students—to question the status quo in many high school classrooms. As we saw in Chapter 2, I constantly encounter teachers who insist, "It's not fair to students who were successful on their first try if others get to do the assignment or the test over again!" Such thinking is an artifact of the "sift and sort" function of schooling—a mission that is no longer acceptable in the information age. In today's schools, where producing high-quality work must be a requirement, not an option, teachers and students must redefine the concept of fairness. "Fair" does not mean that the teacher covers the material once, in the same way for everyone, and then tests student understanding once, in the same way, for all students. "Fair" must be redefined as "equity of opportunity." And because different students have different strengths and needs, instruction, assessment, and grading must be responsive to these differences. Who among us would complain "It's not fair!" when we learn that our neighbour had to take his or her in-car driving test three times before passing it? It's the contrary; we are more likely to insist that our neighbour continue to practise and take the test as many times as it takes in order to become a proficient driver with whom we must share the road!

Such thinking must become the norm in all of our classrooms—classrooms where different students are at different places in their learning, are perhaps practising different skills, are receiving different levels of support—but classrooms where *all* students are working toward an agreed-upon set of essential skills and enduring understandings that have been clearly articulated and communicated to them and their parents.

WHAT ROLE DOES THE EDUCATIONAL ASSISTANT PLAY?

The educational assistant (EA) performs a key role in today's integrated classroom. This role must be clearly defined to ensure that the EA *supports* students in their quest to learn but does not unintentionally distort the assessment picture that emerges by *completing* work for the student.

Darlene is assigned to work with several students who are fully integrated into the regular program. The following case study outlines what she shared with me about her perspective on her role.

▲ The educational assistant (EA) performs a key role in today's integrated classroom.

Darlene Bowles, from the Simcoe-Muskoka Catholic District School Board, Ontario, explains her role:

I see my role as Educational Assistant as having several key responsibilities:

- I assist the teacher in delivering the curriculum, or a parallel curriculum, for students with special needs.
- I assist with orchestrating social environments that will enable these students to develop friendships.
- I model and initiate coping strategies to decrease students' anxiety in the classroom.
- I suggest instructional tools that will enhance students' confidence, facilitate their learning, foster understanding of concepts, and lead to significant accomplishments.

Ultimately, my role is to support the development of these students so they can become more independent.

As an educational assistant, I do not have the depth of knowledge of course content possessed by the teacher. But I can assist the teacher by suggesting how to present course material in a modified format. This may involve accommodating or modifying expectations, chunking information, lowering the level of vocabulary, or producing simplified notes that students can read and use to follow along with their peers. As a team, the teacher and I have strengths in different areas, and by working together we can foster a sense of belonging and promote success for all students in the classroom.

At the beginning of each semester, I meet with the teacher whose students I will be assisting. At

this time, I become familiar with the course outline, as well as the specific materials to be taught. We also discuss any novels, movies, assignments, and course culminating tasks that may need to be modified. From there, I share with the teacher my knowledge of the students' interests, strengths, and needs. I also introduce and demonstrate any computer programs that may assist in delivering the program to the students in question. We discuss how such programs may promote students' attention and understanding. Planning ahead is really the key to everyone's success in the end; it reduces frustration for the teacher, for the educational assistant, and, most importantly, for the student.

The use of technology has become such an important tool for so many students; it assists them in developing the essential skills that can make the difference in succeeding alongside their peers in the classroom. Here are some of the common challenges that can be met by the use of technology:

- ***fine motor challenges:*** using adaptive technology may be the only way a student is able to commit thoughts and ideas to paper.
- ***spelling challenges:*** these can seriously jeopardize a student's ability to create a sentence or paragraph. Using word-prediction software, the student can become more independent, and this in turn builds self-esteem.
- ***reading/vocabulary/studying challenges:*** Kurzweil is a software program that enables the student to independently scan a set of notes, a novel, or a test given by the teacher. The program reads the material, highlights words, facilitates the student's

answering questions, and then generates a printout for the teacher to assess.

- **brainstorming and organizing ideas:** this is a complex set of skills. By using webbing software that utilizes graphic organizers, students are supported as they generate ideas for paragraphs, stories, and longer projects.

In addition, PowerPoint software is a wonderful tool for introducing a unit since it allows for the importing of visuals that promote understanding for all students. It provides an easy-to-use substitute for traditional cue cards and enhances student creativity. It also fosters interaction between students and the teacher.

As I observed Darlene working with her students, her dedication and passion were evident in the strategies she employed as well as in her interaction with the students. But just as important was her unwavering commitment to developing the independence of the students.

GRADING AND REPORTING FOR STUDENTS WITH SPECIAL NEEDS

The biggest trap that educators fall into when communicating about learning with students with special needs and their parents is to confuse effort with achievement. When teachers are fearful about further damaging students' self-esteem, they often assign grades that reflect how much effort the student has demonstrated, despite the fact that little achievement is evident. In other cases, a student may have received significant support in order to accomplish a task, yet the assigned mark and anecdotal comment make no mention of this. The result in each case is miscommunication as reflected by invalid grades: neither the student nor the parent has clear or accurate information about what the student has accomplished. And, as a teacher who has worked with eighteen- and nineteen-year-olds who, though they were bright, could neither read nor write, I can assure you that a *true* sense of self-esteem never comes from a *false* sense of achievement!

Students with special needs know when they are being rewarded for merely trying hard, and they also know when they have been socially promoted. Our goals when assessing, grading, and reporting on the achievement of all students must be accuracy, clarity, simplicity, and transparency.

I sometimes begin my workshops by asking teachers to identify the number-one burning issue that they would like me to address during our time together. Inevitably, the question, *How do I grade the achievement of special education students?* is among the issues identified. Related questions that are usually raised include:

- Do I need to use different rubrics for students with special needs?
- How can an A, a B, or a C mean the same thing for my students with special needs as it does for my other students?

Assuming that a standards-based, criterion-referenced grading structure is in place, there are a number of key principles that will help clarify all grading questions relating to exceptional students:

Principle 1: Performance standards, as represented by rubric levels, letters, and percentage grades must represent *consistent measures* of achievement for *all* students.

Principle 2: The curriculum *grade level* at which a student is working must be clearly communicated to the student and parents.

Principle 3: The amount of *support* provided to enable a student to achieve success on a given task or during a term must be made clear to the student and must be communicated to parents. (See Chapter 9: Grading and Reporting.)

To better understand these principles, we need to review the distinction between content standards and performance standards. Content standards comprise the curriculum—the concepts and skills that students are expected to acquire. Performance standards measure *how well* students have learned these concepts and skills as demonstrated through various assessment tasks. Performance standards are communicated through tools such as rubrics and scoring guides, as well as report card grades. Think of a performance standard as the equivalent of a metre stick: we cannot change its length! To do so would render it useless as a measuring device. It's the same with rubric levels and grades; if we change what these symbols mean, depending on which students' achievements they are used to describe, we render them useless. Instead, we must ensure that the curriculum grade level—the content standards—on which a student is working is appropriate to his or her current knowledge and skills. In other words, we adjust the content standards, *not* the performance standards.

Whether the student is working at grade level or below grade level, the teacher must also document how much support the student requires to achieve success. Support may include more in-class assistance than other students are receiving; it may involve the scaffolding of an assessment task (e.g., a series of prompts to simplify a problem-solving task); or there may be other interventions deemed necessary by the teacher to enable the student to succeed. But because the ultimate goal of teaching must be to have students work independently, the degree of support provided must be documented to inform the student and parents about progress toward this goal.

Summary

In this chapter, we focused on three groups: students with learning disabilities, students with behavioural disorders, and English Language Learners. We stressed the need for early assessment of these students in order to identify areas of need that can be addressed in our instruction planning. We examined some myths about students with special needs to dispel the idea that "special needs" automatically means limitations. A differentiated classroom—and differentiated assessment—means being responsive to students' different strengths and needs, while maintaining the integrity of course content. As with all learning environments, the goal is to have students develop understanding, proficiency, skills, and independence.

End-of-Chapter Activity

Focus on one of your students with special needs and complete this form: Classroom Observation of a Student with Special Needs (pictured below, and included on the DVD). Once you have completed this task, determine how effective you were in assessing that student's strengths and needs based on what you saw and heard. You might also consider these activities:

- Reread the case study of the educational assistant (page 142) and assess your current or past understanding of the EA's role and responsibilities. Identify changes you wish to make regarding the respective roles you and EAs play in working with your students.

- Working from an existing unit of study, use the strategies described in this chapter to differentiate the unit for an individual or a group of students with similar needs.

Classroom Observation of a Student with Special Needs

Complete the following anecdotal record for one of your special needs students. When finished, determine how effective you were in assessing that student's strengths and needs, based on what you saw and heard.
To maximize the reliability of your observational assessment, complete this record during the first few days that you are working with a student. Repeat the process periodically throughout the term.

Name: _____   Class: _____   Date: _____

Observations and Notes

Response to texts:	Response to assigned tasks:
Persistence with tasks:	Organization (self, time, materials):

TOOL 1.5

Classroom Observation of a Student with Special Needs

A modifiable version of this tool can be found on the DVD.

6. Assessment is a collaborative process that is most effective when it involves self-, peer, and teacher assessment and when it helps students to be reflective learners who take ownership of their own learning.

7. Performance standards are an essential component of effective assessment. In a standards-based system they must be criterion-referenced (absolute), not norm-referenced (relative).

8. Grading and reporting student achievement is a responsive, human process that requires teachers to exercise their professional judgment.

GATHERING EVIDENCE AND COMMUNICATING ABOUT LEARNING

Grading and reporting practices must be carried out according to school or district policies. This section offers guiding principles and approaches to ensure that grading and reporting procedures are fair, responsive, and consistent.

Chapter 8: Assessment Tools and Technology looks at a range of assessment purposes and corresponding tools. It includes an examination of effective rubrics. This chapter also provides an overview of current technology, such as handheld devices, and their potential for facilitating assessment. Rubric templates appear in the Tools section of the DVD.

Chapter 9: Grading and Reporting examines performance standards and how to communicate them to students and parents. It also offers practical guidance on methods for scoring student work and determining grades.

CHAPTER EIGHT

ASSESSMENT TOOLS AND TECHNOLOGY

> **BIG IDEA 6**
>
> Assessment is a collaborative process that is most effective when it involves self-, peer, and teacher assessment and when it helps students to be reflective learners who take ownership of their own learning.

> **BIG IDEA 7**
>
> Performance standards are an essential component of effective assessment. In a standards-based system they must be criterion-referenced (absolute), not norm-referenced (relative).

WHAT IS AN ASSESSMENT TOOL?

This chapter addresses these frequently asked questions:

- *How do I know when to use a rubric and when to score work in a more traditional way?*
- *How do I know if the rubrics and checklists I use are of high quality?*
- *Can new digital, hand-held devices make assessment more efficient?*

An assessment tool is any device that enables an assessor—teacher or student—to assess the quality of a given task or performance. Rubrics, checklists, and scoring guides are all assessment tools. Assessment strategies, on the other hand, are the actual tasks and performances that students are required to undertake. They include projects, assignments, tests, role-plays, debates, and so on. The chart on the next page illustrates some common assessment strategies and their corresponding assessment tools.

▲ Communicating performance standards to students is an essential component of effective assessment.

Common Assessment Strategies and Corresponding Tools

Assessment Mode and Strategy	Purpose for Assessment	Assessment Tool
Oral Communication • Conference • Informal discussion • Oral questioning	• Provide feedback on work • Assess skills (e.g., reading) • Assess depth of understanding	Anecdotal record/Rubric
Performance Assessments • Skills demonstration • Design project • Inquiry/investigation • Media product • Simulation • Presentation • Role-play	• Assess level of performance of skills • Assess application of knowledge and skills • Assess depth of understanding • Assess understanding and communication skills	Checklist/Rubric/ Rating scale Checklist/Rubric

Written Assignments
 	
• **Quizzes/Tests**
  – selected response
  – short answer
  – extended response
 	
• **Graphic organizers**
  – mind map
  – word web
 	
• **Extended writing**
  – article
  – personal essay
  – expository essay
  – review
 	
  – journal
 	
  – portfolio
	
	• Assess knowledge
	
	• Assess knowledge and understanding
	
	• Assess depth of understanding
	
	• Assess depth of understanding
	
	• Assess understanding and communication skills
	• Assess metacognition
		
		Scoring guide
		Scoring guide
		Marking scheme
		
		Rubric
		
		Rubric/Checklist

Assessment Tools and Technology

Assessment tools are of critical importance to both teachers and students. A good assessment tool enables a teacher to gather and record data about how well a student performs on a given task. As we saw in Chapters 4, 5, and 6, such data may be used for diagnostic, formative, or summative purposes. But a well-designed assessment tool, such as the one below, also communicates to students the standard of quality that is required for an assessment task. In other words, an effective assessment tool such as a rubric or scoring guide tells students what criteria will be assessed by the task, as well as "how good is good enough" for each of these criteria.

Rubric for Desktop Digital Video				
Criteria	**Level 1 (Limited)**	**Level 2 (Fair)**	**Level 3 (Proficient)**	**Level 4 (Excellent)**
Understanding of video production techniques	• video reflects a **superficial understanding** of production techniques	• video reflects a **partial understanding** of production techniques	• video reflects a **solid understanding** of production techniques	• video reflects a **deep understanding** of production techniques
Quality of video	• video reflects **ineffective or inappropriate use** of available software	• video reflects **somewhat effective use** of available software	• video reflects **appropriate use** of available software	• video reflects **innovative and highly effective use** of available software
	• video has **limited** visual elements, textures, and colours	• video has **somewhat effective** visual elements, textures, and colours	• video has **effective** visual elements, textures, and colours	• video has **highly effective** visual elements, textures, and colours
Use of equipment and images	• showed **limited understanding** of appropriate equipment use	• showed **fair understanding** of appropriate equipment use	• used equipment **appropriately**	• used equipment **expertly**
	• showed **limited understanding** of security and fairness issues	• showed **some understanding** of security and fairness issues	• showed **solid understanding** of security and fairness issues	• showed **deep understanding** of security and fairness issues
Communication	• **had difficulty** in creating a storyboard	• created a **somewhat effective** storyboard	• created an **effective** storyboard	• created a **highly effective** storyboard
	• provided **superficial documentation** of the stages of production	• provided **partial documentation** of the stages of production	• provided **solid documentation** of the stages of production	• provided **thorough documentation** of the stages of production

▲ Students need to know the standard of quality that is required for an assessment task.

As students work on their video projects in Information and Communications Technology, as represented in the preceding rubric, they know they must pay attention to the four criteria: demonstrating understanding of the techniques taught in the unit; the quality of their video; ability to use equipment and images correctly; and their ability to plan and document the stages of their video, in writing. Furthermore, they know that each of these criteria must be demonstrated at Level 3 or above to meet the expected performance standard.

Teachers often point out that words such as *appropriately* and *somewhat effective* are vague, and that is why they feel the need to quantify all indicators on a rubric. This is the wrong approach. (See Rubrics Are Qualitative Assessment Tools, later in this chapter, page 162.) The solution is to discuss the rubric with students when a task is introduced, and also to discuss samples of student work reflecting the levels, in order to clarify understanding about quality work.

In all but one of the rubrics presented in this chapter, the achievement levels run from low to high. I acknowledge that many teachers find it more beneficial to use a high-to-low format. My rationale here is simply a matter of consistency. Note that the rubrics on the DVD are modifiable, and you can reverse the order to suit your own preference.

TYPES OF TOOLS: PURPOSES, PROS, AND CONS

As part of the assessment planning process, teachers need to match assessment strategies with the appropriate tools. For example, short-answer tests require a scoring key; students can use checklists to ensure that they have met all required elements before submitting their work for marking; complex performance tasks require rubrics for adequate assessment; anchors plus rubrics help students understand the targets they are aiming for, and also help to improve the reliability of teachers' assessments. The chart on the next page lists the most commonly used assessment tools and includes the pros and cons associated with their use.

Assessment Tools: Purposes, Pros, and Cons

Assessment Tool	Purpose	Pros (+) and Cons (−)
Anecdotal record—ongoing written observations about students' progress, collected over time	tracks growth in specific skills by highlighting areas of strength and need	+ useful for providing detailed information to students and parents − time-consuming
Anchors—student work samples that correspond to the performance levels set out in a rubric **Exemplars**—samples within the anchor set that represent the expected standard or quality	when used in conjunction with a rubric, help teachers and students see what a set of performance standards look like in practice	+ provides teachers and students with models of quality work − can limit student creativity if used inappropriately or if only one sample is provided for each performance level
Checklist—a list of specific skills to be demonstrated during a performance task or attributes required in a product	used for self-, peer, or teacher assessment; determines whether a specific performance or product contains all of the required elements	+ makes expectations clear to students; effective and reliable for self- and peer assessment − informs students about deficits but not how to improve
Frequency scale—a scale used to measure how frequently a desired behaviour or attribute occurs	used to inform students how frequently they demonstrate a required behaviour or exhibit a desired attribute	+ efficiently assesses behaviours and learning skills − inappropriate if quality rather than quantity is the variable to be scored
Rating scale—a scale that assigns a numerical value to one or more assessment criteria	used to inform students of the extent to which they met a criterion	+ efficiently matches a score to a desired criterion − does not inform students how to improve
Rubric—a set of criteria and performance indicators arranged according to expected levels of performance	communicates to teachers, students, and parents what is expected in a given performance or product before it occurs; is also used to assess the quality of the performance or product once it has been completed	+ clarifies for teachers, students, and parents what quality work looks like − poorly written rubrics may focus on quantity as opposed to quality − can limit the range of student performance if poorly written
Scoring guide—a precise explanation of how marks are awarded for specific questions on a test or for specific performance indicators on a product	used to increase the reliability of marking; may also be used to clarify expectations for students	+ fosters discussion among teachers about their expectations for quality work − can narrow the possible range of student responses

WHAT KIND OF TOOL TO USE, WHEN

Different types of assessment generate different kinds of information about student learning. For example, consider the following quiz. It yields data on whether students have memorized facts about electric, gravitational, and magnetic fields. A scoring key is used to determine the number of correct responses and to generate a numerical score. The student's knowledge in this case may be quantified and expressed as a fraction such as 14/20.

Physics Electrostatics and Waves Quiz

Name: _____

Part A: Quantity Warm-up [8 marks]
Fill in the non-shaded areas of the following table with appropriate information.

Quantity	Description	Related Equation	Units
			N•s
			eV
Voltage or Electric Potential			
Electric Field			

Part B: Fill In the Blanks [6 marks]
Fill in the blanks in each question with the appropriate text or numerical answer.
1. Radio waves travel at the speed of light. Travis is listening to WPHY (96.3 MHz on the dial) and is 300 km away from the radio transmitter.
   a) The wavelength of the radio waves is _____. [1]
   b) The number of wavelengths that fit between the transmitter and Travis is _____. [1]
2. Sulogna is in a satellite at an altitude of 300 km above the earth's surface. ($m_{SATELLITE}$ = 2200 kg). Assume that the satellite is motionless and just about to fall!
   a) The gravitational potential energy of the satellite is _____. [1]
   b) The amount of total energy needed to escape orbit is _____. [1]
3. Chris and Shane create a longitudinal wave in a Slinky. One wave is comprised of a compression and a _____. [1] After much experimentation, they find that the only factor that affects the speed of the wave is _____. [1]

Later in the unit, however, students may be asked to complete a complex performance task in which they design an experiment to illustrate either Coulomb's law or Newton's law of universal gravitation. This kind of task calls for the use of a rubric like the following to clearly identify for students the criteria to be assessed and the desired level of performance for each criterion.

Rubric: Physics Fields Laws Experimental Design

Criteria	Level 1 (Limited)	Level 2 (Fair)	Level 3 (Proficient)	Level 4 (Excellent)
Application of the universal law(s) in the experimental method	• experimental method has only a limited connection to the physical phenomena being explored	• experimental method has some connection to the physical phenomena being explored (e.g., demonstrates or measures some, but not all, quantities involved in the law)	• experimental method has a considerable solid connection to the physical phenomena being explored and demonstrates all quantities involved	• experimental method is highly connected to the quantities in the law being explored and strongly demonstrates the relationship between them
Use of scientific vocabulary	• terminology and conventions are used with limited effectiveness, such that the experiment is difficult to understand	• terminology and conventions are used with some effectiveness, providing some clarity in the experiment	• terminology and conventions are used with considerable effectiveness, contributing to a clear description of the experiment	• terminology and conventions are used with a high degree of effectiveness, contributing to a succinct and clear description of the experiment

Assessment Tools and Technology   **153**

A rubric is a qualitative tool, not a quantitative tool. While it's true that a rubric may be used to generate one or more levels of performance according to a four-point scale, the richness of a rubric is in the descriptive indicators for each level. These descriptors inform students about their current strengths as well as the areas needing improvement. A well-constructed rubric, then, is as much an instructional tool as an assessment tool.

As a reporting period approaches, teachers are usually required to combine quantitative and qualitative data into an overall grade. But that is a grading challenge, not an assessment issue. The point I am stressing here is that different assessment tasks yield different kinds of data.

How do teachers know whether a given task should be assessed quantitatively or qualitatively? In other words, "How do I know when to use a rubric?" Common sense and experience both come into play to answer this question. In workshops I say to teachers, "*If you can score a task numerically, using a 'total out of …' score and feel confident about defending such scores, then do so. If, on the other hand, you find yourself asking 'How can I score this task reliably and with confidence using a numerical score?,' then you probably need a rubric.*"

The figure below shows the relationship among curriculum targets, assessment tasks, and assessment tools. Notice that the more important the curriculum target, the more complex the assessment task, and the greater the likelihood that a rubric is the appropriate assessment tool.

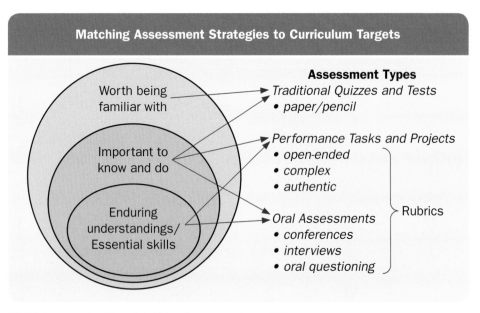

SOURCE: Adapted from Grant Wiggins & Jay McTighe, *Understanding by Design*, 1998

In my early years as a high school English teacher, I lived in fear of students or parents demanding that I defend the percentage scores that I assigned to lengthy essays. The fact is, I could not have explained why one paper received a 73 percent and another a 75 percent! Had rubrics been available to me back then, I would have felt much more confident about the marks I assigned.

CASE STUDY 1	**Completeness and Quality Require Different Assessment Tools**

Recently, I was chatting with a high school social studies teacher about problems he was having with assessment. Here is part of our conversation:

Andrew: Damian, I'm having problems with the rubric that I'm using to assess written reports in my History classes. On the rubric, students get a Level 3 if most of the elements I'm looking for are included. But the hardest-working students who always include everything that's required are discouraged by this. Any ideas?

Damian: It's critical that you distinguish between assessing work for **completeness**—in other words, inclusion of all of the required elements—and the **quality** of the work reflected in each of those elements.

Andrew: How do I do that?

Damian: For these reports, you need to explain clearly to your students that all the required elements of the report must be included before they can be considered ready for marking by you. To do this, give students a "Yes/No Checklist" that identifies all the required elements. Before students submit the reports to you for marking, ask them to independently check their reports for completeness. Then have them get a peer to check the report for completeness. Then, and only then, are the reports ready for you to assess. And your assessment will be to determine the **quality** of the reports, given that the students themselves have already assessed for **completeness**. This is one simple strategy to convince students that a report is not even acceptable unless all the required elements are there.

Andrew: So just to clarify, the checklist is used by the students—first self, then peer—to check for completeness. Then I use the rubric to assess for quality, right?

Damian: That's it. Let me know if this approach makes a difference.

Following are a rubric and corresponding checklist. Students use the checklist every time a personal or persuasive essay is due. Before submitting their work, they use the checklist, first for self-assessment, followed by a peer assessment, to determine whether their essay meets all the required criteria. This simple classroom strategy, when implemented routinely, can dramatically improve the quality of work submitted to the teacher for marking.

TOOLS 5.7 & 5.8

Personal/Persuasive Essay Rubric and Checklist

Modifiable versions of the tools on the next page can be found on the DVD.

Assessment Tools and Technology

Rubric: Personal/Persuasive Essay

Note: Select only those categories/criteria that are appropriate to the assigned task.

Categories/ Criteria	Level 1 (Limited)	Level 2 (Fair)	Level 3 (Proficient)	Level 4 (Excellent)
Knowledge/ Understanding	• demonstrates **limited** understanding of information, ideas, concepts, or themes	• demonstrates **some** understanding of information, ideas, concepts, or themes	• demonstrates **solid** understanding of information, ideas, concepts, or themes	• demonstrates **thorough and insightful** understanding of information, ideas, concepts, or themes
	• stylistic devices are **lacking** or **ineffective**	• stylistic devices are **somewhat** effective	• stylistic devices are **effective** (e.g., use of exaggeration, repetition, parallelism)	• stylistic devices are used **artfully**
Thinking/Inquiry	• includes **little** information to support main ideas/personal interpretations	• includes **some** information to support main ideas/ personal interpretations	• includes **sufficient** information to support main ideas/personal interpretations	• includes **rich and detailed** information to support main ideas/personal interpretations
	• **has difficulty** analyzing and synthesizing ideas and information, and communicating them	• analyzes ideas and information in **simple** ways, and communicates them	• **analyzes** ideas and information, synthesizes them, and communicates them	• analyzes ideas and information in **insightful** ways, synthesizes them **skillfully**, and communicates them

SOURCE: ADAPTED FROM *NELSON ENGLISH LANGUAGE AND WRITING 11 TEACHER'S GUIDE*, 2002

Student Self-Assessment Checklist for Personal/Persuasive Essay

Name: _____ **Term:** _____

Record the date each time you use this checklist.
Make a check mark under the date when you are able to reply "Yes" to the question.

	Date										
Have I demonstrated a solid understanding of the information, ideas, concepts, or themes in my text?											
Have I used stylistic devices that are effective (e.g., exaggeration, repetition, parallelism)?											
Have I included sufficient information to support the main ideas and personal interpretations in my essay?											
Have I analyzed and synthesized ideas and information, and communicated them?											
Have I anticipated alternative viewpoints?											
Have I explained the relationship between a personal viewpoint and the culture or society to which one belongs?											
Have I compared different ideas, concepts, or themes?											
Is the logic of my argument consistent?											
Is my thesis clearly stated?											
Does my conclusion summarize my thesis effectively?											
Is the overall organization of my essay effective (e.g., effective transitions within and between introduction, body, and conclusion)?											
Have I used diction, tone, and language level that is appropriate for my audience and purpose?											
Have I used language conventions correctly and effectively (i.e., spelling, grammar, usage, and mechanics)?											

SOURCE: ADAPTED FROM *NELSON ENGLISH LANGUAGE AND WRITING 11 TEACHER'S GUIDE*, 2002

TASK-SPECIFIC AND GENERIC RUBRICS

You may remember that in Chapter 1, I identified the two goals that drive my work:

Goal 1: To ensure that assessment benefits all students.

Goal 2: To assist teachers in making their assessment practices more effective and more efficient.

Many teachers feel overwhelmed by the sheer amount of assessment they feel compelled to do. One factor contributing to this problem is the profusion of different rubrics teachers may be using. This raises the question of whether it is preferable to use generic or task-specific rubrics. A generic rubric may be used to assess a wide variety of similar tasks; for example, a generic rubric for assessing student understanding may be used in any subject area.

Teachers using generic rubrics are able to manage with a relatively small number of rubrics to assess the full range of complex tasks for a given course. Students benefit when the same rubric is used by teachers of different subjects to assess similar skills—they are more likely to "hit the target when it stays still," to paraphrase Rick Stiggins. The only drawback to this approach, for both teachers and students, is the lack of precision in describing the attributes of quality work.

Partial Generic Rubric for Assessing Knowledge and Understanding				
Criteria	**Level 1 (Limited)**	**Level 2 (Fair)**	**Level 3 (Proficient)**	**Level 4 (Excellent)**
Knowledge	• demonstrates limited knowledge of key facts and terms	• demonstrates some knowledge of key facts and terms	• demonstrates sufficient knowledge of key facts and terms	• demonstrates thorough knowledge of key facts and terms
Understanding	• demonstrates limited understanding of key concepts, principles, and theories	• demonstrates some understanding of key concepts, principles, and theories	• demonstrates sufficient understanding of key concepts, principles, and theories	• demonstrates thorough understanding of key concepts, principles, and theories

A task-specific rubric, such as the partial rubric on the following page, is designed to assess only one task. The problem for teachers favouring task-specific rubrics is the need to have a much larger number of assessment tools. And while task-specific rubrics communicate to students a more precise performance target, students, too, may become overwhelmed when presented with a separate rubric for each assessment task.

Partial Task-Specific Rubric for Assessing Knowledge and Understanding: Political Systems

Criteria	Level 1 (Limited)	Level 2 (Fair)	Level 3 (Proficient)	Level 4 (Excellent)
Define the political system; give examples	• definition shows a limited understanding of the political system • gives only a few examples, with limited effectiveness	• definition shows a fair understanding of the political system • gives some examples, with some effectiveness	• definition shows a solid understanding of the political system • gives sufficient, appropriate examples	• definition shows a thorough understanding of the political system • gives several insightful examples
Explain and illustrate the structure of the political system	• explains the structure of the system to a limited extent	• explains the structure of the system in some detail	• explains the structure of the system in detail and illustrates it	• thoroughly explains the system in great detail and provides a highly effective illustration of it
Explain how the political system works	• has difficulty explaining how the system works	• explains fairly well how the system works	• clearly explains, with details, how the system works	• thoroughly explains, with insightful illustrations, how the system works

So what is the answer to this apparent dilemma? As a compromise between the two approaches, I recommend that teachers use a small number of well-crafted generic rubrics that may be customized to suit the demands of a specific task. This is accomplished by adding task-specific examples to the generic rubric, as shown in the following example.

Generic Rubric for Assessing Knowledge and Understanding with Task-Specific Examples

Criteria	Level 1 (Limited)	Level 2 (Fair)	Level 3 (Proficient)	Level 4 (Excellent)
Knowledge	• demonstrates limited knowledge of key facts and terms	• demonstrates some knowledge of key facts and terms	• demonstrates sufficient knowledge of key facts and terms; *e.g., defines characteristics of each political system; uses all key terms such as democracy and autocracy correctly*	• demonstrates thorough knowledge of key facts and terms
Understanding	• demonstrates limited understanding of key concepts, principles, and theories	• demonstrates some understanding of key concepts, principles, and theories	• demonstrates sufficient understanding of key concepts, principles, and theories; *e.g., explains how a political system emerges and evolves using specific examples from Europe in the 20th Century*	• demonstrates thorough understanding of key concepts, principles, and theories

Note that it is not necessary to provide examples at all levels; the generic qualifiers serve to differentiate achievement at each level. Teachers could produce large versions of their generic rubrics, laminate them, and display them prominently in the classroom. When a specific task is introduced, class discussion can lead to customizing the rubric, using markers or sticky notes. Alternatively, teachers could project the generic rubric using an interactive whiteboard or data-projector and insert the task-specific examples during a class discussion.

▲ Rubrics for assessment tasks should be displayed prominently or distributed to students.

ANALYTIC AND HOLISTIC RUBRICS

Rubrics are often classified as being either *analytic* or *holistic*. Typically, an analytic rubric has several distinct criteria; for example, a Planning criterion is handled separately from a Communicating criterion. Each criterion is accompanied by a set of indicators that describe levels of performance for each criterion. Holistic rubrics, on the other hand, contain a general set of indicators for each achievement level. They don't indicate levels of performance for each criterion; they indicate a level of performance based on multiple criteria. Most of the rubrics used in this book are analytic, and most teachers use this type more frequently than the holistic.

The following is an example of an analytic rubric for a scientific inquiry.

Rubric: Scientific Inquiry				
Categories/ Criteria	**Level 1 (Limited)**	**Level 2 (Fair)**	**Level 3 (Proficient)**	**Level 4 (Excellent)**
Questioning/ Hypothesizing	• has difficulty generating hypothesis	• generates a questionable hypothesis	• generates a valid hypothesis	• generates an insightful hypothesis
Planning	• identifies and controls few variables	• identifies and controls some variables	• identifies and controls most major variables	• identifies and controls all major variables
Conducting/ Recording	• follows procedures in a limited way	• follows procedures with some competence	• competently follows procedures	• selects and follows appropriate procedures
Analyzing/ Interpreting	• provides limited analysis of data	• provides some analysis of data	• provides sufficient analysis of data	• provides rich analysis of data
Communicating	• has errors that interfere with communication	• has some errors but not sufficient to interfere with communication	• has minor errors	• has few, if any, errors

The following is an example of a holistic rubric. Holistic rubrics are often too vague and generic to be used to coach students toward excellent performance—and that is not their intended purpose. Furthermore, they typically do not isolate individual traits but instead feature an overall description of each performance level. They are often used to score large-scale assessments. The following example is from a provincial writing assessment.

HOLISTIC WRITING RUBRIC

5	4	3	2	1
This writing has a strong central focus and is well organized. The organizational pattern is interesting, perhaps original, and provides the piece with an introduction that hooks the reader and carries the piece through to a satisfying conclusion. The writer has chosen appropriate details and established a definite point of view. Sentences are clear and varied. Word choice is appropriate. If there are errors in mechanics, they are the result of the student taking a risk, with more complex or original aspects of writing.	This writing has a clear and recognizable focus. A standard organizational pattern is used, with clear introduction, transitions, and conclusions. A point of view is established and a sense of audience is clear. The writer has used appropriate details, clear and correct sentence structures, and specific word choices. The few errors in mechanics do not impede communication or annoy the reader unduly.	This piece of writing has a recognizable focus, though there may be superfluous information provided. The organization pattern is formulaic, and may be repetitive, but is clear and includes a basic introduction and conclusion. The point of view is clear and consistent. The word choices and sentence structures are clear but not imaginative. The mechanics show less effort and attention to proofreading than in the high levels.	This piece of writing has an inconsistent or meandering focus. It is underdeveloped and lacks a clear organization. Incorrect or missing transitions make it difficult to follow. There may be an introduction without a conclusion, or the reverse, a conclusion with no introduction. The point of view is unclear and there are frequent shifts in tense and person. Mechanical errors interfere with the reader's understanding and pleasure.	This piece of writing lacks focus and coherence. No organizational pattern has been chosen and there is little development of the topic. Point of view may shift in a confusing way. Mechanical errors are abundant and interfere with understanding. The piece must be read several times to make sense of it. It is not apparent that the writer has cared to communicate his or her message.

SOURCE: Adapted from *English Language Arts 10 Teaching and Learning Strategies Writing: Assessment of Writing*, Saskatchewan Education

Teachers generally do not need separate analytic and holistic rubrics. It is preferable to have a rubric that can be used analytically when coaching students (assessing *for* learning), and holistically when conducting assessment *of* learning. Such multi-purpose rubrics strike a balance between being too vague or too detailed. The following is part of a rubric for assessing an oral presentation.

Partial Rubric: Formative Assessment of an Oral Presentation

Criteria	Level 1 (Limited)	Level 2 (Fair)	Level 3 (Proficient)	Level 4 (Excellent)
Communication of Ideas	• ideas are few, simple, and lack clarity	• ideas are clear and simple	• ideas are clear, original, and reflect some complexity	• ideas are clear, original, and sophisticated
	• audience is indifferent	• audience is occasionally engaged	• audience is engaged	• audience is moved
	• little evidence of adapting vocabulary to situation and audience	• vocabulary is usually appropriate to the situation	• vocabulary is appropriate to situation and audience	• vocabulary is skillfully selected to match situation and audience
	• responses to questions are insufficient	• responses to questions are brief and/or insufficient	• responses to questions are clear and complete	• responses to questions are thorough and insightful

The indicators that the teacher observed during one student's first attempt have been circled. You could use this rubric during a one-on-one conference to point out to the student areas of strength and areas needing improvement. This would be using the rubric *analytically*. Because the feedback is formative, you would not need to summarize the assessment into an overall score.

The same rubric is used much later in the term when the teacher needed to determine a summative score for the same performance. This time (see below), the teacher looked at the pattern of observations and asked (while recognizing that the performance did not fall exclusively into one level): *What set of indicators best captures the overall level of performance at this time?* This is using the same rubric *holistically*. In this case, the teacher uses professional judgment and determines that Level 3 represents the most consistent level of performance for this student at this time.

TOOL 5.1

Formal Presentation Rubric

A generic, modifiable rubric similar to the ones on this page can be found on the DVD.

Partial Rubric: Summative Assessment of an Oral Presentation

Criteria	Level 1 (Limited)	Level 2 (Fair)	Level 3 (Proficient)	Level 4 (Excellent)
Communication of Ideas	• ideas are few, simple, and lack clarity	• ideas are clear and simple	• ideas are clear, original, and reflect some complexity	• ideas are clear, original, and sophisticated
	• audience is indifferent	• audience is occasionally engaged	• audience is engaged	• audience is moved
	• little evidence of adapting vocabulary to situation and audience	• vocabulary is usually appropriate to the situation	• vocabulary is appropriate to situation and audience	• vocabulary is skillfully selected to match situation and audience
	• responses to questions are insufficient	• responses to questions are brief and/or insufficient	• responses to questions are clear and complete	• responses to questions are thorough and insightful

Assessment Tools and Technology

RUBRICS ARE QUALITATIVE ASSESSMENT TOOLS

As explained earlier, I consider well-designed rubrics to be qualitative tools—meaning, a rubric is necessary only when the product, process, or performance to be assessed is complex, involving multiple criteria. Such complex tasks—rich problems in mathematics or science, design projects in technology, drama productions, visual arts products such as paintings and sculptures, and so on—all require the assessor to make professional judgments using sets of descriptors or "performance indicators" associated with several levels of performance ranging from "novice" to "expert." It is a serious mistake to believe that all of the valued attributes or "criteria" for such assessments can be scored with 100 percent accuracy according to an absolute scale. In the words of Dylan Wiliam:

> *The trouble with such 'objective' approaches is that while many things can be measured, there are also many important things that cannot, and the danger is that the things that can be measured easily come to be regarded as more important than those that cannot.... We start out with the aim of making the important measurable, and end up making only the measurable important....* (Wiliam, 2001).

Video Clip 9

Common Assessments and Collaborative Marking (16:57)

Assessment using rubrics is an activity undertaken by human beings, examining complex performances, products, and processes generated by other human beings. It requires professional judgment and will always include measurement error. Such error may be reduced by ensuring that rubrics are of high quality and by teachers participating in shared or "moderated marking." In this process, teachers of the same course design a common assessment task for students to undertake. The teachers then meet to assess the work. They engage in blind marking, in which student names are replaced by codes. This reduces the possible impact of bias. Using a rubric, the teachers first separate student work into "satisfactory" and "unsatisfactory" piles. The "satisfactory" work is then separated into "high" and "low" piles. Finally, if a four-level rubric is being used, the "highs" are separated into Level 4 and Level 3 work, while the "lows" are separated into Level 2 and Level 1 work. By engaging in moderated marking once or twice a year, teachers can significantly increase the reliability of their assessments.

All too often I encounter rubrics that include the least important yet most easily measured attributes of a task. Why? Because many teachers, fearing that their assessments will be challenged by students and their parents, create rubrics that enable them to quantify each of the criteria. The following rubric illustrates this problem. Students were assigned an authentic task in Art class that required them to write a review of a show at a local gallery. The review was intended to appear in a newspaper or magazine. The task included conducting research into the artist whose work was displayed; hence the references to concepts, technique, and style. The "thesis" refers to the student taking a position with respect to the significance of the artist's work. There is no separate mark allocation for the thesis, since students were instructed to develop their argument throughout the review. Consequently, the task was "marked out of 40."

Art Show Review Rubric 1							
Parameter	**A+ A**	**B**	**C**	**D**	**E**	**Mark**
Evidence of research (of artist's concepts, techniques, style)	about 8 pieces of evidence				2 or less pieces of evidence	/15
Understanding/use of art terms and vocabulary	about 8 clear examples					/15
Style and organization	very clear, concise					/10
Defence of thesis	well-defended argument					
TOTAL						/40

A more appropriate rubric for this task is shown below. This "qualitative" tool describes levels of performance for each criterion, instead of merely "quantifying" them. Furthermore, the rubric serves as an instructional tool, because the descriptors coach students toward excellent performance.

Art Show Review Rubric 2				
Criteria	**Level 1 (Limited)**	**Level 2 (Fair)**	**Level 3 (Proficient)**	**Level 4 (Excellent)**
Evidence of research (of artist's concepts, techniques, style)	• review shows limited evidence of research • provides few references to concepts, techniques, and style, and the references are random and unclear	• review shows some evidence of research • provides some references to concepts, techniques, and style, to some effect	• review shows clear evidence of research • provides effective references to concepts, techniques, and style	• review shows very strong evidence of research • provides insightful and sophisticated references to concepts, techniques, and style
Understanding/ use of art terms and vocabulary	• shows limited understanding of art terms and vocabulary	• shows some understanding of art terms and vocabulary; uses some terms inappropriately	• uses art terms and vocabulary effectively and appropriately	• uses art terms and vocabulary expertly
Style and organization	• review shows limited clarity and organization	• review reflects some clarity and organization	• review is clear and well organized	• review shows high degree of clarity and is very well organized
Defence of thesis	• thesis lacks support	• thesis is supported to some extent	• thesis has sufficient support and reasoning	• thesis is strongly supported with insightful reasoning

*Generic Rubric for
Mathematical Thinking,
Inquiry, and Problem Solving*

A generic, modifiable tool
similar to the one below
can be found on the DVD.

DIFFERENT VARIABLES FOR PROCESSES, PRODUCTS, AND PERFORMANCES

Rubrics need to be designed according to the demands of the assessments to which they apply. Learning processes such as inquiry and problem solving require rubrics that allow for the assessment of students' skills over time. Following is a Process rubric that is designed to assess improvement over time in students' mathematical problem solving.

	Rubric: Mathematical Problem Solving			
Criteria	**Level 1 (Limited)**	**Level 2 (Fair)**	**Level 3 (Proficient)**	**Level 4 (Excellent)**
Think: Understand the Problem	• shows **limited** understanding of the problem (e.g., is unable to identify sufficient information or to restate problem)	• shows **some** understanding of the problem (e.g., is able to identify some of the relevant information but may have difficulty restating the problem)	• shows **complete** understanding of the problem (e.g., is able to identify relevant information and to restate the problem)	• shows **thorough** understanding of the problem (e.g., is able to differentiate between relevant and irrelevant information and is able to rephrase the problem)
Plan: Make a Plan	• shows **little or no evidence** of a plan	• shows **some evidence** of a plan	• shows evidence of an **appropriate** plan	• shows evidence of a **thorough** plan
Do: Carry Out the Plan	• uses a strategy and **attempts** to solve problem but **does not arrive at a solution**	• carries out the plan **to some extent**, using a strategy, and develops a **partial and/or incorrect solution**	• carries out the plan **effectively** by using an **appropriate** strategy and **solving the problem**	• shows **flexibility** and **insight** when carrying out the plan by **trying** and **adapting**, when necessary, **one or more** strategies to **solve the problem**
	• shows **little evidence** of revising plan when necessary	• shows **some evidence** of revising plan when necessary	• shows **strong evidence** of revising plan when necessary	• revises plan in **insightful ways**, if necessary
	• use of procedures includes **major errors and/or omissions**	• use of procedures includes **several errors and/or omissions**	• use of procedures is mostly correct, but there may be a **few minor errors and/or omissions**	• use of procedures includes **almost no errors or omissions**
Review: Look Back	• **has difficulty** identifying either errors or omissions in the plan or in the attempted solution	• shows **some ability to check** the plan and attempted solution for errors and/or omissions	• **checks** the plan and solution for procedural errors and omissions	• **thoroughly reviews** the plan and solution for effectiveness of strategies chosen and for procedural errors and omissions
	• draws **faulty** conclusions based on **insufficient** evidence	• draws **partial** conclusions based on **some** evidence	• draws **appropriate** conclusions based on **sufficient** evidence	• draws **thoughtful** conclusions based on **all available** evidence
Communicate	• provides a **limited** explanation of the strategy/solution that **lacks clarity** (e.g., uses very little mathematical language; makes **very little** use of mathematical representations—models, diagrams, graphs, tables)	• provides a **partial** explanation of the strategy/solution that shows **some clarity** (e.g., uses some mathematical language correctly; makes **some** use of mathematical representations—models, diagrams, graphs, tables—as required, as necessary)	• provides a **complete** and **clear** explanation of the strategy/solution (e.g., uses mathematical language correctly; makes **appropriate** use of mathematical representations—models, diagrams, graphs, tables—as required, as necessary)	• provides a **thorough, clear**, and **insightful** explanation of the strategy/solution (e.g., uses precise mathematical language correctly; makes **most appropriate** use of mathematical representations—models, diagrams, graphs, tables—as required, as necessary)

Notice that a Process rubric includes indicators that describe what *students* are doing. Furthermore, because Process rubrics are designed to assess skills, the variables that are reflected in the indicators across the performance levels relate to growth in skills. These variables include mastery, fluency, frequency, and ability to self-monitor.

Rubrics designed to assess the quality of products and performances should focus on the attributes of those *products* and *performances*, *not* on the students producing them. Following is a Product rubric illustrating this important principle.

TOOL 5.26

Rubric: Creating a Web Page

A modifiable version of the tool below can be found on the DVD.

Rubric: Creating a Web Page				
Categories/ Criteria	**Level 1 (Limited)**	**Level 2 (Fair)**	**Level 3 (Proficient)**	**Level 4 (Excellent)**
Content and Clarity	• information presented is **limited**, with **excessive use** of graphics	• information presented is **somewhat effective**, but with **too much dependence** on graphics	• information presented is **appropriate** and **to the point**, with **appropriate** use and number of graphics	• information presented is **thorough** and **highly relevant**, with **thoughtful** use and number of graphics
	• page **lacks** simplicity and clarity, with an overly "busy" look	• page **has some degree of** simplicity and clarity, but is somewhat "busy"	• page is **effective** in its simplicity and clarity	• page is **highly effective** and **inviting** in its simplicity and clarity
Consistency of Elements	• shows **limited consistency** in style of background, format, and colour throughout the whole	• shows **some consistency** in style of background, format, and colour throughout the whole, **with some randomly chosen elements**	• shows **consistency** in style of background, format, and colour throughout the whole, **with appropriate and effective variation**	• shows high degree of consistency in style of background, format, and colour throughout the whole, **with creative and highly effective variation**
Understanding of Structure/ Navigation	• shows **limited** understanding of effective structure and navigation	• shows **some** understanding of effective structure and navigation; site is **somewhat difficult** to navigate	• shows **strong** understanding of effective structure and navigation; site is **easily navigable**	• shows **thorough** understanding of effective structure and navigation; site is **easily and intuitively navigable**
Audience and Conventions	• word choice, level of language, and design elements reflect a **limited sense** of the intended purpose or audience	• word choice, level of language, and design elements **attempt to suit** the purpose and audience	• word choice, level of language, and design elements are **appropriate** to the purpose and audience	• word choice, level of language, and design elements are **very well suited** to the purpose and **highly appealing** to the audience
	• **has a high number** of errors in grammar and spelling	• has **three to four** spelling or grammar errors	• has **one or two** spelling or grammar errors	• has **no** spelling or grammar errors
	• **few** resources are documented properly	• **most** resources are documented, with **some errors**	• resources are documented with **only one or two errors**	• **all** resources are documented **thoroughly and correctly**

The variables that differentiate the levels on a Product or Performance rubric include work quality, depth of knowledge demonstrated, and suitability to purpose.

▲ Developing and refining rubrics needs to be an ongoing, year-to-year process.

Q'S AND A'S ABOUT RUBRICS

Here are the questions I am asked most frequently about rubric design and use, as well as my typical responses:

Q. – Who should create rubrics?

A. – Rubric development requires a high degree of assessment literacy. Few teachers have had the opportunity to learn the skills necessary for developing high-quality rubrics. Unfortunately, many of the rubrics appearing in published resources are seriously flawed. So the short answer to this question is "assessment experts with bags of classroom experience." That said, when teachers collaborate on the design of a rubric, levels of assessment literacy can soar. Hence, when either developing a rubric or selecting rubrics developed by others, teachers should use the Rubric Checklist on page 170 to assess their quality.

Q. – Should I develop rubrics with my students?

A. – It is worthwhile to have students identify the criteria for a complex assessment task before they begin work. This requires students to think deeply about the essential elements of the task and thereby better understand the demands of the task. For example, engage students in a class discussion about the essential elements to consider when designing a backyard deck, prior to assigning this task in math or building technology class. However, I strongly advise against having students develop the indicators for each criterion. Such work is complex, time-consuming, but, most importantly, demands a deep understanding of the gradations of performance from *Novice* to *Expert* or from *Limited* to *Excellent*. These decisions require a thorough understanding of local, provincial, or state performance standards.

Q. – Should students use rubrics to assess their own work?

A. – Yes, but with two caveats. First: self- and peer assessment should only be for the purposes of "assessment *for* learning" (see Chapter 6). Second: checklists are much simpler for students to use than rubrics. Train students to self- and peer-assess their work using a checklist before expecting them to use a rubric.

Q. – How can I make my assessment less subjective when it is based on a rubric?

A. – Assessment of complex tasks will always include measurement error and will always require a degree of professional judgment. Collaborating with other teachers in developing a rubric will lead to greater understanding of and agreement on those criteria that are difficult to define. Collaboration must include the examination of student work samples. Yes, this does present a "chicken-and-egg" problem insofar as students should have the rubric before they work on the task. The solution? The developing and refining of complex assessment tasks and rubrics needs to be an ongoing, year-to-year process—but it has to start at some point. (See also the explanation of moderated marking, on page 162 in this chapter.)

> **Video Clip 9**
>
> *Common Assessments and Collaborative Marking* (16:57)

Q. – Doesn't a rubric limit what students are going to produce by telling them what I'm looking for?

A. – Not if the rubric is well designed, and if it contains performance indicators that are clear, without being overly prescriptive. What's more important is that students need to see two or more anchors that represent work at the upper levels on the rubric. The anchors for a given level must be as different as possible to communicate to students the full range of work deemed to meet that level. Tell your students that there is no ceiling to excellence; some of them may redefine what it looks like on a given task.

Q. – How do I know if the rubrics I'm using are of a high quality?

A. – Apply the Rubric Checklist (see page 170) to each of the rubrics you are planning to use.

Q. – How do I know if the levels I assign to student work are accurate?

A. – This question is about standard-setting. First of all, teachers of the same course need to collaborate in the development of rubrics. Through their experience and the examination of student work samples, they need to discuss and reach agreement regarding the range of "acceptable" or "passable" performance for a given task. (Depending on the rubric to be developed, "work samples" may include video footage of processes, products, or performances.) They then need to agree on the gradations or levels of performance within this range, with the highest level representing superior achievement and the lowest level representing what is minimally acceptable. Once a rubric has been developed, it requires validation through classroom use to verify that it does, in fact, represent the intended range of performance. This field testing may lead to the revision of some or all of the indicators.

Q. – Should students see the rubric before they begin work on a task?

A. – Absolutely!

Q. – Should I use pluses and minuses at each of the levels?

A. – This question applies only when a rubric is being used for "assessment *of* learning" (summative) purposes (see Chapter 4). There is no "right and wrong" to this question. In many cases, local assessment policy will dictate whether each level represents a discrete "cut point" or whether pluses and minuses may be used to describe work that bridges two levels.

Q. – Should a rubric include descriptions of failing performance?

A. – My response to this question is a categorical "No." Why would we spend time describing non-achievement when excellence is the goal? Furthermore, non-achievement looks very different from student to student, so why waste time trying to define it?

Q. – Does Level 1 on my rubric mean "Fail"?

A. – The more important question is "What does the lowest level on a rubric represent? Is it a minimally acceptable performance or a failing performance?" In Ontario, I frequently encounter rubrics whose Level 1 indicators describe unsatisfactory performance—yet Level 1 achievement is rewarded with a passing grade. For example, in a rubric for a visual presentation, some Level 1 indicators might be "Labels are too small or no important items were labelled" and "Graphics do not relate to the topic." All rubrics developed in Ontario should contain Level 1 indicators that reflect *limited but passing performance.*

Q. – On a four-level rubric, should the scale move from lowest to highest, or highest to lowest performance?

A. – Again, there is no definitive answer to this question. Many jurisdictions advocate placing the highest level of indicators on the left of a rubric so that students are drawn to descriptions of excellence. The tradition of placing the lowest level first is just that: the tradition of moving from lowest to highest.

Q. – What if a student performs above the highest level on my rubric?

A. – Great! Make it clear to the student that he or she has exceeded the highest level on the rubric and award Level 4^{++}!

Q. – What overall mark do I assign when a student gets several different levels for each of the criteria on a rubric?

A. – Let me first stress that a rubric's most important purpose is to help students improve the quality of their work during instruction—in other words, using the rubric as an assessment *for* learning tool. However, a well-designed rubric may also be used as an assessment *of* learning tool. When using a rubric to summarize a student's overall performance on a single task, the critical question is *What level best reflects this student's achievement at this point in time?* Whether one uses the mean, median, mode, or estimates the overall achievement level, the process requires professional judgment, *not* a simple numerical calculation. (See Chapter 9 for more information.) It is imperative, however, that all teachers of a given course, within a department, or ideally across a school discuss and agree upon how such professional judgments are made. In other words, ongoing discussion about best practice in assessment should include teachers sharing strategies about rubric use.

Q. – How do I convert rubric levels into percentage grades?

A. – As we saw earlier, there are reasons why a rubric is preferable to numerical scoring when assessing complex tasks. Converting from levels to percentages should only occur as a reporting period approaches. While there is no perfect way to convert a 4- or 6-point scale into a 100-point scale, many jurisdictions employ a "pegged scale." (Chapter 9 deals with summarizing rubric levels and numerical scores into grades; see especially page 205.)

Q. – Should I adjust rubrics for my special needs students?

A. – A rubric is similar to a metre stick in that it should serve as a fixed and known measurement device, albeit a qualitative rather than a quantitative one. It is therefore inappropriate to change the meaning of the levels on a rubric to suit students with special needs. What may need to change is the curriculum; some students may need to work on learning outcomes from a different grade in order to experience success. Or it may be necessary to adapt the assessment task for some students by providing scaffolding or rendering it less challenging in some other way. The measurement tool—the rubric—must not change.

Q. – How do I convince parents that rubrics are useful?

A. – In my experience, parents of students in Grades 1 to 6 are highly supportive of rubrics because they help their children understand what quality work looks like and help them improve their work. From my perspective, the resistance to greater rubric use in secondary schools originates more from within schools than from without. That said, we all need to help parents understand that much of the important work that students are required to do demands the kind of descriptive, qualitative assessment that rubrics provide, as opposed to simple numerical scores.

Rubric Checklist

Use the following checklist to assess the quality of commercially produced and locally developed rubrics, or to examine rubrics that you have developed with your colleagues.

	YES	NO
1. Is it clear whether the rubric is designed to assess a product, a performance, or a process?		
2. Is there a manageable number of criteria—four to six?		
3. Do all of the criteria identify the essential elements of the task?		
4. Are all of the criteria observable? (Avoid criteria that involve inferences, e.g., "Attitude toward task—student approaches task with confidence." Such criteria lead to biased observations.)		
5. Is the rubric appropriate for student use? (uses age-appropriate vocabulary)		
6. Does the rubric clearly communicate to students how to improve? (Refer to samples on pages 163 and 164.)		
7. Are the key words used to identify attributes of products or performances clear and used consistently? (e.g., *thesis* is used consistently and not sometimes replaced with *argument*)		
8. Does each row of performance descriptors describe only one observable indicator? (This is crucial, because multiple indicators combined as one descriptor prevent reliable teacher judgments.) Consider the following example: "Has difficulty accessing information sources and uses only one source." A student may have difficulty accessing information from sources but may use several sources.		
9. Are the same modifiers used throughout the rubric to convey a sense of "Level 1-ness," "Level 2-ness," and so on? (e.g., *limited, sufficient, complete, exhaustive* are used to denote progression on all criteria)		
10. Do the levels provide an appropriate and consistent range of performance from novice to expert, or from limited to excellent?		

TOOL 1.6

Rubric Checklist

A modifiable version of this tool can be found on the DVD.

11. Does each row of performance descriptors progress logically from level to level? (This will be more likely if the appropriate variable has been identified. See page 164 for explanation of process and product variables.) For example, from Level 1 to Level 4, a student's skill in formulating a research question is described as follows: "Has difficulty formulating a question; formulates a tentative question; formulates a clear question; formulates an insightful question."		
12. Does the lowest level reflect minimally acceptable performance? (see page 168 in previous Q's and A's section)		
13. Does the highest level represent superior performance? (Note: this does *not* mean that a student must achieve beyond grade level.)		

14. Are the variables that distinguish the levels appropriate?
  • process rubric—fluency, autonomy, frequency, etc.
  • product/performance rubric—depth and breadth of content, accuracy, etc.		

15. Are the increments in achievement or performance from level to level appropriate and equal? (This can be achieved by developing or revising the rubric during a collaborative or moderated marking session.)		
16. Could a performance be considered excellent, based on a teacher's knowledge and experience, yet receive a low mark, based on the rubric?		
17. Could a performance be considered weak, based on a teacher's knowledge and experience, yet receive a high mark, based on the rubric?		
18. Does the rubric clearly describe quality without being overly prescriptive? (See page 157 for discussion of generic and task-specific rubrics.)		
19. Do I feel confident using this rubric to assess student work?		
20. Do I feel confident sharing this rubric with students and parents to communicate my expectations for quality work?		

Before you begin, consult your local and provincial curriculum documents and also Chapter 3: Planning with the End in Mind. Then work through the following steps as a team.

1. Decide on the task or performance you wish to assess. The example I'm using here is written for a Phys. Ed. task requiring students to create a physical fitness program that uses technology (such as an exercise or dance program in the form of a video game, DVD, or suitable for a PDA or interactive whiteboard).

2. If available, gather student samples from previous years. For my example, I would gather sample programs from last year's class.

3. Examine your samples and ask: *What are the critical elements (criteria) we need to assess?* Start by brainstorming all possible criteria. Then reduce the total number of criteria to between four and six essential elements of the task or performance. This is hard work, and may lead to disagreements! But that's part of the dialogue necessary to increase your understanding of assessment.

Rubric: Physical Fitness Program				
Criteria	**Limited**	**Fair**	**Proficient**	**Excellent**
Effectiveness of Program				
Understanding of Program Benefits				
Use of Technology				
Safety				

4. Look again at the samples of student work and ask: *Based on these criteria, which samples represent a proficient level of achievement?* Use these samples to help you begin writing performance indicators.

5. Choose one criterion and write a set of point-form performance indicators that describe a Proficient performance for this criterion.

Criteria	Limited	Fair	Proficient	Excellent
Effectiveness of Program			• program is **effective** for improving fitness level • program is **engaging** for user group	
Understanding of Program Benefits				
Use of Technology				
Safety				

6. Write the Proficient performance indicators for the rest of the criteria. Keep referring to the samples of student work to ensure that you're capturing valid indicators of quality.

Criteria	Limited	Fair	Proficient	Excellent
Effectiveness of Program			• program is **effective** for improving fitness level • program is **engaging** for the user group	
Understanding of Program Benefits			• shows **solid** understanding of physiological benefits of the program (strength, endurance, and energy)	
Use of Technology			• program uses technology **effectively** and **efficiently** • technology is **suitable** for the user group	
Safety			• program includes **effective** and **appropriate** warm-up and cool-down activities • program features **appropriate** procedures for safe participation and use of equipment	

Be consistent with your phrasing; for example, use the present or past tense consistently, or if one indicator begins with *program,* they all should, though there may be some variation.

7. Working from the Proficient level, write the performance indicators for the Excellent, Limited, and Fair levels. It is critical to be clear about whether Limited represents the *minimal* level of acceptable work or *unacceptable work.* With the former case, you may expect many students to perform below the Limited level; with the latter case, Limited will represent the lowest level of performance you expect to see from any of your students. This issue is usually dictated by provincial or local standards.

Criteria	Limited	Fair	Proficient	Excellent
Effectiveness of Program	• program has **limited effectiveness** in improving fitness level • program has **limited appeal** to the user group	• program is **fairly effective** in improving fitness level • program may engage **some** of the user group	• program is **effective** in improving fitness level • program is **engaging** for the user group	• program is **highly effective** in improving fitness level • program is **creative** and **highly appealing** to the user group
Understanding of Program Benefits	• shows **limited** understanding of physiological benefits of the program (strength, endurance, and energy)	• shows **some** understanding of physiological benefits of the program (strength, endurance, and energy)	• shows **solid** understanding of physiological benefits of the program (strength, endurance, and energy)	• shows **thorough** understanding of physiological benefits of the program (strength, endurance, and energy)
Use of Technology	• program's use of technology is **limited** • technology **lacks suitability** for the user group	• program uses technology **somewhat** effectively • technology is **fairly suitable** for the user group	• program uses technology **effectively** and **efficiently** • technology is **suitable** for the user group	• program uses technology **skillfully, creatively,** and **to its full potential** • technology is **highly appropriate** for the user group
Safety	• program has **very few** warm-up and cool-down activities • attention to safe participation and use of equipment is **limited**	• program includes **some** warm-up and cool-down activities • procedures for safe participation and use of equipment are **somewhat evident**	• program includes an **appropriate** number and variety of warm-up and cool-down activities • procedures for safe participation and use of equipment are **evident**	• program includes **highly appropriate** and **varied** warm-up and cool-down activities • procedures for safe participation and use of equipment are **highly evident**

8. Review the draft of your rubric using the Rubric Checklist, then revise the rubric as necessary.

9. Field-test the rubric with your students to validate it for quality before using it for summative (assessment *of* learning) purposes. Using the rubric for diagnostic or formative assessment is one way to conduct this validation.

10. Share the polished rubric with other teachers, students, and parents to help everyone understand the standards of quality for the particular task or performance.

BASED ON IDEAS OF GRANT WIGGINS

In the performance indicators, avoid using highly subjective words such as good *or* nice *as well as overly pejorative words such as* poor *and* weak.

ASSESSMENT TECHNOLOGY

HANDHELD DEVICES IN THE CLASSROOM

Today's Smartphones, personal digital assistants (PDAs), and other mobile devices have the potential to change assessment in dramatic ways. The evolution of hand-held power and convenience opens up many possibilities for in-class, on-the-fly assessment. The portability and convenience of such devices enable teachers and students to capture and store assessment data as a natural part of their classroom interaction. This can increase the reliability of observational assessment, and reduce after-class time spent by teachers transferring data to their records.

The following chart outlines some of the new technology, its potential to change assessment practice, and some pros and cons associated with each device.

> ▶ Video Clip 10
>
> *Using Technology to Support Assessment* (8:55)

Digital Assessment Technology: Pros and Cons			
Assessment Technology	**Assessment Use**	**Pros**	**Cons**
Web browsers are common on higher-end devices, especially those with higher-resolution, larger displays and wireless capability (i.e., providing a full-featured mobile surfing experience).	• web-based assessment software can be accessed and used directly in the classroom • can pull up student data and notes, add comments, and manage assessment tasks and grades directly on the mobile device, in class	• recorded evidence will be immediately available in the primary assessment tracking system; no need to copy or transfer data later	• if the device and school have wireless capabilities, web access will be virtually free; otherwise, data charges for web access will likely be incurred • some devices have limited web browsing capability

(continued)

Assessment Technology	Assessment Use	Pros	Cons
The capability to run **mobile versions of assessment software** may be available for certain devices, depending on the software vendor and the device.	• features of the mobile version will be somewhat limited compared with the full version, but in-class entry of student assessment data, anecdotal observation, and review of existing data may be available	• transfer of assessment data from the handheld device to the official records (wherever they are stored) will be simpler and faster than using paper/pencil methods	• mobile client software usually involves an added cost • transferring data back to the main system can be inconvenient
Notetaking or a word-processing application can be found on any PDA.	• can record anecdotal notes or observations from natural interactions with students or student–teacher conferences	• can capture key learning moments and observations as they arise and then use these snippets for later feedback or to inform report card comments	• small screen and tiny keyboards may be inconvenient for some
Spreadsheets and charting capability is available on some full-featured devices.	• can maintain a class list in chart form, allowing recording of marks, rubric levels, or brief observations over time in the classroom • can set up multiple columns with dates to track progress over time for a key learning or skill. • can enter anecdotal comments into the spreadsheet as per the Notetaking section above	• entering data in spreadsheet cells makes it simple to track and record a number of numerical marks • various measures of "most consistent" can be applied using spreadsheet functions • spreadsheets are an efficient tracking tool when a teacher is not using any other assessment software	• if the teacher is using other assessment software, then after-class data transfer may be required • numerical data on its own will not help students' progress, so teachers must be sure to give written and verbal descriptive feedback to supplement marks

(continued)

Digital Assessment Technology: Pros and Cons *(continued)*

Assessment Technology	Assessment Use	Pros	Cons
Media capture capability (photography, audio recording, and/or full video) is available on most phones and other handheld devices.	• can capture samples of oral communication for later review; can compare these with other samples from the same student to determine progress, especially for performance tasks • can photograph exemplars (samples of student work) for use with future classes • can shoot video of student work or presentations for later review Note: In all cases, student permission should be sought before recordings are made. Further, if a recording is to be used for any purpose beyond private assessment by the teacher, then permissions must be sought, using an official district permission form.	• video or audio exemplars (student work samples) are invaluable in helping students understand assessment criteria when a teacher is introducing an assigned task • recordings can be excellent discussion starters for parent interviews and for other in-school team discussions • teacher and student can review recorded performance tasks together to provide feedback • students can self- or peer-assess their own performance as captured on a recording	• handheld devices may have limited capacity for video (although audio and photograph capability may be extensive) • reviewing audio and video out of class may be time-consuming

AUGMENTING CLASSROOM ASSESSMENT ON THE WEB

Today, classroom websites are an important adjunct to face-to-face learning and are rapidly becoming as ubiquitous as the twentieth-century blackboard. Even in districts that do not provide staff with web hosting and maintenance tools, educators are making use of free online services to create web content for parents and students. Hosting services have evolved in simplicity so that new content and existing files can be assembled online with no html, ftp, or other skills required.

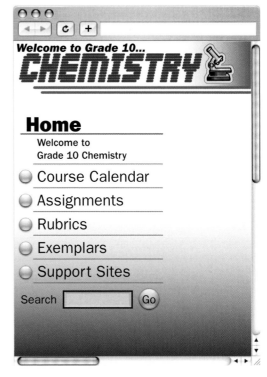

The most common information posted on teacher or class websites are course outlines and other basic program information. Teachers also typically provide up-to-date homework lists and due dates. Far less common—at present—are classroom handouts for downloading at home by students and parents. These provide the greatest potential for augmenting classroom assessment online as they leverage an underutilized support for student learning—the parent! Providing parents—as well as students—with the essential assessment tasks for a course, as well as the criteria that describe success for each task, can dramatically increase success rates for students. I therefore encourage all teachers to post not only due dates and assignments, but also to upload original versions of classroom handouts and assessment tools such as rubrics, checklists, and exemplars to their websites. Providing clear, detailed information that describes success aids learning and guides students' work powerfully, both at home and in school.

Assessment *for* learning advantages aside, websites also reduce confusion for students and parents about classroom activity and augment existing formal and informal communication (i.e., interviews, phone calls, and report cards). Finally, class websites are efficient, effective ways for assisting students who lose course materials and helping students who have missed classes.

◀ Posting materials on a classroom website invites parental involvement, which can dramatically increase student success. Assessment tools such as rubrics, checklists, and exemplars can all be uploaded to the site.

Some teachers will see maintaining website information as an added burden. But if teachers take the simple yet powerful step of making their web documents the single, original source of content for their course, the task is not onerous. Editing course material can be done simply by updating the website alone. Handouts, as well as any other materials for class use, are thus printed from the website. When combined with a reliable backup system, teachers can free themselves from the hassles of traditional file management via school servers, personal hard drives, or USB sticks. As new assessment tasks and rubrics are developed, these are naturally created directly on the website so that students and parents will always have the "latest and greatest" version of information. Finally, teachers who use interactive whiteboards in the classroom can export lessons, notes, student examples, annotated exemplars, and other in-class, on-the-fly material in .html or .pdf file format for later uploading to the class website.

To augment these online assessment supports, teachers may also post progress updates, including assignment and mark information, by creating password-protected pages and/or code names that protect the anonymity of student data. This is typically done only when a separate web-based assessment software system is not being used. See page 220 in Chapter 9 for more details about web-based assessment software.

Whenever I meet with educators and talk about communication, I ask everyone present to put up their hands if their own children are in the school system. I then ask them to put their hand *down* if they would prefer *not* to have access to detailed information about what is going on in the classroom. So far, nobody has ever put down a hand!

▲ Today's digital technology facilitates student learning and the demonstration of assessment strategies and tools.

Summary

This chapter looked at assessment tools—their suitability for various types of tasks and their pros and cons. The chapter had a particular focus on rubrics—highly effective assessment tools because of the way they communicate to students the standard of quality required for an assessment task. And, in recognition of today's technological capabilities and potential, the chapter ended with an overview of technological tools that can assist teachers with their assessment practices.

End-of-Chapter Activity

Using the information you've taken from this chapter—the Rubric Development Toolkit in particular—work with a group of colleagues to create a rubric. You can then self-assess your work by applying the Rubric Checklist on page 170, also available on the DVD. Alternatively, use the Rubric Checklist to assess a set of rubrics that you are currently using.

You may wish to run a workshop with your colleagues to increase knowledge and skills related to the variety of technological devices that can be used to improve assessment practices.

TOOL 1.6

Rubric Checklist

A modifiable version of this tool can be found on the DVD.

GRADING AND REPORTING

BIG
IDEA
8

Grading and reporting student achievement is a responsive, human process that requires teachers to exercise their professional judgment.

PERFORMANCE STANDARDS

This chapter addresses these frequently asked questions:

- *What method should I use to summarize a set of marks into an overall grade? I've heard that the mean isn't fair to some students.*
- *I keep hearing that we should emphasize students' most consistent achievement while paying more attention to more recent work. If so, how should I weight marks when determining grades?*
- *What are some suggestions for helping me defend report card grades at parent-teacher interviews?*

When I began my teaching career in the 1970s, I had little knowledge about grading theory. In my teacher training, discussion about grading had been limited to the statistical features of the normal curve. The prevailing approach at that time reflected a belief that success in school, like one's IQ, was a function of one's gene pool. I don't recall ever questioning, or being asked to question, the practice of comparing one student's achievement with that of others.

In my early years as a high school English teacher, I routinely identified the range of achievement within a given class at the beginning of a term by noting which students produced the best work and which students produced the weakest work, and then scoring the rest of the class's work according to this range. In other words, I assumed the following:

- Standards used to judge the quality of work are relative from year to year and class to class, depending on the quality of work produced by a given group of students.
- Criteria for excellent work will emerge from the work of the strongest students in the class; in other words, "I'll know an 'A' when I see it."
- Regardless of my teaching, I should reasonably expect that my top students will remain my top students, my average students will remain my average students, and my weak students will remain my weak students.

In my classes, I felt no need or pressure to communicate performance targets to my students. Students and parents rarely if ever asked me to explain how I had determined the letter and percentage scores that I assigned to individual pieces of work or the overall (aggregate) grades that I entered on report cards. There was an implicit acceptance that, as a secondary teacher, I had been anointed with the ability to determine marks and grades in a reliable manner. Assessment and grading were, in the words of Rick Stiggins, "the land of myth, mystery, and magic" (personal communication, 2007).

How times have changed! In today's climate of accountability, standards that fluctuate from class to class and year to year are unacceptable. Teachers must now, as part of their routine practice, discuss with colleagues the standards for quality work—performance standards. They must then develop clear, concise, and easy-to-use tools to communicate these standards to students. These same tools must then be used by students and teachers to assess the extent to which student work meets these standards.

THE ROLE OF STANDARDS IN EDUCATION

Let's take a moment to review the origins of the standards-based movement in education. In the 1990s, the education community, in its quest to define standards more clearly, turned to the "Total Quality Management" (TQM) approach—a business management strategy that had revolutionized the Japanese automobile industry. It was argued that educators had hold of the wrong end of the stick when they wrote curriculum and program in terms of the teacher's objectives. Instead, they were urged to write curriculum in terms of student outcomes. In other words, it didn't matter how well a teacher had covered the curriculum; if students hadn't learned what was taught, then the teaching was unsuccessful. This premise seemed to me to be perfectly reasonable. But coming as it did from industry, the TQM model also addressed the issue of quality control. Not only were teachers told to rethink their mission in terms of student outcomes, but they were also encouraged to specify precisely what those outcomes were to look like. At this point, I became a little nervous.

A manufacturing business is successful when it develops a quality product and then replicates it hundreds, thousands, or millions of times, without lapses in quality—an admirable mission if producing consumable goods such as automobiles, cameras, or computers. But educators are charged with the unique task of nurturing and developing the potential of individual human beings. Surely, I thought, our goal is to produce uniqueness, not sameness! Not long after reaching this conclusion, I met Grant Wiggins for the first time. He had just produced the superb resource *Standards, Not Standardization*, in which he argued strongly for publicly known standards of quality but also cautioned against cookie-cutter models of curriculum, instruction, and assessment.

More than a decade later, I continue to implore teachers to tread carefully when implementing standards-based assessment practices. Teachers must resist those forces that seek to standardize education in the mistaken belief that sameness can lead to excellence.

HOW SHOULD PERFORMANCE STANDARDS BE SET?

In typical norm-referenced assessment contexts, the standard for a given task is set according to the work produced by students. This is the case in both large-scale normative assessments and in classroom situations. With large-scale assessments, test designers use a set of sophisticated norming procedures to establish the reference scale for a given test. Tests are periodically "re-normed" to reflect changes in the student population for whom the test is intended. In the past, as I described earlier, on page 182, teachers often established classroom norms based on the work produced by their students. Consequently, the standard for "A" work one semester could differ quite markedly from "A" work in another semester.

In standards-based, criterion-referenced classrooms and schools, the standard for excellence for a given task must be set, agreed upon, and made public before students set to work. Notice that I said "must be." For teachers of a given course, agreement on the essential assessment tasks as well as on the assessment criteria for each task is a prerequisite to instruction. These criteria and associated performance indicators comprise the "performance standards" that must be communicated to students as the targets they are expected to hit.

One could argue that a norming process still operates in a criterion-referenced classroom in terms of how standards are set. This is true in that teachers identify

A reminder:
Norm-referenced assessment *is assessment that compares students' performances with a normed sample of student performance.*
Criterion-referenced assessment *is assessment that measures students' performance against a set of predetermined performance criteria.*

In British Columbia, provincial performance standards have been established for reading, writing, numeracy, and social responsibility. The standard-setting process involved the gathering of thousands of student work samples generated in response to specific prompts for each of these strands. Teams of educators then developed descriptive criteria, based on these samples, which in turn became the provincial performance standards for each task.

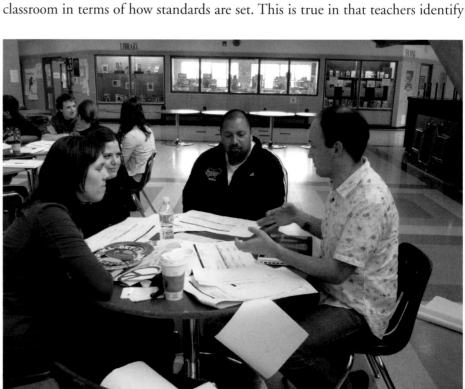

▲ Teachers of a given course need to agree on the essential assessment tasks and the assessment criteria for each task.

the criteria for assessing a given task, examine or discuss samples of work that have been produced over time in response to this task, and then create rubrics for assessing the task. By gathering samples of student work over time, they are able to anchor the standards reflected in the rubric and to periodically adjust the rubric. The important departure from norm-referenced practice is the communication of the performance standard for the task *before* students begin work.

HOW ARE PERFORMANCE STANDARDS COMMUNICATED TO STUDENTS?

How do standards differ from standardization in classroom practice? First, while teachers must ensure that rubrics and checklists are of a consistently high quality, they must also ensure that students are shown two or more exemplars or anchors for a given level of achievement; furthermore, they must expect and be open to students redefining what excellence looks like—in other words, some students will exceed the exemplar. (See the Glossary for definitions of *exemplar* and *anchor*, and also see page 98 in Chapter 6.)

Rubrics and checklists have the potential to communicate in clear and powerful ways the criteria and indicators that are the hallmarks of quality work and performance. Yet all too often these tools emphasize only the conventions and structural elements that are quantifiable—and, hence, easy to mark. As we saw in Chapter 8: Assessment Tools and Technology, checklists and rubrics must be developed by teams of teachers working collaboratively as they examine samples of student work or performance. I have often sat through dull, uninspired, formulaic presentations that received the highest possible scores as determined by a rubric, while another presentation that was captivating, original, and creative received a poor score. As Wiggins points out (1998), when this occurs, the rubric is targeting the wrong criteria. And more often than not, such criteria focus on formulaic models that emphasize structure and conventions.

Why must teachers ensure that they have two or more anchors for a given achievement (rubric) level? Because with only one sample, students and teachers will conclude that a piece of work or a performance must exactly replicate the anchor in order to be scored at that level. Again, compare the purpose of education with the goal of a manufacturer—"standards, *not* standardization." When teachers select anchors to reflect a given level of achievement or performance, they must identify at least two samples that are as different as possible from each other, while still meeting the indicator associated with that level. Consider the following example.

Task: Students chose two measures of the human body (e.g., foot size, stride length, height, arm length, etc.), analyzed the relationship between them, and then communicated their findings. Students were allowed to choose their own method of representing and analyzing the data and communicating their findings during the investigation.

Rubric: The teacher decided to focus on the "data analysis and communication" aspects of the task. The following rubric describes a range of achievement for these two aspects.

Rubric: Data Analysis and Communication				
Criteria	**Level 1 (Limited)**	**Level 2 (Fair)**	**Level 3 (Proficient)**	**Level 4 (Excellent)**
Validity of conclusion in analyzing a data trend (or lack thereof)	• makes an ineffectual or inaccurate conclusion, with limited support	• makes a semi-valid conclusion, with some support	• makes a valid conclusion, with considerable support	• makes a strongly valid conclusion, with highly effective support
Effectiveness of data description	• describes the data set with limited accuracy and thoroughness, omitting details or using vague terms	• describes the data set with some accuracy and thoroughness, referring to some details (e.g., range, spread) and using mathematical terms	• describes the data set with considerable accuracy and thoroughness, referring to most or all details present and using appropriate mathematical terms	• describes the data set with a high degree of accuracy and thoroughness, referring to all details and using highly effective mathematical terms
Use of mathematical vocabulary	• uses very little mathematical vocabulary, and with lack of clarity	• uses some mathematical vocabulary, with some clarity and precision	• uses mathematical vocabulary, with considerable clarity and precision	• uses a broad range of mathematical vocabulary, with a high degree of clarity and precision

Anchor 1, Level 3

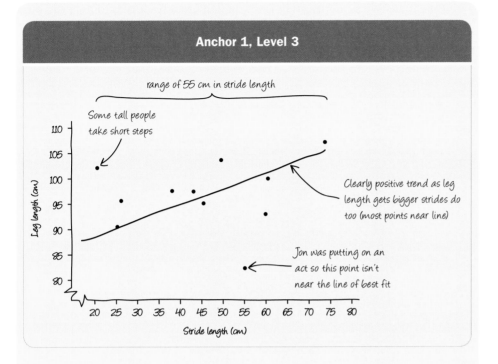

This student has described most aspects of the data using appropriate mathematical terms (e.g., "near the line of best fit" and "range"). The student's finding of a "clearly positive trend" is consistent with the data, and the student has drawn a line of fit illustrating this increase. The student has supported the conclusion by explaining the outlying points as well (e.g., "Jon was putting on an act").

Anchor 2, Level 3

"I think people with long legs had longer strides. When you first look at the points plotted, you see them spread out a little bit, with a spread from 20 cm to 75 cm in stride length. The leg length ranged from 80 to 107 cm. I think there was some measuring errors because some people stepped too little and one person tried to overdo their step. That means some of these points might be a bit off. But if you look at the slope for the people with longer legs, then 5 cm more in leg length means about 20 cm more stride (except one). So my hypothesis was correct."

This student has used terms like *spread* and *range* and described many aspects of the data. The student has hypothesized that leg length and stride are related in a positive way, and supported this with a rough measure of slope as well as an explanation of the erroneous data.

While these two students produced quite different responses to the task, both samples meet the indicators associated with performance at Level 3.

A final word about communicating performance standards to students and the use of anchors and exemplars: There must be no arbitrary performance-level ceiling set for a task. Some students can and will redefine excellence, and teachers must always be open to this possibility.

▲ These models of the respiratory system are exemplars that help teachers set performance standards and help students see the standards they are expected to aim for.

THE PURPOSE OF GRADES

While grades serve a variety of purposes, (Stiggins, 2004; O'Connor, 2002) one purpose is of paramount importance in the secondary school context: *Grades must indicate student proficiency in the essential knowledge and skills associated with a given course of study.*

Implicit in this purpose is the assurance to the student, parent, and next-grade teacher—for all grades except 12—that the student is prepared to undertake work at the next grade level in a given subject. For this reason, there are major problems inherent in current procedures for granting high school credits. First of all, most Canadian provinces use 50 percent as their pass/fail cut-point. Knowing 50 percent of the material taught can hardly be considered "proficient." Nobody wants to fly with a pilot who scored 50 percent on his or her exams at flight training school! Pass/fail cut-points of 50 percent are an outdated relic of norm-referenced approaches to grading. Secondly, cases involving students who fall short of the 50 percent cut-point typically come before promotion committees who ask the question "Should we award Anton an extra 3 percent? His grade in this course is currently 47 percent."

This is, quite simply, the wrong question! The correct question is "Has Anton demonstrated the necessary knowledge and skills to indicate that he is prepared to undertake work at the next grade level?" And of course a grade of 47 percent would indicate that he has not. We are not helping students, teachers, parents, or society at large by deceiving students into thinking that a final grade of 50 percent is worth anything. Given the increasing complexity of high school programs from grade to grade, students achieving a grade of 50 percent in Grade 9 are probably destined for failure in Grade 10.

One solution to this problem is replacing single summary grades for a course with standards-based grades. For accreditation, students must demonstrate proficiency in all of a course's "standards." In science, for example, Anton's report card might contain the following information:

Standards-Based Grades in a Science Course	
Ability to relate science to technology, society, and the environment	61%
Scientific investigation skills, strategies, and habits of mind	50%
Understanding of science concepts	30%

These grades communicate to Anton and his parents his proficiency—or lack thereof!—in each of the major learning goals of this science course.

Where, currently, is the educational community in regard to reporting on proficiency in the ways just described? The answer is that we have a long way to go. Many districts I have worked in recently are beginning to experiment with standards-based grading; however, most projects I have seen are at the pilot stage. But even if your school's report card does not include standards-based grades, such grades may be communicated to students and parents via informal interim reports. The good news is that almost everywhere I travel, educators are talking about the need to change grading and reporting practice in these ways.

WHAT GOES INTO THE GRADE?

While discussion of the elements that should comprise students' grades is critical, I shall make only a few brief comments here since my colleague Ken O'Connor's two books *How to Grade for Learning* (2002) and *A Repair Kit for Grading: 15 Fixes for Broken Grades* (2007) explore the topic thoroughly. Grades must present students, parents, and college and university admissions departments with accurate, clear, concise, and current information about achievement. To meet these criteria, grades must not represent a stew of achievement, behavioural, and attitudinal data, and then be further distorted by the inclusion of late penalties and zeroes for work not submitted. Consider the following report.

This misleading blend of achievement and behavioural data...

Item	Achievement
Attendance	D–
Punctuality	F
Participation	D+
Group Work	B
Test 1	B+
Test 2 (missed)	F
Test 3	A–
Project 1	A+
Project 2 (late)	B
Presentation	A

... leads to a misleading grade:

Final Grade	C–

Effective reporting formats should contain information about all the elements listed in the above example, but they must be communicated *separately* so that students and parents receive information about each one, discretely. To illustrate: a parent, a potential employer, or a university or college admissions board all need to know how well a student has acquired the essential knowledge and skills associated with a given course. But they also need separate information about the student's generic work habits, such as the ability to get along with others, to produce work on time, and to demonstrate initiative. Hence, reporting formats such as the one on the next page are far more useful.

▲ Information about students' work habits, such as getting along with others and demonstrating initiative, are more useful if reported separately.

Ontario

**Provincial Report Card
Grades 9–12**

Semester	Report Period	Date

Student		Grade	Principal	

Address — School Council Chair

School — Telephone — Board

Address — Fax — Address

To parents or guardians and students: This copy of the report should be kept for reference. The original or an exact copy has been placed in the student's Ontario Student Record (OSR) folder and will be retained for five (5) years after the student leaves school.

Courses IEP = Individual Education Plan ESL = English As a Second Language ELD = English Literacy Development These boxes appear for each course where appropriate	Report Period	Percentage Grade	Course Median	Credit Earned	Comments Strengths/Areas for Improvement/Next Steps	Attendance			Learning Skills E = Excellent, G = Good S = Satisfactory N = Needs Improvement					
						Classes Missed	Total Classes	Times Late	Works Independently	Teamwork	Organization	Work Habits/Homework	Initiative	
Course Title: _____ Course Code: _____ Teacher: _____ ☐ IEP ☐ ESL ☐ ELD	First													
	Final													
Course Title: _____ Course Code: _____ Teacher: _____ ☐ IEP ☐ ESL ☐ ELD	First													
	Final													
Course Title: _____ Course Code: _____ Teacher: _____ ☐ IEP ☐ ESL ☐ ELD	First													
	Final													
Course Title: _____ Course Code: _____ Teacher: _____ ☐ IEP ☐ ESL ☐ ELD	First													
	Final													
Student's Average					To view provincial curriculum documents, visit the Ministry of Education's website: www.edu.gov.on.ca.									

▲ In this reporting format, achievement data is separated into two types of information. Data about essential knowledge and skills related to the courses is recorded on the left. Recorded separately, on the right, is information about learning skills, such as the student's ability to work independently, his or her organizational skills, and teamwork skills. These are largely behavioural skills.

SOURCE: ONTARIO MINISTRY OF EDUCATION

REPORTING ON LEARNING SKILLS

Gathering data to inform achievement grades is complex, as the data typically includes a combination of scores, rubric levels, and perhaps letter grades. But gathering data on learning skills can, and should, be simple and efficient. These skills are largely behavioural, so the frequency with which students demonstrate them is the most important variable to be assessed. For example, when looking at data about completing work on time, an employer wants to know if a student is *consistently* punctual, not just during the first month of school. If a college admissions board is selecting candidates for an engineering program, they want evidence that a student *routinely* shows initiative. For these reasons, learning skills should be reported using a frequency scale such as this:

Learning Skills Assessment: Computer Studies

Student: _____

Assessing *how* people work is just as important as evaluating what is produced. Scores from one (1) to four (4) in each category of the self-evaluation will be given according to the following guidelines.

SCORE	DESCRIPTION	COMPARISON TO "THE STANDARD"	CONSISTENCY	DESCRIPTORS
4	Excellent	exceeds the standard for this learning skill; outstanding in this area	routinely	independent, disciplined, leader...
3	Good	meets the high standard for this learning skill, but still room for improvement	frequently	limited help needed, effective...
2	Fair	approaching the standard for this learning skill; consistency or quality should be improved	sometimes	when helped, able to...
1	Needs Improvement	below standard for this learning skill; much more effort is needed	rarely	major support needed, limited skill/effort...

Fill in the following table according to the instructor. Remember **TOAD (Truth, Objectivity, Accuracy, Discretion).**

Marker	Time Period/ Date(s)	Independence (attends on time, works alone, on-task, meets timelines...)	Teamwork (participates, listens, helps, questions, shares, cooperates...)	Organization (records due dates, plans, brings stuff, schedules...)	Work Habits/ Homework (works outside class time, puts quality in, uses time effectively...)	Initiative (curious, explores, challenges self, inquires, solves problems, takes risk, self-directed...)
Self	1st 1/2					
Peer	1st 1/2					
Teacher	1st 1/2					
Self	2nd 1/2					
Peer	2nd 1/2					
Teacher	2nd 1/2					
Most Recent, Common Score						

Notes for Improvement

The key for teachers when gathering classroom data about students' learning skills is to balance efficiency with reliability. Shelley has a simple system to achieve such a balance.

CASE STUDY 1	**Shelley's Records for Homework Completion**

Shelley assigns homework most days because she believes that practising what they have learned in the day's lesson helps students to consolidate their learning. She doesn't collect the homework, but uses it to determine how well students understood the lesson. At the beginning of each class, students immediately begin work on a review activity that Shelley has written on the board. They know they are expected to leave their completed homework open on their desks for Shelley to check. Each day, she checks the homework of 10 students by simply recording "Done" or "Not Done" on a tracking chart. The next day, she checks the homework completion of another group of 10 students. By the first reporting period, she has checked each student's homework four times in order to provide summary data to the student

and parents regarding one aspect of "Responsibility," which is a key learning skill.

- four checks and four times "Done" earns the summary descriptor "Routinely"
- four checks and three times "Done" earns the summary descriptor "Frequently"
- four checks and twice "Done" earns the summary descriptor "Sometimes"
- four checks and once "Done" earns the summary descriptor "Rarely"

Following this "Completion" check, Shelley instructs students to work with peers to check each other's homework, make corrections, and identify which areas posed difficulties. Shelley then examines these difficult areas with the class before introducing new material.

ORGANIZING GRADES BY LEARNING TARGET, NOT BY ASSESSMENT TASK

Traditionally, secondary teachers have organized their marks according to assessment tasks. As a reporting period approached, summary grades were calculated as an average of these marks, as in the following example from a Grade 12 Physics course. (Note that there is a column for "weight"; weighting will be discussed in more detail later in the chapter.)

In the Tools section of the accompanying DVD, you will find samples of checklists for gathering data related to learning skills.

Sample 1: Grades Organized by Assessment Tasks

School: Newton DHS

Class: Grade 12 Physics
Student: N. Isaac

Overall Grade: 71%
Class Average: 77%

#	Item	Date	Unit	Weight	Actual Mark	Mark (%)	Class Avg. (%)	± Class Avg. (%)
1	Grade 11 Review Test	Sep. 5	1	10	59/100	59	81	−22
2	Forces Quiz	Sep. 17	1	5	20/30	68	64	4
3	Friction Lab	Sep. 21	1	6	33.5/50	67	65	2
4	Force Problems Worksheet	Sep. 27	1	3	58/100	58	68	−10
5	Dynamics Test	Oct. 1	1	10	59/100	59	74	−15
6	Energy Quiz	Oct. 2	2	5	20/25	79	75	4
7	Momentum Lab	Oct. 10	2	6	28.5/30	95	70	25
8	Homework and Review	Oct. 17	2	3	34/50	68	82	−14
9	Energy Test	Oct. 28	2	10	95/100	95	88	7
10	Fields Quiz	Oct. 29	3	5	59/100	59	74	−15
11	Electric Magnetic Lab	Nov. 1	3	6	34/50	68	75	−7
12	Electromagnetism Quiz	Nov. 3	3	5	15/25	59	79	−20
13	Fields Test	Nov. 6	3	10	59/100	59	76	−17
14	Light Quiz	Nov. 13	4	5	24/30	79	76	3
15	Dual Slit Lab	Nov. 19	4	6	47.5/50	95	79	16
16	Light Test	Nov. 26	4	10	68/100	68	75	−7
17	Exam Review	Dec. 10	5	8	98/100	98	88	10
18	Homework Review	Dec. 15	5	5	14.5/25	58	60	−2
19	Lab Test	Jan. 10	5	10	59/100	59	77	−18
20	Exam	Jan. 24	5	20	136/200	68	78	−10

Standards-based grading requires teachers to gather and organize assessment data according to essential learning targets or achievement categories. This necessitates the creation of assessment plans that reflect these targets. In the following example (Sample 2 on the next page), a science teacher has created an assessment plan based on four grading categories: Knowledge and Understanding; Thinking and Inquiry; Communication of Learning; and Application of Learning. (Note that the wording and number of categories/strands/broad outcomes varies in different provinces/states.) Each assessment task has been designed to provide achievement evidence in one or more of these categories. At any time, the teacher is able to examine her data or communicate data to the student and parents, according to achievement in a given category or on a given task. Data organized in this way provides critical information about successes and, more importantly, about areas requiring immediate attention. See Access to Students' Grades later in this chapter, for cautions concerning parental access to grades.

▲ A quiz would be part of a Knowledge and Understanding (or similarly worded) grading category. Organizing assessment plans by category allows teachers to examine and share data according to achievement in a given category or task.

Sample 2: Grades Organized by Learning Targets

School: Newton DHS

Class: Grade 12 Physics
Student: N. Isaac

Overall Grade: 71%
Class Average: 77%

#	Assessment Task	Date	Unit	Category	Weight	Actual Mark	Mark (%)	Level
1	Show What You Know	Sep. 5	1	Know/Und	3.0	59/100	59	1+
2	Forces in the Real World	Sep. 17	1	Appl'n	3.5	20/30	68	2+
3	Friction: Quel Drag!	Sep. 21	1	Think/Inq	3.0	33.5/50	67	2+
4	The Force Be With You	Sep. 27	1	Comm'n	3.8	58/100	58	1+
5	Dynamics Test	Oct. 1	1	Know/Und	6.1	59/100	59	1+
6	Energy Quizzignment	Oct. 2	2	Know/Und	2.4	20/25	79	3+
7	Puck on Thin Ice	Oct. 10	2	Think/Inq	3.1	28.5/30	95	4++
8	Mechanics Mini-Conference	Oct. 17	2	Comm'n	3.8	34/50	68	2+
9	Energy Demonstration	Oct. 28	2	Appl'n	8.9	95/100	95	4++
10	Outstanding in the Field	Oct. 29	3	Know/Und	2.4	59/100	59	1+
11	Electromagnetic Invest.	Nov. 1	3	Think/Inq	3.1	34/50	68	2+
12	Doorbell Analysis	Nov. 3	3	Appl'n	3.6	15/25	59	1+
13	Fields Report	Nov. 6	3	Comm'n	6.1	59/100	59	1+
14	Light Quiz	Nov. 13	4	Know/Und	2.4	24/30	79	3+
15	Interference Experiment	Nov. 14	4	Think/Inq	3.1	47.5/50	95	4++
16	Light Quest	Nov. 16	4	Think/Inq	6.3	68/100	68	2+
17	Exam Group Review	Nov. 19	5	Know/Und	4.9	98/100	98	4++
18	Lesson Presentation Q&A	Nov. 23	5	Comm'n	5.0	14.5/25	58	1+
19	Lab Carousel	Nov. 26	5	Appl'n	8.9	59/100	59	1+
20	Final Exam (multiple choice and short answer)	Dec. 1	5	Know/Und	6.1	68/100	68	2+
21	Final Exam (extended response)	Jan. 25	5	Think/Inq	6.3	88/100	88	4

Category Analysis

Category	Number of Entries	% of Grade	Mark (%)	Level
Application	4	25	73	3
Communication	4	25	60	2–
Knowledge and Understanding	7	25	73	3
Thinking and Investigation	6	25	80	4–

Most secondary-school subject areas include both knowledge and skill targets. For example, the physics course represented in the preceding example includes the following learning targets:

Enduring Understandings

- Forces acting on an object will determine the motion of that object.
- Interactions involving the laws of conservation of energy and conservation of momentum can be analyzed mathematically.
- Gravitational, electric, and magnetic fields share many similar properties and can be described mathematically.
- Light has properties that are similar to the properties of mechanical waves and can be described mathematically.

Essential Skills

- Analyze and evaluate technological applications involving force, energy fields, and light for their impact on society and the environment.
- Develop inquiry and research skills including initiating and planning; performing and recording; analyzing and interpreting; and communicating.

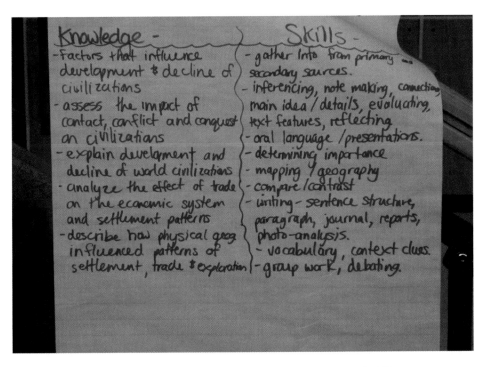

▲ Most secondary-school subject areas include both knowledge and skill targets.

Enduring Understandings Summarized by Unit/Term

While enduring understandings are discrete to each unit of the course, students are required to demonstrate the same set of essential skills throughout the course. From a grading standpoint, this may require the teacher to summarize the data separately for each of these two domains, as shown in the following chart. She would determine a summary Knowledge/Understanding grade for each unit and then an overall summary Knowledge/Understanding grade for the term; for the essential skills, she would determine only an overall summary grade for the term or the course.

Knowledge/Understanding Data Summarized by Unit and by Term

TERM 1

Unit Title	Unit Number	Category	Mark (%)	Level
Show What You Know	1	Know/Und	64	2
Dynamics Test (Knowledge)	1	Know/Und	72	3–
Force Conference	1	Know/Und	78	3+
UNIT SUMMARY			**71**	**3–**
Energy Test (Knowledge)	2	Know/Und	68	2+
Kinetic Conference	2	Know/Und	71	3–
Energy Quizzignment	2	Know/Und	79	3+
Energy Concepts Mindmap	2	Know/Und	85	4–
UNIT SUMMARY			**76**	**3**
Outstanding in the Field	3	Know/Und	59	1+
Electromagnetic Conference	3	Know/Und	71	3–
Electromagnetism Diagram	3	Know/Und	90	4
Electromagnetism Report	3	Know/Und	98	4++
UNIT SUMMARY			**80**	**4–**
Light Quiz	4	Know/Und	58	1+
Wave/Particle Conference	4	Know/Und	69	2+
Light Test (Knowledge)	4	Know/Und	74	3
UNIT SUMMARY			**67**	**2+**
TERM 1 SUMMARY			**74**	**3**

Essential Skills Data Summarized by Term Only

The following marks have been summarized for the essential skill *"Develop inquiry and research skills including initiating and planning; performing and recording; analyzing and interpreting; and communicating."* Note that emphasis has been given to more recent evidence of this skill in the determination of the term grade. As the skill was demonstrated and practised throughout the course, the student has improved somewhat in proficiency and so earlier evidence carries less weight.

Essential Skills Data By Term

TERM 1

Title	Unit	Category	Level
Forces in the Real World (research)	1	Appl'n	3–
The Force Be With You	1	Comm'n	2+
Friction: Quel Drag!	1	Think/Inq	1+
Energy Demonstration	2	Appl'n	2+
Mechanics Mini-Conference	2	Comm'n	2+
Puck on Thin Ice	2	Think/Inq	4
Doorbell Analysis (analysis & interp.)	3	Appl'n	3+
Fields Report	3	Comm'n	3
Electromagnetic Investigation	3	Think/Inq	2+
Interference Experiment	4	Think/Inq	4–
Light Quest (research)	4	Think/Inq	4–
Lab Carousel	5	Appl'n	3–
Lesson Presentation Q&A	5	Comm'n	3+
Final Exam Open	5	Think/Inq	4
Term 1 Summary			**4–**

HOW MUCH DATA IS NECESSARY FOR GRADING PURPOSES?

In Chapters 4 and 6, we saw the importance of distinguishing between assessments *for* learning—assessments that are specifically designed to improve learning—and assessments *of* learning—those that are designed to determine how well a student has acquired essential understandings and demonstrated essential skills by the end of an instructional period, such as a unit, term, or semester. To help clarify this distinction, I described assessments *for* learning as practices and assessments *of* learning as games. To take that analogy further: we can't assess the success of a sports team on the basis of one game; we have to look at the trend throughout a whole season—and it's the same with assessing student achievement. Teachers must ensure that the conclusions they reach about student achievement are based on a sufficient number of assessments *of* learning. Is there a magic number or a formula for gathering sufficient evidence of achievement for grading and reporting? No—but there are some important guidelines, which are listed below and then explained in more detail. The sample of evidence for reporting must:

- include triangulated data (a minimum of three pieces of evidence) for each major learning target
- *not* include diagnostic evidence
- *not* include formative evidence if triangulation is possible with summative evidence

GUIDELINE 1: TRIANGULATE THE DATA

See the Triangulation of Data diagram in Chapter 4, page 57.

I introduced triangulated data in Chapter 4. To review briefly, it means using three or more pieces of evidence for each major learning target. A major learning target may be a strand, such as Geometry, Cell Theory, or Art History, or it may be a broad skill set, such as Expository Writing, Mapping Skills, or Inquiry Skills. Regardless of how curriculum is organized, teachers should strive to base grades for each major learning target on at least three pieces of summative evidence. The principle of triangulation is important in increasing the validity of a grade—that is, the extent to which inferences based on assessment evidence actually represent what a student knows or can do. If grades are based on only one piece of evidence, the potential for drawing invalid conclusions is high, depending on whether the student had a good day, bad day, cheated, plagiarized, etc. The problem with two pieces of data is that one piece may suggest the student "gets it" while the other piece may suggest the student does not. A third piece of data enables teachers to make an inference on the basis of two out of three.

GUIDELINE 2: DON'T USE DIAGNOSTIC EVIDENCE

To return to the sports analogy, data from initial or diagnostic assessments is the equivalent of the tryout. This type of data is to be used purely to help the teacher decide upon entry points for instruction. In short, *no* data gathered prior to instruction must ever be used for grading and reporting purposes.

GUIDELINE 3: DON'T USE FORMATIVE EVIDENCE IF TRIANGULATION IS POSSIBLE WITH SUMMATIVE EVIDENCE

What about including formative assessment evidence in student grades? Generally, since formative assessments represent "practices," they should not comprise part of a student's grade. That said, teachers sometimes find that they have insufficient summative evidence to be able to triangulate the data, especially when determining interim grades. In this case, it may be necessary to dip into the formative data bin for a third piece of data. When doing so, formative data should be weighted less heavily than summative data. The following chart illustrates this situation: the checklist is a formative assessment; the interview and project are summative.

Grade 11 Communication Technology: Use video techniques in response to a communications challenge or problem				
Item	**Date**	**Mark**	**Level**	**Weight**
Camcorder and editing suite "Launch Checklist"	Sept. 9	5/10	1–	2
Partner video interview	Sept. 16	NA	2+	4
Stream of photos project	Oct. 10	NA	3	8
Summary Interim Grade			**3–**	

In the example above, the summary interim grade is determined as follows: the mark for the "Launch Checklist" is weighted minimally since it is a formative assessment occurring early in the term. The video interview and photos project are both summative; however, given the weights assigned, the photos project is deemed the more significant based on the evidence of learning it provides and because this evidence represents more recent achievement.

REPORT CARD GRADES AND MEASUREMENT ERROR

Report card grades are, at best, a crude summary of large amounts of information about student achievement. We know that a grade is a symbol we use to periodically identify a student's current achievement relative to a known standard. But we need to recognize that *behind* the grade lies important information—information that identifies areas of strength and of need. Grades—these mere symbols—seem to get far more attention than does information about learning. I advise teachers to expect every grade they enter on a report card to be challenged by the student or parent. Far from becoming defensive about such challenges, teachers should welcome the opportunity to discuss all the information that the grade represents.

We would also do well to recognize that every grade contains measurement error. This is not a weakness of grades; it is just the reality of the process. A grade is not an accurate measure of everything that a student knows about a given subject. It is only a summary, based on a sample of evidence, that allows teachers to make inferences about what a student appears to have learned. A useful analogy may be made to opinion polls. When a polling firm wants to determine how Canadians feel about an issue, they determine the necessary sample size and then interview the sample in order to make inferences about the population as a whole. When results are published, the polling firm reminds Canadians that the results are subject to measurement error. For example, the firm may report "These results may be considered accurate 19 times out of 20, with an error of 3 percentage points." There are at least two reasons for such measurement error: the responses of some people in the sample may not represent what they actually feel or believe; and the results are based on only a sample, not the whole population.

Report card grades are similar to opinion polls in terms of the two reasons for measurement error. The scores that a student receives on the set of assessments comprising the grade may not fully or accurately represent what that student actually has learned about the learning targets in question. Also, grades are based on only a sample of evidence of learning and may not reflect all that a student has learned about a set of learning targets.

I make these observations because, unlike polling firms, teachers do not publicize the measurement error associated with grades. (Note that commercial test publishers *do* provide this information about their products.) In fact, we often suggest by our words and actions that there is *no* measurement error inherent in our grading practices. I believe that teachers, students, and parents would all benefit from acknowledging that all educational assessment, grading, and reporting are subject to measurement error. While it can be minimized by using clear, public performance standards and teacher practices such as moderated marking, it is nevertheless an unavoidable part of what we do.

▲ Grades are based on only a sample of evidence of learning and may not reflect all that a student has learned about a set of learning targets.

PERCENTAGE GRADES, LETTER GRADES, AND ACHIEVEMENT LEVELS

Most grading systems in Canada and the United States use letter or percentage grades to summarize student achievement on report cards. Some systems use achievement levels, most notably the International Baccalaureate program, which uses a seven-point grading scale.

Most of the grading dilemmas I face when working with teachers reflect the incompatibility of using percentage grades to report on achievement in standards-based systems. To illustrate: the majority of teachers I meet these days are using rubrics to assess the quality of more complex student products and performances. Usually these rubrics describe four levels of performance. Teachers also use numerical scores, expressed as fractions (48/50, 18/25), to assess knowledge and skills on simpler assessments such as quizzes and selected response tests. The problems occur when teachers are required to combine rubric levels and numerical scores into percentage grades. The simplest and best solution is, of course, to abandon percentage grades! However, this decision often rests with individuals who are more concerned with politics than with pedagogy, as reflected in statements such as "Parents demand percentage grades." I should point out that in the many parent information sessions I have conducted in recent years, not one parent has made this demand. I should also add that I provide parents with compelling reasons why rating their children's achievement against clear and consistent performance standards provides far more useful information than percentage grades that sift and sort their children as being bright, average, or weak!

In districts where letter grades are used, the conversion of a set of numerical scores and rubric levels into an overall grade is relatively straightforward, as shown in the following conversion chart.

Grade Conversion Chart			
Rubric Descriptor	**Rubric Level**	**Numerical Score**	**Letter Grade**
Excellent	4	8–10	A++
			A+
			A
			A–
Proficient	3	7	B+
			B
			B–
Fair	2	6	C+
			C
			C–
Limited	1	5	D+
			D
			D–
	Below 1	0–4	

Note: This is a sample chart. Grade equivalents will vary according to local policy.

CONVERSION TO PERCENTAGE GRADES

In jurisdictions where percentage grades are required, this conversion represents a significant challenge for teachers. The challenge lies in having to convert marks based on a four- or five-point scale to grades based on a 100-point scale. Each rubric level can be subdivided to align with ranges on the percentage scale. The problem arises when local policy requires teachers to assign a precise percentage grade.

PEGGED SCALES

A common solution to this problem is to use a pegged scale in which the 100-point scale is reduced to a 12- to 15-point scale.

	Grade Conversion Chart Including Percentages				
Rubric Descriptor	**Rubric Level**	**Letter Grade**	**Numerical Score**	**Percentage Range**	**Percentage Points**
Excellent (Expert)	4	A++	8–10	80–100%	100
		A+			95
		A			90
		A–			85
Proficient (Practitioner)	3	B+	7	70–79%	78
		B			75
		B–			71
Fair (Apprentice)	2	C+	6	60–69%	68
		C			65
		C–			61
Limited (Novice)	1	D+	5	50–59%	58
		D			55
		D–			51
	Below 1		0–4	Below 50%	

Note: This is a sample chart. Grade equivalents will vary according to local policy.

While some measurement experts may argue that this pegged scale is not a true percentage scale, solutions like this represent the kind of "work-arounds" that are necessary as the educational community struggles to shift from norm-referenced to criterion-referenced practice.

THE PROBLEM WITH ZERO

The use of percentage grades is also problematic when teachers have to respond to students not submitting assessment tasks. In workshops, I am frequently asked, "What should I enter in my marks program when a student doesn't complete an assignment?" As Guskey and Bailey (2001), O'Connor (2002), and Reeves (2004) have said, zero is *not* an appropriate response to work not submitted. Furthermore, the idea that assigning zeroes motivates students to change their behaviour is not only unsupported by research, it is also damaging.

CASE STUDY 2   Alex

Alex's world revolved around cars, especially the high-performance variety. School had always been a struggle for Alex because of his learning disabilities. The technical options he had selected for his first year in high school were going to be Alex's only salvation—or so he thought. Though very intelligent and an excellent problem-solver in situations requiring mechanics, Alex exhibited serious deficits in reading and writing. He was fortunate to encounter Mr. Hansen from the Special Education Department, who, having been assigned Alex as part of his caseload, would provide support and monitor Alex's progress in all his classes.

Unfortunately, the high school Alex began attending in September was brand new. The equipment for the transportation technology course had not been delivered in time for the school's opening, and it didn't arrive until late in the fall term. Instead of hands-on projects, students were required to read long sections of the textbook, answer questions, and complete written assignments. And while

Mr. Hansen had succeeded in winning Alex's trust to the point that Alex was producing short pieces of writing for him, Alex was determined not to be embarrassed in his transportation technology class. He chose not to complete the written tasks in that class.

On Parents' Night, after the interim report cards had been sent home, Alex's mother came to see Mr. Hansen. As she entered his room, she began to cry. When he asked what was upsetting her, she showed him Alex's report card, as well as the computer printout from transportation technology (see below).

Mr. Hansen explained that, as far as he knew, the equipment had now arrived, and he asked Alex's mother if she had visited the transportation technology teacher that evening to ask whether Alex could make up the missing practical projects. "I just came from there," she replied. "He told me that if he allowed Alex to make up the missing projects now, it would mess up his class average."

#	Assessment Task	Date	Mark
1	Ch. 2 reading: Engine	Sep. 2	6/10
2	Safety Questions	Sep. 9	0/10
3	Ch. 3 reading: Chassis	Sep. 16	4/10
4	Ch. 4 reading: Electrical	Sep. 23	0/10
5	Fuel and Oil Types quiz	Oct. 7	5/10
6	Chapter review assignment	Oct. 10	0/10
Interim Grade		**Oct. 10**	**15/60 = 25%**

Yes, this is a true story! The use of zeroes is not an appropriate response to any student who does not submit work, but it can be especially harmful for students like Alex. Furthermore, as Reeves has shown, in percentage-based grading systems, assigning zero for work not done is indefensible on the basis of rudimentary mathematics. He writes:

> On a 100-point scale, the interval between numerical and letter grades is typically 10 points, with the break points at 90, 80, 70, and so on. But when the grade of zero is applied to a 100-point scale, the interval between the D and F is not 10 points but 60 points. Most state standards in mathematics require that fifth-grade students understand the principles of ratios—for example, A is to B as 4 is to 3; D is to F as 1 is to zero. Yet the persistence of the zero on a 100-point scale indicates that many people with advanced degrees, including those with more background in mathematics than the typical teacher, have not applied the ratio standard to their own professional practices. To insist on the use of a zero on a 100-point scale is to assert that work that is not turned in deserves a penalty that is many times more severe than that assessed for work that is done wretchedly and is worth a D (Reeves, 2004, p. 324).

HANDLING INCOMPLETE ASSIGNMENTS

So what *is* an appropriate response when students do not complete one or more of the assessments that provide essential evidence of learning? As we saw in Chapter 4, from the point of view of student learning, teachers need to establish a plan that will see the work completed. The plan should include home contact, a completion contract, and should temporarily deprive the student of free time by assigning him or her to a supervised study area during lunch or after school. From a grading standpoint, "Incomplete" should be entered into the grading record. By the time the first or interim reporting period occurs, if the student still has not completed one or more of the essential assessment tasks, then "Incomplete" should appear in place of a summary grade on the report card. Anecdotal comments should identify the specific assessment tasks that have not been completed. At this time, it may be necessary to revisit the completion contract, with both the student and parents present.

If, at the end of the course, one or more of the essential assessments have still not been completed, then this question must be asked: "Does the sample of achievement evidence that the student *has* completed provide sufficient evidence of his or her learning in this course?" Remember that the question of proficiency must be answered in terms of the student's preparedness for work at the next grade level, not in terms of arbitrary cut-points such as 50 percent. If the sample of evidence is deemed to reflect proficiency, despite the missing evidence, anecdotal comments should still indicate work that has not been completed.

Is there any situation in which assigning zero is appropriate? Yes, when the work submitted is worth nothing—in cases of plagiarism or cheating. But in such cases, the zero must *not* be factored into the computation of the summary grade. Academic dishonesty is an attitudinal and a behavioural issue and must be dealt with as such. Contact with parents and documentation in anecdotal records are appropriate responses. Furthermore, if the assessment task in question is one that represents evidence of essential learning, then the students must complete an alternative task. These tasks should not require additional work for the teacher. Part of effective assessment planning involves generating, over time, alternative forms of major assessment tasks for situations such as student absence and academic dishonesty.

DETERMINING GRADES—GUIDING PRINCIPLES

How grades are determined—including any weighting of tasks—should be communicated to students at the outset of the course or term.

Before discussing the most appropriate method for determining grades, we need to ask what we want report card grades to represent. As we saw at the beginning of this chapter, a single grade used to represent achievement in a given subject area can be, at best, only a crude, symbolic summary of what is actually a large amount of information. We also saw that a letter grade generally provides a more accurate summary than a percentage, if the marks comprising that grade have been determined using standards-based assessments. In jurisdictions where policy still dictates that the summary grade be expressed as a percentage, despite the use of rubrics and other standards-based tools, teachers are faced with the formidable challenge of converting marks based on a four- or six-point scale to grades based on a 100-point scale. The following guidelines apply to determining both letter and percentage grades. However, given the inherent problems of translating marks derived from four- and six-point scales into percentage grades, the guidelines are of particular importance in this situation.

1. **A report card grade should capture the trend in student achievement over time—that is, the most consistent achievement.**

   Since report card grades are generally used only two or three times during a course to communicate achievement, they must provide the best possible summary for a given instructional period. However, grades must summarize achievement on summative tasks; they should not include marks from diagnostic or formative tasks. (See page 201, Guideline 3, for an explanation of when formative marks may need to be included.)

◄ A report card grade should capture the trend in student achievement over time.

2. **A report card grade should not be skewed by extreme scores; rather, it should reflect the student's most consistent achievement.**

   For a report card grade to represent the trend in achievement, it must not be skewed by one or two extreme scores. Since such scores may occur due to extraneous circumstances, teachers must use their professional judgment when deciding to include or exclude them.

3. **A report card grade should attribute greater emphasis to more recent achievement.**

   Assuming that students' depth of understanding and level of skill should improve over time, grades should attribute greater weight to assessments occurring toward the end of a given unit or reporting period. If grades are based on the marks from summative tasks only, then the tasks occurring in later units of study should be assigned greater value. If teachers don't feel comfortable with estimating a series of grades to achieve this, then software or a spreadsheet can be used to assign more weight to more recent work (e.g., Summative Task 1 = Weight 1; Summative Task 2 = Weight 2, etc.). Teachers of the same course need to agree on the appropriate range of weighting to ensure that each task carries an appropriate weight in terms of the final grade. See the following graphic.

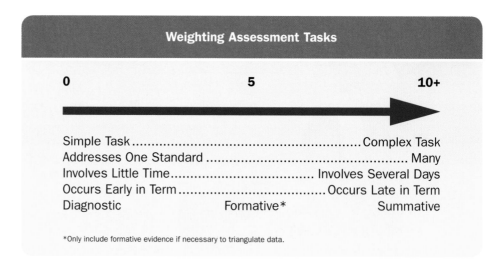

Weighting Assessment Tasks

0	5	10+

Simple Task..Complex Task
Addresses One Standard .... Many
Involves Little Time..................................... Involves Several Days
Occurs Early in Term......................................Occurs Late in Term
Diagnostic   Formative*   Summative

*Only include formative evidence if necessary to triangulate data.

Alternatively, if all summative tasks are scored using fractional scores (e.g., 25/30) and the weight of each score is determined by the denominator, then making later tasks "out of" a greater value will also increase their emphasis. In other words, a later task could be marked out of 60 rather than out of 30. See the boxed text, Using "Mark Out of…" Weighting to Simplify Grade Combinations, page 212, for further explanation.

4. **When determining grades, either by calculation or by estimation, great care must be taken to avoid unintentional weighting of specific tasks.**

When a series of assessments have been scored numerically, each with a different denominator, there is a danger that some of them may be attributed greater weight than intended. For example, in the Incorrect Grade Determinations charts that follow, the grade includes scores from a 75-item short-answer test as well as a major project scored using a four-point rubric containing four criteria. While the teacher had intended the project to carry far greater weight than the test, her failure to convert all scores to a common scale before weighting them caused unintentional skewing of the overall grades. Had she followed this guideline, the data would have resulted in the chart called Correct Grade Determination.

Incorrect Grade Determination	
Item	**Mark**
Short-answer test	42/75
Major project	Level 4 (4-point rubric)
Simple Total (incorrect)	**46/79 = 58%**

In this first calculation, the teacher has simply added 4 to 42 and 75, resulting in a skewed overall grade.

Incorrect Grade Determination		
Item	**Mark**	**Percentage**
Short-answer test	42/75	56%
Major project	Level 4	90%
Simple Average (incorrect)		**73%**

In this case, the teacher has failed to convert the scores to a common scale. The test and the project have different denominators. Again, the result is a skewed overall grade.

Correct Grade Determination				
Item	**Mark**	**Percentage**	**Weight**	**Weighted Contribution**
Short-answer test	42/75	56%	2.5	140 (percentage figure × weight)
Major project	Level 4	90%	10	900 (percentage figure × weight)
Weighted Average			**12.5**	**1040/12.5 = 83% (Level 4–)** (add the two figures above and divide by the weight at left to get the percentage)

This example shows that the teacher has converted the scores to a common scale and calculated the weighting to arrive at a weighted average.

The mathematics involved in combining individual items into categories using a weighted average and combining categories into final grades using another weighted average may lead to confusion or, at worst, outright errors. Furthermore, using grading software to do this does not solve the problem if the teacher cannot easily explain the mathematics behind the final grade.

A simpler option is to record all marks using whatever method is appropriate (e.g., rubric level, percentage, mark out of..., etc.) and then to convert each mark into a fractional score with a denominator that represents the intended weight for the item. Thus the amount that the item is "out of" represents the weight. The overall grade can then be determined using a simple total.

This method provides a powerfully simple way to weight tasks and to combine marks into overall grades—by *simply adding all the numerators and denominators*. Most students and parents will understand this method themselves. The result? Transparency and clarity regarding the determination of grades. Here is a simple illustration using just two marks:

Using "Mark Out of..." Weighting to Simplify Grade Combinations		
Item	**Mark**	**"Out of" Score**
Short-answer test	42/75	14/25
Major project	Level 4	90/100
Simple Total		**104/125 = 83% (Level 4–)** (simply add the numerators and the denominators)

5. **A report card grade should not be a surprise to the teacher who determines it, nor to the student and parent who receive it.**
   Report cards are only one of many communication devices that inform students and parents about achievement. While frequent communication with all parents is desirable, teachers need to ensure that they make contact early in the semester or term if students are experiencing significant difficulties. Whether the communication is by phone, e-mail, or face-to-face contact, the report card must *not* be the first indication of the problem.

6. **In some cases, the teacher's professional judgment may need to supersede a calculated grade.**

When teachers determine report card grades by mathematical calculation, they must be aware of whether the resulting grade accurately represents the trend in achievement they have observed. Discrepancies typically occur as a result of absence from school, a single poor score on a major summative assessment, or examination anxiety. Whatever the cause, we must be cognizant that assessment and grading are human processes used to describe the achievements of adolescents. As professionals, we are sometimes called upon to use our experience and good judgment to adjust a grade to ensure that it represents a fair summary of a student's achievement at a point in time.

Having considered these six guidelines, let's now examine the most common approaches to calculating percentage grades. (Note that the term *calculating* is used here to differentiate this process from *estimating*, a method often used when determining letter grades that summarize a series of rubric scores. See page 218 for further explanation.)

DETERMINING GRADES: THE MEAN AND WEIGHTED MEAN

The mean, or average, is often criticized in the literature on grading (O'Connor, 2002 and 2007) since it can lead to a skewed grade when there are one or two extremely low scores. The mean is not a fair method for determining grades when all marks that a student has received are included. Consider the following graph.

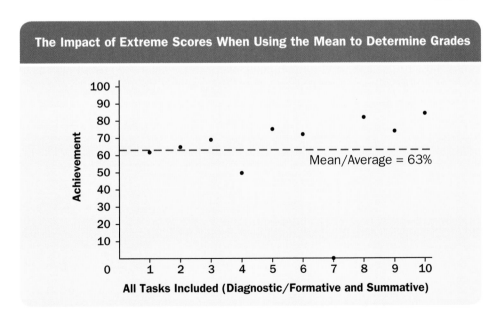

The Impact of Extreme Scores When Using the Mean to Determine Grades

In the preceding graph, Assessment Tasks 1, 4, and 7 were diagnostic/formative. The student did not complete Task 7, and a score of zero was assigned. It is clear from this sample graph that the mean does not accurately reflect the trend in the student's achievement.

The mean is also "mean" to students when all marks are weighted equally, regardless of when the assessments took place—or when the purpose of different assessments is ignored. This problem is also illustrated in the preceding graph.

However, if teachers create assessment plans that differentiate diagnostic and formative assessments from summative assessments and weight them appropriately, the mean *may* be used to determine the grade, as shown in the following graph.

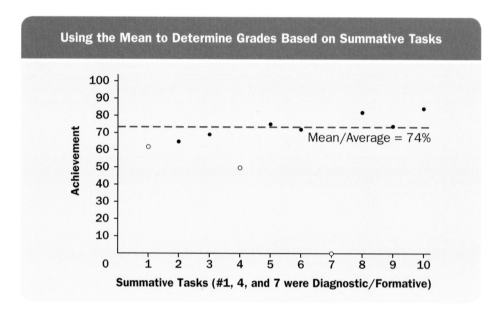

Using the Mean to Determine Grades Based on Summative Tasks

Mean: *The arithmetic mean, or average, is the sum of a set of values divided by the number of values.*

Median: *The central or middle point of a set of values.*

Mode: *The value that occurs most often in a set of values.*

In this example, the overall grade, as determined by the mean, is a better reflection of the student's achievement because it does not include data from diagnostic, formative, and missed assessments. However, the grade does *not* reflect the steady improvement demonstrated by the student over time. Taking *more recent* evidence into account, a grade of 80 percent or even higher would better represent the student's achievement. Typical student progress often follows this pattern of steady, if sometimes erratic, improvement, so the emphasis on more recent evidence when determining grades is important.

DETERMINING GRADES: THE MEDIAN

The median, or middle value in a series of scores, is described more favourably in the literature since it is not affected by extreme scores (O'Connor, 2002). However, this feature of the median may also be problematic, because if several scores are either high or low, the median will not reflect them. Consider, for example, the median for the following set of marks:

69, 70, 72, 72, **74**, 84, 92, 99, 99

The median is simply the middle score in any series of sorted scores. If there is an equal number of scores in the series, the average of the two middle scores is considered the median. In the set of marks above, the median score is 74 percent. However, using the median as a summary grade ignores the high marks this student achieved (92, 99, 99). Had the teacher used the *mean* as the summary grade, the student would have received a grade of 81 percent!

DETERMINING GRADES: THE MODE

The mode is the most frequently occurring value in a series of scores. This method is most often associated with representing a trend in student achievement. For this reason, the mode is the preferred method for determining grades in jurisdictions where policy dictates that grades must represent the "most consistent level of achievement" (*The Ontario Curriculum, Grades 9–12: Program Planning and Assessment*, 2000). While the mode is of little use as a summary when marks are spread out over many intervals, it is appropriate when rubric levels or letter grades are used. For example, a four-point rubric scale or a +/– letter grade scale will typically provide the teacher with enough marks to arrive at a most-frequently-occurring value—a value that provides a meaningful representation of student achievement.

Occasionally, a bi-modal distribution may occur—in other words, two "most frequently occurring scores." This is illustrated in the following graph.

Interval: The number of possible score points on a scale; e.g., 10 on a 10-point scale; 100 on a percentage scale.

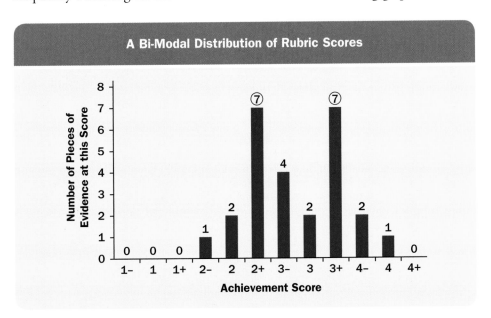

In the situation in the preceding graph, two modes appear: there are seven scores at Level 2+ and seven scores at Level 3+ In this case, the teacher may select the mode that represents the student's more recent achievement.

DETERMINING GRADES: BLENDED MEDIAN

Given that standards-based grading often yields several grades (e.g., one grade for each of several categories, strands, or broad learning outcomes), the median may be used to determine the grade for each of these program elements. Since the median minimizes the impact of extreme scores, it is the preferred method to determine the category/strand/broad outcome grades. An overall grade may then be determined by averaging the category grades. As with the tasks within the categories, the categories themselves can be proportionally weighted (if need be) within the final grade. Grading software—and an understanding of the computations operating within the software—is a key tool when using methods such as these to determine final grades.

▲ Standards-based grading often yields several grades—one grade for each of several categories, strands, or broad learning outcomes.

Blended Median			
Item	**Category**	**Mark**	**%**
Forces Quiz	Knowledge	56	56
Mechanics Quiz	Knowledge	85	85
Kinematics Quiz	Knowledge	87	87
Electromagnetism Quiz	Knowledge	74	74
Friction Quiz	Knowledge	84	84
Knowledge Category Median			**84**
Doorbell Analysis (analysis & interp.)	Application	3+	78
Energy Demonstration	Application	2+	68
Forces in the Real World (research)	Application	3–	72
Lab Carousel	Application	3–	74
Application Category Median			**73**
Fields Report	Communication	3	75
Lesson Presentation QA	Communication	3+	78
Mechanics Mini-Conference	Communication	2+	68
The Force Be With You	Communication	2+	68
Communication Category Median			**71.5**
Electromagnetic Investigation	Thinking	2+	68
Final Exam Open	Thinking	4	90
Friction: Quel Drag!	Thinking	1+	58
Interference Experiment	Thinking	4–	86
Light Quest (Research)	Thinking	4–	86
Puck on Thin Ice	Thinking	4–	86
Thinking Category Median			**86**

This table shows the median for each of four categories (or strand, or broad outcome). An overall grade can then be determined by averaging the category grades.

DETERMINING GRADES: CALCULATION VERSUS ESTIMATION

Traditionally, grading has been viewed as a mathematical process. High school teachers have relied upon calculators and, more recently, grading software to determine grades using one of the methods described in the previous sections of this chapter. Mathematical calculation has been necessary because summary grades have included dozens of marks. Three fundamental shifts in grading practice have made it possible for teachers to estimate summary grades without the use of digital technology.

1. We now understand that fair and appropriate summary grades should be based on only a subset of all the work that students have completed.
2. The use of four- or, at most, six-level rubrics has made it possible to estimate grades by eyeballing the summary grade.
3. The most consistent level of achievement—the mode—is increasingly being viewed as the preferred measure of central tendency.

The following graph is an example of how to estimate a summary grade. In this case it is clear that the student has most consistently performed at Level 3–. Note, however, that if the final twenty assessments in the course were scored at 3–, 3, 3+, 4–, and 4+, then a final grade higher than 3– may be more appropriate to reflect this improvement.

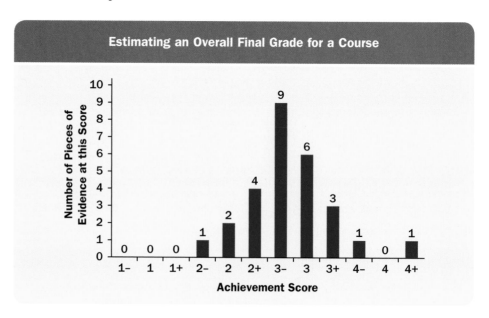

Estimating an Overall Final Grade for a Course

DETERMINING GRADES: CONCLUSION

Regardless of the method used to determine report card grades, an overriding principle is the need to explain the grading process to students and parents in a clear and transparent manner. Given that most students and many adults struggle with basic numeracy, using complex weighted categories and combinations of scoring methods, while pedagogically appropriate, may ultimately confuse everyone. Simpler practices such as the "mark out of …" method (see page 212) or the exercise of professional judgment can, at the end of the day, prove to be the most effective.

The variety of approaches to determining grades highlights the importance now given to professional judgment as a legitimate part of the grading process. Grading is not an absolute science. It is a human process, carried out by skilled, caring educators to provide students and parents with critical information about learning.

Report card grades have serious consequences for students in secondary school. It is incumbent upon educational leaders at all levels to ensure consistency in the methods used to determine grades. While there are many aspects of teaching that require individual teacher creativity, grading is *not* one of them! We owe students and their parents the assurance that grades are determined fairly and consistently. At the very least, there must be consistency in grading practice among all teachers in a given school; preferably, there is consistency among all schools in a given district; ideally, there will be consistency among all districts in a given province or state.

ACCESS TO STUDENTS' GRADES

Parent access to student grading information is increasing as grading software becomes more sophisticated and home Internet use becomes the norm. One unfortunate consequence is parents' increased preoccupation with their sons' and daughters' overall grades. I frequently encounter parents checking grades on a daily basis! This trend runs counter to the research, cited throughout this resource, about the vital role of assessment *for* learning—which should *not* be graded. What is the solution?

First, let me emphasize the need for transparency with respect to communication about student learning. But transparency can include informing parents about the importance of both initial and formative assessments. Parents need to fully understand that there are different purposes for assessment and that not all assessments should be included in report card grades.

From a technical standpoint, as O'Connor (2002) recommends, the averaging or summarizing function that generates overall grades can be suppressed until a formal reporting period. Furthermore, teachers need to explain to parents why initial and formative assessments are weighted at "0." As always, the more consistently such practices are implemented across a school or district, the more accepting parents will be.

Selecting Grading Software

Managing marks and grades electronically can save time and contribute powerfully to student learning. However, the selection of grading software must be based on criteria that reflect sound pedagogy, fairness, accuracy, clarity of communication, and user-friendliness. Too often, grading software is developed by IT experts with little input from assessment experts and teachers, and is purchased on the basis of cost and political expedience.

Grading programs are merely tools to help teachers manage their work. As such, they must be designed to *match* sound assessment policies and practices—not to *dictate* policy and practice. Teachers must become highly skilled in using grading software to the best effect; this requires a deep understanding of the ways a grading program manipulates, blends, and communicates data and information about student achievement.

The following considerations will help individual teachers, principals, and district leaders select grading software that is both pedagogically and technically sound. These questions are listed according to priority.

1. Does the software support best practices in assessment?

The following features align with the principles and practices outlined in *Talk About Assessment*. Although a particular program may not meet all of these requirements, it should meet most of them in order to be considered for school use. The provision of features must also be balanced with ease of use, because even the best feature will be ineffective if the software is overly complex.

The software should:

- provide assessment planning tools that will help teachers plan for a balanced variety of approaches and methods
- allow for creation and/or association of rubrics and other assessment tools that link achievement with data
- allow for a variety of assessment tasks and corresponding mark-entry methods (e.g., percents, levels, "marks out of...," etc.)
- provide details of how the program arrives at the summary grades
- support robust anecdotal comments and other notes for conferencing and providing feedback to students and parents

- accommodate standards-based categories for clustering work based on learning targets
- provide for the separate collection and analysis of achievement and behavioural data
- provide weighting methods both for individual assessments and for broad learning targets or categories
- allow for more recent evidence of learning to be emphasized
- differentiate diagnostic, formative, and summative assessments so that certain data can be stored but not included in the calculation of final grades
- flexibly handle missed work so that items may be excluded from grade calculations rather than counting as a zero
- use mark aggregation methods to compute grades that support the principle of "most consistent" achievement (e.g., mode, median, blended methods, and estimating)
- provide a range of analysis tools (numerical and graphical) for identifying trends in student progress, disaggregating categories, and determining the impact of various weighting and aggregation methods
- provide robust reporting tools for individual student reports, class reports, automatic e-mail reports, etc., which enhance communicating with and providing feedback to students and parents
- support in-class mark entry and retrieval for use with handheld devices or a laptop in the classroom as part of ongoing evidence gathering and feedback

2. Does my district or school mandate a particular grading program?

Mandated systems eliminate personal choice, but this inflexibility is offset by the additional support, training, and customization—such as import/export with the student information system—that will likely be provided locally. In a situation in which a software system is mandated by a district but the software does not adequately support student learning as described above, advocating change is a better response than complicity!

3. Is the software web-based?

Managing grades with a web application (i.e., where teachers can work through a web browser rather than installing software on any particular computer) provides a number of key advantages and is quickly becoming the norm. Unless Internet access is limited by geographical location or the software has a limited set of features that inhibits best practice, web-based applications are generally preferable to installed software for the following reasons:

- Parents and students can be given live access to assessment data and grades rather than the teacher having to periodically print, e-mail, or post information on a web page ("pull" communication rather than "push" communication). Because the data is stored online, any addition to or editing of assessment data occurs automatically and immediately, making that updated information available for students and parents. Student success is supported when frequent, ongoing, informal communication occurs between reporting periods. Teachers may take some time getting used to the heightened level of transparency, but this transparency will generally promote more defensible, effective practices described elsewhere in this resource.
- Teachers can work from any Internet-connected computer rather than ferrying files back and forth on a memory stick or worrying about whether files stored on a school server will be accessible at home.
- No installation is required anywhere; software updates are automatically applied and any operating system (e.g., Windows, Mac, Linux) can be used as long as it has a compatible browser.

4. Other important questions to consider:

- What level of support, training, and additional resources are provided by the software vendor?
- Is there an established market and history of usage by teachers for the product that will ensure it is usable and well tested?
- Does the software company have a solid financial background that ensures the product will be supported well into the future?
- Is the software compatible with district or school student information and reporting systems?
- Is the software compatible with district report card systems for ease of exporting marks, grades, and comments for reporting?
- What additional features are provided (e.g., provision of class lists, seating plans, loaned items)?

If you are currently using grading software, you might wish to formulate some simple explanations of how the software determines the grades. You could keep these on hand to assist you in explaining the process—and the math—to students and parents.

Summary

In this chapter we examined grading and reporting, particularly:

- performance standards and how to communicate them to students
- the purpose of grades and how to organize them
- measurement error in report card grades and other grading dilemmas
- guiding principles for determining grades
- approaches to calculating percentage grades
- tips for selecting grading software

Much of grading and reporting is necessarily about the rather cold facts of scoring methods, calculations, and numeracy. But the main guiding principle for teachers to remember is that grading is a human process requiring fairness, consistency, and professional judgment.

End-of-Chapter Activity

Use Assessing My School's Grading and Reporting Practice to examine your school or district's current practices. This tool allows you to consider strengths, areas of concern, and issues to raise with your principal or other administrators.

TOOL 1.7

Assessing My School's Grading and Reporting Practice

A modifiable version of this tool can be found on the DVD.

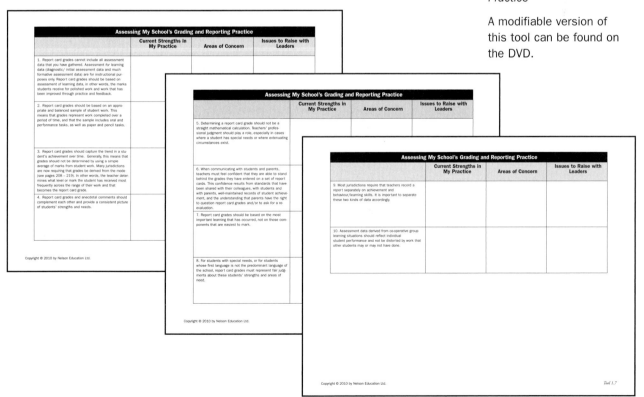

Section 5

IMPLEMENTING CHANGE

Chapter 10: Lessons from the Field, the concluding chapter, returns to the reality of change in education. The chapter discusses the need for assessment reform and provides case studies that show how such change has been effected. I outline steps for reforming assessment at three levels: system, school, and individual teacher. Four conditions for sustainable assessment reform—focus; support and accountability; collaboration; and staying the course—are described.

CHAPTER TEN

LESSONS FROM THE FIELD

A WORD ABOUT IMPLEMENTATION

Chapters 1 through 9 have focused on the need to examine assessment practices to ensure that all students maximize their learning potential. This final chapter shifts the focus to implementing assessment reform at the classroom, school, and district levels. While teachers will certainly benefit from my suggestions regarding the change process at each of these levels, school administrators and district leaders will find the strategies for site-based and system reform to be of particular interest.

EXAMINING OUR PRACTICE

Implementing change in education is difficult, as it should be. The education of children and adolescents is far too important to be swayed by fad, whim, or fancy. That's not to say that education is immune to marketing messages that promise miracles. Open any issue of the most widely read educational journals and you will find numerous promises and claims, particularly in the realm of assessment. But teachers—the second most important people involved in education (I don't have to identify the most important!)—are typically wary of change, especially if they suspect a fad or a magic bullet. So when I say that implementing change is difficult, I mean that it usually occurs slowly because, despite a plethora of workshops and other professional learning programs, many teachers continue to do what they know best once they close the classroom door.

But as we saw in Chapter 2, which dealt with changes in education and assessment, the world is a very different place than it was when many of us graduated from teachers' colleges. The mission of schools has changed. Young people have changed. The workplace has changed, and continues to change at a dizzying speed. This is why I begin my workshops by inviting educators to be professional. I usually say, "Today is an opportunity to do what professionals in all fields must do: to examine our current practice, to learn what research is telling us, and to consider ways in which we might become even better at our craft."

Talk About Assessment: High School Strategies and Tools has presented a wealth of strategies, supported by extensive research, that have the potential to improve the learning of all students. This chapter will explore the "how" of assessment reform at the district, school, and individual teacher level. Again, we will merely scratch the surface in terms of change theory and practice. Elmore, Fullan, Hargreaves, Sparks, and others are the experts in this field. I shall simply share some of the approaches that I have found effective and highlight some specific examples.

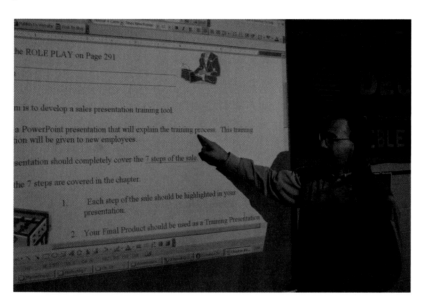

▲ The workplace has changed, and continues to change at a dizzying speed.

WHY THE NEED TO CHANGE?

Why is it necessary to change teachers' current assessment practices? The obvious answer is "to improve student learning." But how do we actually measure improvement in a teacher's assessment practice? We need to look at two kinds of improvement: observable changes in teachers' practices and measurable gains in student learning. For many teachers, the biggest obstacle to changing their current assessment practice is the attitudinal one, which we explored in Chapter 2. This is why, in my work, I introduce the question "Why do I need to change my practice?" in terms of two questions that are more concrete:

1. What do my assessment practices need to look like to help all students learn?
2. How can I change my assessment practices in ways that save me time, as well as improve student learning?

Both of these questions are designed to highlight for teachers the *need* to reflect upon their current practice in order to identify areas they may wish to change.

IMPLEMENTING SYSTEM-WIDE CHANGE

As an educator who lived in Ontario from 1995 to 2003, I certainly know how *not* to approach system-wide improvement. Threats, budget cuts, teacher testing, intimidation, and humiliation tend not to work very well! But then neither did placing faith in the capacity of school systems to "re-culture" themselves, with little regard for accountability. Andy Hargreaves—who also lived in Ontario during the "Common Sense Revolution"—advocates combining culture with contract:

> *We need a more sophisticated understanding of how cultures and contracts can contribute to reinventing public education...so that it combines the mutual personal trust of relationships with the professional trust and accountability of performance contracts* (2004).

Professional learning communities (DuFour & Eaker, 1998) have quickly become the preferred model for implementing educational change. Hargreaves tells us:

> *Professional learning communities use evidence and intuition in order to work and talk together to review their practices and to increase their success.... In a professional learning community, the culture changes— everyone sees the big picture and works for the good of the whole community. Professional learning communities bring together culture and contract. They value both excellence and enjoyment* (2004).

DuFour (May 2004) has identified three essential attributes of a professional learning community:

- a commitment to student learning
- a culture of collaboration
- a focus on results

In her quest to identify the most effective professional learning practices globally, Linda Darling-Hammond, adviser on education to the Obama administration in Washington, and her colleagues have discovered some common elements:

- daily time for professional learning and collaboration among teachers
- ongoing professional development that is embedded within subject content
- extensive formal and informal in-service opportunities
- supportive induction programs for new teachers
- school governance structures that directly involve teachers in decision making about curriculum, instruction, assessment, and professional development (Chung Wei, Andree, & Darling-Hammond, 2009, pp. 28–33)

▲ In effecting change, teachers shouldn't have to try to "do it all"; it's the principal's job to provide the focus for improvement.

FOUR CONDITIONS TO EFFECT SUSTAINABLE ASSESSMENT REFORM

Based on my own work throughout North America as well as abroad, I have identified four essential conditions for successful and sustainable improvement in assessment practices: focus; support and accountability; collaboration; and staying the course.

1. Focus

We all know the fate of overly ambitious school improvement plans that are an inch thick and accomplish nothing. When implementing assessment reform, as with any other educational change, the first step must be to identify the most pressing needs. And these needs must be identified with reference to data—student achievement data, teacher and administrator observational data, survey data, and teacher self-report data, for example.

Ironically, these days, having too much data is a more common problem than having too little data! Often, when visiting a school, I barely make it through the front door before the principal is ushering me in to a locked room to view the data wall! But as the assessment *for* learning research has shown, increasing the frequency of testing does nothing to improve achievement. It's what happens between tests—targeted instruction to address areas of need—that increases learning. So while district and school administrators automatically think "test scores" when I mention data, I am more interested in data that measures what teachers are currently doing *between* tests. If, for example, test scores indicate poor reading achievement in Grade 9 across a district, I immediately want to gather data about the instructional and formative assessment strategies currently being used by all Grade 9 teachers. This would require a combination of teacher self-report data gathered through questionnaires, as well as classroom observational data gathered by school administrators. What can emerge from this data-gathering phase is a focused plan for addressing a district-wide need.

As another example, let's assume that a school system has identified a problem with inconsistency in grading and reporting practices across its secondary schools. A system-level improvement plan for assessment reform must be of at least three years' duration. It must also be a "design-down" plan. In other words, the plan must begin with system leaders developing a vision of the ideal state. For example, they might ask: "What do we want grading and reporting to look like in all of our secondary schools three years from now?" Such questions must initially be answered with *no* limitations or restrictions, if a true vision of the ideal state is to be identified. Inevitably, as the planning process unfolds, conflicting agendas will likely cause the "ideal state" to be scaled back and pared down, certainly to the "desired state" and eventually, to the "achievable state." But if, as educational leaders, we don't dare to dream, we will never take the kinds of brave but essential steps to create a system that really does prepare students for the 21st century.

Here is a model for system-wide improvement that I have used with senior district administrators as part of a strategic planning process:

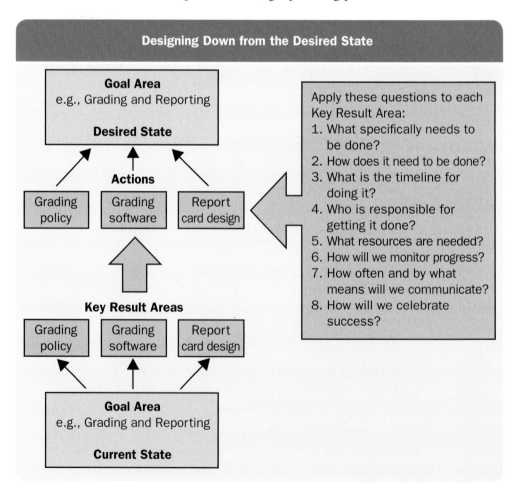

The Designing Down model is a generic one, suited to system-wide improvement in all areas. But when focusing exclusively on assessment, I suggest to senior administrators the following blueprint for designing a plan to implement assessment reform across a district. I invite you to discuss it, play with it, and adapt it to suit your own local needs.

Blueprint for System-Wide Assessment Reform

1. Senior administrators must agree on the need for assessment reform as part of the district's strategic plan.

2. Current policies and procedures must be examined for congruence with the assessment reforms, and be revised if necessary.

3. Current systems and software for grading, reporting, and storing student achievement data must be examined for alignment with the assessment reforms. Plans to revise, develop, or purchase technologies must be established.

4. A professional development plan must be created to support the assessment reforms at all levels: system leaders, school leaders, teachers, and parents. An assessment handbook describing how to implement changes in practice should be produced and given to every teacher.

5. Support staff must be thoroughly trained in the strategies and procedures associated with the assessment reforms, i.e., district-level consultants and key teachers receive in-depth training.

6. A common message about the critical elements of the assessment reform is delivered system-wide through keynote sessions, webcasts, school websites, parent communications, etc. This ensures that everyone in the system is aware of the initiative, albeit with differing levels of understanding and commitment to it.

7. Training of school teams by system support staff takes place. School teams must include teachers from all subject areas, as well as a school administrator.

8. School-level administrators meet to discuss approaches to implementing the assessment reforms; for example, creative solutions to finding planning time, and fostering collaboration within and between subject areas.

9. System-level Instructional Technology leaders meet with school representatives to brainstorm ways to use new technologies to support the initiative (see Collaboration, on page 233). Examples are: using the Intranet as a medium for sharing best practices, and developing units of study or rich performance tasks and rubrics. The goal is to create a district-wide database of excellent materials to support the initiative.

(continued)

10. System and school leaders monitor progress in a systematic way and make adjustments to the plan as necessary.

11. As new priorities emerge, the assessment initiative is integrated with them, not abandoned.

12. Successes are celebrated as they occur through, for example, district and school websites, district professional development days, and teacher presentations at local and provincial/state conferences.

13. The transfer of school administrators from school to school is planned strategically to ensure that the initiative is sustained at each school.

2. Support and Accountability

I see plenty of evidence of the support provided by school districts to assist teachers in improving their assessment practices. Workshops, keynote addresses, print and video resources, consulting opportunities—support takes many forms. But examples of district-wide accountability are rare. And because change is uncomfortable and challenging at the best of times, many teachers will not embrace it unless they are held accountable. Accountability should not be threatening or coercive. Instead, it must be seen as a supportive reminder to busy teachers to do the things that everyone has agreed will work and will improve teaching and learning. Just as I demand that my editorial staff hold me accountable for meeting writing deadlines, educators should expect that supervisors will hold them accountable for doing the things that lead to constant improvement. What does this kind of accountability look like in the context of system-wide assessment reform? Here is one example:

Initiative: All schools are required to implement "assessment *for* learning" strategies in all classes.

Plans of Action:

- *All* school principals will ensure that "assessment *for* learning" is one of their schools' three improvement goals for the next three years.
- A certain percentage (designated by the particular system) of professional learning resources for the next three years will be allocated to "assessment *for* learning."
- An Intranet will be used to facilitate the creation and sharing of exemplary "assessment *for* learning" resources.
- All schools will be required to contribute to these resources.
- All schools will share classroom-level success stories during principal meetings.

Accountability measures like these are designed to improve teaching and learning by making sure that all teachers across a district continue to grow as professionals in ways that benefit students. Implemented in a supportive and collegial way, they can increase teachers' pride in their work and sense of accomplishment.

3. Collaboration

When an initiative is deemed so important that all schools are required to implement it, system-wide resources must be harnessed to facilitate professional learning and implementation. This means using today's digital technologies to delegate tasks. Why, for example, do I so often encounter groups of science teachers in different schools spending their valuable time developing almost identical performance tasks for the same course? Why are communications technology teachers in one high school spending their limited planning time developing a rubric for assessing website design and gathering exemplars while their colleagues across town are doing the very same thing? I am describing common practice! With so little planning time available and so much vital work to be accomplished, we must harness the power of web technology to "work smarter, not harder." In the example cited in the earlier Focus section concerning poor achievement in the Grade 9 students' reading (see page 229), the reading experts in the district must be mobilized to provide training and coaching to all Grade 9 teachers. While very few high school teachers consider it part of their role to teach reading, if students cannot read well enough to understand high school texts, then *everyone* must become a reading teacher! And such work must be undertaken collaboratively, with models of best practice made available across the district.

▲ Use the power of web technology: performance tasks and rubrics can be developed collaboratively and shared both within schools and among schools across cities and districts.

4. Staying the Course

Significant, sustainable improvement in teacher practice that leads to improved student learning takes at least three years to accomplish. Yet all too often, changes in senior personnel see the abandonment of costly initiatives long before their promise has been realized. Strong district leadership is visionary, wise, and strategic. In other words, it is based on a vision of just how great teaching and learning can be, it is grounded in the wisdom of experience, and it is implemented through a strategic plan that features specific actions, measurable results, and a clear chain of responsibility.

As an independent consultant, I must confess to having been involved in a number of "parachute drops"—one-day visits to districts to deliver upbeat, motivational keynote addresses with no follow-up whatsoever. But I am also proud to say that I continue to be involved in numerous multi-year, district-wide improvement initiatives that reflect all of the elements I am describing in this chapter. One such case involves the Ottawa-Carleton District School Board, in Ontario. I will leave it to Jennifer Adams, Superintendent of Curriculum, Instruction, and Assessment, to tell of her experience in the following case study.

CASE STUDY 1   A Superintendent's Perspective

Like most school jurisdictions in Canada, throughout North America, and indeed around the world, the Ottawa-Carleton District School Board's number-one priority is improving student achievement. As the largest school district (70,000 students) in the nation's capital, simply put, student achievement matters.

The district has made bold instructional moves within the primary and junior divisions (Junior Kindergarten to Grade 3, and Grades 4 to 6) throughout the past five years. Research-based instructional practices (e.g., balanced literacy) were identified as a district expectation in every primary and junior classroom in every school in the district. Instructional coaches, selected from current teaching staff, led the way in providing job-embedded professional learning. In schools, teachers collaborated, sharing experiences and ideas that resulted in significant payoffs for students. Over this five-year period, provincial assessment scores for Grade 6 soared from 44 percent to 63 percent in reading; 54 percent to 64 percent in writing; and 51 percent to 67 percent in mathematics (compared with provincial gains of 7 percent in reading; 8 percent in writing; and 4 percent in mathematics).

So where does assessment and evaluation come in? In 2006–2007, the district's annual report on student achievement revealed the need to identify a vehicle to move practice forward, not only in primary and junior division classrooms, but in all classrooms, K to 12. While instructional practice had been a focus in elementary schools, assessment

and evaluation was deemed to be a natural next step. In secondary schools, assessment and evaluation was already a hot topic, with practice varying both within schools and across schools.

We began with a revision to the district policy and procedure on assessment, evaluation, and reporting. The intended purpose was to align district policy with Ministry direction, to move to research-based practices in all classrooms, and to build consistency of practice throughout the district. Needless to say, the topic attracted a lot of attention!

From start to finish, it took eighteen months for the policy and procedure to be revised, approved, and implementation to begin. But it was worth it! A plan was presented to the Board of Trustees describing the process and timelines and seeking approval for consultation. This step was important not only from an approval standpoint, but also because it announced publicly that this work would begin in the district.

A small writing team of elementary and secondary teachers and administrators was formed to write the first draft of the policy and procedures. First steps included a search of assessment and evaluation policies in other jurisdictions, a review of current research, and a review of Ministry documentation. A gap analysis was undertaken to determine where the current policy stood and where the new policy needed to go.

Communication and consultation with staff and the community began with the first draft of the revised policy and procedure. Principals were asked to meet with staff and school councils to engage in discussions and to submit feedback. All Board advisory committees had similar opportunities.

What did the consultation process tell us? Well, it's safe to say that there were strong opinions from both staff and the community, identifying the need for a support document for teachers and administrators to help with implementation of the revised policy and procedure. Teachers and administrators would need time to discuss, debate, and ultimately to develop school policies describing what these practices would look like in their school.

The revised policy and procedure has been in place since September 2008. Upon arrival at school, every teacher and administrator in the district received a copy of *The Educators' Resource Guide: Assessment, Evaluation and Reporting of Student Achievement*, an extensive support document describing best practice in backward design planning, assessment of/for/as learning, and reporting. Principals and vice-principals received significant training and a compendium of activities to use with teachers throughout the school year. The district designated A & E as the focus for the first professional development day. There has been a renewed involvement of department heads' councils with this as a common focus across all subject areas. Things are moving forward—but not without challenges along the way.

One secondary principal told me that there's been more discussion of pedagogy in his staffroom than he's heard in the past decade. Another secondary principal said that it's a combination of large group discussions and one-on-one conversations that are making the difference. And we're beginning to hear about the success stories:

- One secondary school has established the concept of a series of "clemency" weeks in each semester. Students who have missed assignments are identified, the information is communicated to parents, and throughout this week, students may hand in late or missed assignments. This approach works because the pre-planning allows teachers not to schedule tests or assignments during this week. This means that the teachers are not overwhelmed by the marking. At the end of the first of these weeks, the principal sent out an electronic message to interested parties with a huge "56" with sub-text stating that this was the number of major assignments "recovered" during their week.

- Another principal describes an initiative by a group of volunteer teachers called "Friday Night Lights." Whereas some teachers volunteer to coach basketball teams, these teachers identified students with missing assignments, invited them to spend their Friday evening at school, fed them, and recovered a significant number of missing assignments.

Now *that's* student success. And yes, it's making a difference!

What challenges lie ahead? Administrators will need to continue to work with teachers to develop strategies to manage the challenging parts of the policy and procedure to ensure that teacher workload remains doable. Teachers will continue to need time to share ideas and collaborate in professional learning communities. Our instructional leaders—superintendents, school administrators, and department heads—must continue to expand their knowledge of what good assessment practices look like and encourage teachers to move forward as they conduct "walk-throughs" in their schools. Continued communication with parents and students is essential.

Through this policy statement, the Ottawa-Carleton District School Board has encouraged teachers to find creative ways to allow students to demonstrate their understanding of curriculum expectations. It guarantees that we will not give up on any student. It is an important strategy toward meeting the Board's target of a 90 percent graduation rate. Based on the commitment of teachers and administrators we've seen so far, it certainly seems possible.

– by Jennifer Adams, Superintendent of Curriculum, Ottawa-Carleton District School Board

SCHOOL-LEVEL ASSESSMENT REFORM

While a system-wide approach to assessment reform is advantageous, in my experience the most significant and sustainable improvement occurs at the school level. The school, it would seem, is the optimum environment for change. There are two related reasons for this: first, a school, by virtue of its size, is a more manageable unit in which to make change happen; second, a strong leadership team comprising administrators and department heads has the potential to facilitate significant improvement in practice throughout a school.

Let's apply the same four conditions—focus; support and accountability; collaboration; and staying the course—to examine assessment reform at the school level.

1. FOCUS

When I introduce a school staff to the eight Big Ideas of assessment described in this resource, I quickly point out that they cannot all be addressed at the same time. As we saw in the activity at the end of Chapter 1, the human bar graph (page 11) is one way for teachers to identify what they perceive as assessment practices needing the most attention. But as we saw in Chapter 4 (page 57), triangulation of data is important if we are to feel confident about the conclusions we draw. So in addition to the human bar graph, principals may wish to use their own observations gathered during classroom visits, as well as data gathered at the department level during course and subject meetings to confirm which of the Big Ideas require immediate attention. Having a small, manageable set of improvement targets that are pursued vigorously within a specified time frame is one of the keys to success.

A more formalized tool to gather data about teachers' assessment practices is the Professional Learning in Assessment: Implementation Profile. It may be used to gather "current state" data, as well as to monitor teachers' growth over time.

By examining the responses of all teachers to the "Initial" data-gathering exercise, a school Assessment and Grading Committee can identify current areas of strength, areas of need, as well as potential mentoring teams that will facilitate improvement.

Professional Learning in Assessment: Implementation Profile

Use this profile to track your improvement as you implement new assessment practices. You may wish to assess your practice three times: currently (Initial), after several months (Formative), and at the end of the year (Summative). To record your data, simply write I, F, or S in the space provided under the appropriate column to indicate whether it is an Initial, **F**ormative, or **S**ummative assessment. Ideally, all "S" indicators will be in the last column. Once you've completed the checklist, review the pattern of indicators you have entered. Determine which description best summarizes your practice at this time.

	Beginning I am just beginning to use the following practices and strategies as I try to improve the quality and effectiveness of my assessment practice, but I am tentative and still need a lot of support	On My Way I am feeling more comfortable using the following practices and strategies to improve the quality and effectiveness of my assessment practice, and I need only minimal support	I'm There! I have mastered the following practices and strategies for improving the quality and effectiveness of my assessment practice, and I routinely use them
Planning			
• Design down from big ideas and essential skills when planning units			
• Design down from learning goals when lesson planning			
Assessment *for* Learning			
• Adjust assessment processes appropriately to meet the needs of all students			
• Include regular opportunities for students to demonstrate their learning through performance and oral tasks, as well as written tasks			
• Adjust instruction for groups of students based on assessment data			
• Provide regular and specific feedback to students to help them improve			
• Provide students with assessment criteria before they begin work on a task			
• Provide opportunities for students to redo their work, incorporating feedback			
Assessment *of* Learning			
• Identify a sufficient and appropriate sample of essential learning for purposes of grading			
• Use an effective process for tracking and recording achievement			

2. SUPPORT AND ACCOUNTABILITY

As we saw in the discussion of system-wide improvement, support is a relatively easy condition to put in place; but accountability is a touchy issue. My use of the word accountability is in response to the many teachers who have reacted negatively when I've spoken of the need for "pressure" in the context of assessment reform. Teachers are busy people, and without some degree of accountability in place to move them forward with respect to assessment reform, many will keep doing what they've always done.

So what does accountability look like at the school level? On the next page are three examples, relating to three different initiatives, of how a school principal can hold teachers accountable for assessment reform. (Note that, while responsibility for supervising and monitoring this work may be shared among school administrators and department heads, the goal, of course, is that teachers themselves will implement and monitor this work.)

TOOL 1.8

Professional Learning in Assessment: Implementation Profile

A modifiable version of this tool can be found on the DVD.

- *All* teachers will include implementing "assessment *for* learning" strategies in their personal growth plan for the next three years.
- *All* teachers will submit tangible evidence of their collaborative work, e.g., units of study, common assessments, rubrics.
- *All* teachers will be involved in a mentoring relationship to support the improvement of their in-class oral questioning, with a view to including all students and deepening understanding of course material.

3. COLLABORATION

The structure of secondary schools offers natural contexts for collaboration among teachers. For example, all teachers in a mathematics department may collaborate in developing performance-based assessments to supplement more traditional paper-and-pencil assessments; or teachers of the same course may work collaboratively to implement interactive whiteboard technology to increase student engagement. These teachers may then share their expertise in that technology across all departments in the school. In the United Kingdom, this practice is formalized in the role of a Key Teacher who provides training and support to colleagues throughout the school.

While it's natural to collaborate with a colleague who teaches the same course, it can be just as valuable to work with a teacher in a different department. For example, I visited a school in which a business teacher and a mathematics teacher shared an interest in developing end-of-unit performance tasks. They produced authentic, integrated tasks and were able to share successes and challenges as they occurred in their respective classrooms.

▲ The structure of secondary schools offers natural contexts for collaboration among teachers.

Since I believe that students benefit from the consistent implementation of effective strategies, and that parents like to see consistent practice within the same department, implementing a new approach in all courses in a given subject area can result in significant gains in student learning. However, such broad initiatives should only be undertaken once the bugs have been worked out in pilot projects.

4. STAYING THE COURSE

As was the case at the district level, this fourth condition for effective assessment reform is of paramount importance at the school level. Whenever I am asked to facilitate a "command performance" professional development event, I meet many teachers whose comments and body language scream, "Okay, so what's this year's fad? We did differentiated instruction last year." School leaders must protect their teachers from being overwhelmed by too many initiatives, from being confused by conflicting initiatives, or from becoming disillusioned by short-lived initiatives that create too much work for little or no return. The head teacher at Walkden High School (near Manchester, England—see the following case study) told me that when told he was being transferred to another school after two years into his school's three-year improvement plan, he dug in his heels. He informed his supervisor that he considered it to be in the best interests of staff, students, and parents that he stay at Walkden for at least another year. This enabled him to see the plan through and to ensure that teachers and students had the opportunity to celebrate their successes and receive the recognition they deserved.

As a profession, we don't do "celebration" very well. Yet Fullan (2001) and Schmoker (2001) emphasize how critical recognition and celebration are to teachers. As I visited classrooms and chatted with teachers about the possibility of videotaping their work for the *Talk About Assessment: High School Strategies and Tools* DVD, they radiated excitement! When I suggest to teachers that what they are doing in their classrooms is action research and they should consider submitting their work to educational journals or presenting their work at provincial/state conferences, I encounter a mix of humility, disbelief, and fear. But if conference presentations are too daunting for some teachers, outstanding, innovative teaching and assessment work can and *should* be celebrated on school and district websites and in newsletters, as well as at staff meetings and parent evenings.

I visited Walkden High School, near Manchester, England, in the third year of the "Assessment for Learning: 8 Schools Project." The "AfL 8 schools project" as it was known, was part of the National Strategy for School Improvement, Secondary, sponsored by the Department for Education and Skills in the United Kingdom. It sought to identify what helps pupils to develop as motivated and effective learners, through professional dialogue and collaborative working with teachers, school leaders, and local authorities (LAs).

The following key messages are taken from the final report by the Department for Education and Skills. It should be noted that the key messages were drafted on the basis of observations at all eight schools and not Walkden H.S. specifically.

Key Message 6

To establish AfL whole school, both "top down" and "bottom up" change processes must prevail, as they fulfill different purposes. "Top down" approaches can convey a clear message about expectations and focus for improvement, but this alone does not win the "hearts and minds" of all teachers or build internal capacity.

Key Message 7

AfL practice is most successfully developed where teachers work collaboratively within and across departments, share their practice and learn from what they and their peers do well....

Key Message 8

Senior and middle leaders need to maintain an unrelenting focus on, and support for, the intended change. This includes addressing the issue of competing priorities and the contradictory practices which may stem from these.

Key Message 9

A secure and shared understanding of what effective AfL practice "looks like" is essential for teachers to be able to reflect and develop their practice and for leaders to be able to help them do this. Isolated pockets of good practice can be developed by individual teachers but, for AfL to have significant impact, development needs to be whole school....

– from "The Leadership and Management of Whole School Change," *Assessment for Learning: 8 Schools Project Report*, National Strategy for School Improvement, Secondary, sponsored by the Department for Education and Skills, U.K., 2007

Walkden High School's Assessment for Learning 3-Year Plan targeted a specific goal for each year. The goal for Year One saw the entire faculty learn about and practise providing students with specific, descriptive oral and written feedback to help them improve their work; in Year Two of the project, all staff learned how to make student self- and peer feedback a routine part of each lesson; in Year Three, the focus was on all teachers implementing a research-based model for lesson design.

Although a new focus was added each year, the project was cumulative; i.e., oral and written feedback continued to be a school-wide initiative for all three years, just as the use of self- and peer assessment continued in the third year.

There were a number of key features of the Walkden plan that bear noting:

- The Head and Assistant Head (Principal and Vice-Principal) both taught a class each day. This qualified them as full participants in the implementation of the new strategies. Not only did they provide leadership, they were also able to share their own experiences as teachers struggling to facilitate change with students.

- Eight AfL (Assessment for Learning) Key Teachers worked within and across departments to provide modelling and coaching. The role of these key teachers reflects a strong commitment in the United Kingdom to distributed leadership. Reeves and Marzano cite an ever-growing body of research that identifies the superiority of peer coaching over training by outside experts. (Dr. Reeves and Dr. Allison are the authors of the recent book *Renewal Coaching*, 2009. Marzano's work is from *The Art & Science of Teaching*, 2007.)

- The Key Teachers were allocated one half-day per week to conduct their own research outside the school. This involved visits to other schools and to the local university, online learning, and other professional learning opportunities that related to furthering their knowledge and skills in assessment *for* learning.

- The Head Teacher required every committee operating during the project to have an AfL connection, and every meeting to include AfL on the agenda. For example, all department meetings included progress reports on the project, and all parent–teacher meetings provided updates to the community.

After an early morning meeting with the administrative team at Walkden, I had the opportunity to visit a cross-section of classes at all grade levels. I was impressed by the pervasiveness of the strategies and practices that the Head and Assistant Head had identified as critical to the success of the project. Specifically, I saw an unerring commitment to identifying lesson goals for students. All students understood the purpose of each lesson and how the day's lesson connected to the unit as a whole. All teachers delivered lessons that used a variety of instructional techniques. These included extensive use of new, interactive technologies (interactive whiteboards and laptop computers, for example), student self- and peer assessment of homework and seatwork, games to consolidate understanding toward the end of lessons, the use of students' most common errors and misconceptions to differentiate instruction, and the appropriate use of praise to recognize and celebrate students' contributions and achievements.

But of greater significance than all of these instructional strategies were the student behaviours I observed and the student comments that I heard throughout the school. In every class, students were active, engaged, and often excited participants in their own learning. Generally, students spent more class time speaking than did their teachers; after brief mini-lessons to introduce new material, students worked in pairs or small groups to practise, consolidate, apply, question, or assess their learning. Time-on-task was maximized; busywork was nowhere to be found.

What struck me most about Walkden was that I was witnessing a true "professional learning community," not merely the trappings of one. In the words of Hargreaves, "...the culture changes—everyone sees the big picture and works for the good of the whole community" (2004). For me, this was an example of vision coming to fruition.

TEACHER-INITIATED ASSESSMENT REFORM

While school-wide improvement may be the long-term goal, many projects that I see begin as teacher-initiated pilots. These often occur when one or two teachers return from a conference or workshop, eager to try something new. In the case of one teacher wanting to implement a new strategy, I strongly encourage seeking out a colleague who is willing to collaborate in the project. Planning together, perhaps observing each other teach a class, debriefing what worked and what problems occurred, and then problem solving to refine the strategy are all opportunities for teachers to learn from each other. Furthermore, when teachers collaborate in these ways, they are far more likely to persevere in the face of challenges than if they undertake an initiative alone.

Naturally, there will always be challenges when teachers implement changes to their routines. Michael Fullan speaks about the "implementation dip" (2001, pp. 40–41), the phenomenon that sees things initially get worse in the face of a change in practice. For example, if Elizabeth decides to introduce one-on-one student conferencing during regular class time, she may report, after a couple of weeks, an increase in behavioural problems and a sense that she's not in control of the class. These are natural consequences, but they are problems that can quite easily be solved, especially if Elizabeth is working with a colleague. For example, by chatting with a colleague, and visiting his class during a conferencing session, she gets some excellent ideas for revising her approach. Gradually, as the term progresses, Elizabeth finds that off-task behaviour becomes less frequent, she becomes more used to not having to control the class, and, most importantly, the one-on-one conferences begin to have a dramatic impact on student learning. She and her students have persevered through the implementation dip.

▲ Introducing new approaches such as group conferencing can have a dramatic impact on student learning.

COMMUNICATING CHANGES IN ROUTINES TO STUDENTS AND PARENTS

Some years ago, during a workshop about marking students' work, I had been sharing strategies for teachers to reduce their marking time while at the same time increase student learning. One teacher said at the end of the day, "Great! That pile of marking that I'd planned to take home this weekend can just stay where it is!"

"Hold on a minute," I replied. "It's the middle of the semester. This is *not* the time to make dramatic changes to your marking routines—especially changes that may cause parents to have a fit."

Before implementing changes to current routines, there are a few essential preparatory steps to take that will minimize the potential for parental concern and maximize the likelihood of success:

- Ensure that you have the support of your principal and department head/chair.
- Plan to implement the change at the start of a new semester or term, not midway through an instructional period.
- Ensure that there is a solid research base supporting the change you are about to make. Be ready to cite this research, should the need arise with parents.
- Inform students and parents through a newsletter or e-mail about the proposed change.
- Invite parents to contact you if they have any concerns.

In the classroom, introduce the initiative in a way that clarifies for students their responsibility for its success, as well as your own. For example:

> *We're going to be trying something new this semester. It's called "traffic lighting." It's a fun way to assess your own learning, as well as the work of your peers. Now we shouldn't expect that it will work like a dream from the start. We will all have to work out the bugs. Let me show you what traffic lighting looks like. Then we can discuss any questions you have.* (See the section on Traffic Lights in Chapter 6, page 100.)

Fundamental to the success of this process is the constant use of the pronoun *we*. Teacher and students working collaboratively are equally responsible for a positive learning environment.

As we saw in Elizabeth's case, on the previous page, it is rare that a new approach works well immediately. By monitoring your own and your students' progress, you will be able to make adjustments to a new strategy so that it will become more effective. Yes, this is "assessment *for* learning" with respect to your teaching practice! The Friday Week in Review model described in Chapter 7 can be highly effective for monitoring the success of a new strategy (see page 138).

FAIRNESS AND HUMOUR

Ask a group of high school students to identify the qualities they value most in their teachers and inevitably *fairness* and *a sense of humour* will top the list. We are addressing fairness throughout this resource as we examine assessment practices that benefit students. And while humour does not come naturally to all of us, it is worth putting some effort into "lightening up" if we look at ourselves in the mirror and discover a deficiency in the humour quotient. We can seek out cartoons that are thematically related to units of study; we can make reference to popular media; and we can take the opportunity to laugh at ourselves. Letting students see us as flawed human beings can be intimidating but can also provide encouragement, particularly to students who lack confidence. For example, to help my students identify differences between effective and ineffective oral presentations, I first delivered a very poor presentation and instructed students to list what they saw and heard. I then delivered a quality presentation and again asked students to list what they saw and heard. From their various lists, we developed a composite T-chart to identify what a quality presentation looks like and sounds like. As you can imagine, the bad presentation produced much hilarity as Mr. Cooper made a complete fool of himself! However, important learning followed as we discussed the flaws and then set the stage for the exemplary presentation.

▲ Fairness and a sense of humour are valued qualities in teachers.

Summary

In this concluding chapter, I have reiterated and summarized the need for assessment reform, and explored what it can look like at three levels: district, school, and individual teacher. I hope that the chapter has helped you to examine your own current practice, and that it provides some scaffolding for effecting change, whatever your role.

I hope that this *Talk About Assessment: High School Strategies and Tools* resource as a whole has provided encouragement and guidance in taking the next steps toward making your practice more efficient, more effective, and—always at the heart of it all—beneficial to all students.

Refer to the DVD as you prepare for meetings—or watch clips during meetings—perhaps as a starting point for discussion of assessment experiences or to identify ways to improve practice.

End-of-Chapter Activity

I'd like to recommend a series of action steps:

- Identify areas for improvement through examining the Big Ideas (Chapter 1) and using the Professional Learning in Assessment: Implementation Profile (on page 237 in this chapter and on the DVD).
- Establish a team—see the suggestions in this chapter.
- Create a plan for improvement (see the Designing Down from the Desired State model, page 230 in this chapter). It works at the teacher level, even though it's in the "system-wide" section.
- Have everyone on the team keep a reflective journal to track their progress, successes, and challenges.
- Arrange to meet regularly, using the reflective journals to initiate discussion.

TOOL 1.8

Professional Learning in Assessment: Implementation Profile

A modifiable version of this tool can be found on the DVD.

INTEGRATING ASSESSMENT WITH INSTRUCTION THROUGH STUDENT-DIRECTED RESEARCH PROJECTS

Educators agree that the ability to design and conduct an independent research project is an essential skill for today's high school graduates. Unfortunately, too often, subject-driven content standards dominate curriculum documents and take precedence over such essential skills. In this article, we will examine a model that equips students with a set of essential research and communication skills, while at the same time providing rich opportunities for self-, teacher, and peer assessment. I have named the model *INTU* (meaning, *"I need to understand…."*), a term coined by Carl Bereiter and Marlene Scardamalia (Bereiter and Scardamalia, 1996).

Students begin by formulating their own research question—their INTU. They then undertake an extensive research process in which they seek to answer their question, using books, magazines, newspapers, the Internet, and, if appropriate, one-on-one interviews with peers and adults. Next, they organize their information, acknowledging differing points of view or conflicting arguments, and prepare and deliver a professional presentation on their findings to their teacher and classmates. The final phase involves self-, peer-, and teacher assessment of their work.

INTU-based projects combine assessment with instruction in ways that promote learning across a vast array of learning targets. In the spirit of "backward design" (Wiggins and McTighe, 1998), we will first examine the breadth of curriculum targets that this model addresses; then we will consider how each phase of the process provides opportunities to assess *for* learning (Assessment Reform Group, 1999); we will consider the instruction that needs to occur at each step; and finally, we will explore the INTU as an opportunity for assessment *of* learning.

WHAT RANGE OF CURRICULUM TARGETS DOES THE INTU MODEL ADDRESS?

One of the greatest strengths of the INTU model is the breadth of curriculum standards that it encompasses. We know that teachers everywhere are feeling overwhelmed by the plethora of outcomes or standards they are expected to "cover"—often, as we know, at the expense of fostering student understanding. As you will see in the curriculum table *(see Figure 1)*, the INTU model addresses a huge number of curriculum targets that span several core subject areas.

For the sake of simplicity, we will focus on students in Grade 9, but the INTU model is suitable for students from primary through to college levels. The following is a sampling of the more than forty curriculum targets that students demonstrate as they work through their INTU projects.

	Figure 1

Subject	Curriculum Target (standard, outcome, expectation)
English	• Locate explicit information and ideas in texts to use in developing opinions and interpretations • Use a variety of organizational techniques to present ideas and supporting details logically and coherently • Investigate potential topics by formulating questions, identifying information needs, and developing research plans to gather data • Locate and summarize information from print and electronic sources • Group and label information and ideas; evaluate the relevance, accuracy, and completeness of the information and ideas; and discard irrelevant material • Make constructive suggestions to peers • Plan and make oral presentations to a small group or the class • Analyze their own and others' oral presentations to identify strengths and weaknesses • ….
Science	• Select and integrate information from various sources, including electronic and print resources, community resources, and personally collected data, to answer the question chosen • Gather, organize, and record information using a format that is appropriate to the investigation ….
Social Science	• Demonstrate an ability to collect, organize, and synthesize information from a variety of sources • Select and use appropriate methods and technology to communicate the results of inquiries and present a variety of viewpoints on issues • Develop and use appropriate questions to define a topic, problem, or issue, and use these questions to focus an inquiry • Locate and use effectively materials from primary sources (e.g., field research, surveys, interviews) and secondary sources (media, CD-ROMs, Internet) to research an issue • Demonstrate an ability to distinguish among opinion, argument, and fact in research sources • Describe biases in information and identify what types of information are relevant to particular inquires • ….
Technology	• Share information using media tools and a variety of technologies • Use a variety of software applications, such as word processing, to document projects from conception to completion • ….

What does the INTU model look like as it is implemented in the classroom? To help us explore the four phases of the model, we will observe Freddie and Anna, two Grade 9 students with learning disabilities, who are taking a learning strategies course. We will track their progress as they conduct research into pit bull terriers, a topic they are both very interested in pursuing.

PHASE 1: FORMULATING AN INTU QUESTION

Students need to discover that good research begins with a clear, focused question. I worked as a school librarian many years ago and was confronted daily by students asking, *"Mr. Cooper, do you have any information about ... black holes, Afghanistan, the Olympics, mad cow disease ...?* My reply was always, *"Of course I have information on.... But before we go any further, I want you to go back to your classroom and format a specific, well-worded question that you want to find the answer to."*

When students begin their research with a vague, unfocused topic, they quickly find themselves overwhelmed with information. The result is that they simply begin summarizing whatever they have found. There is no "research" happening—they merely gather and assemble whatever information is most readily available.

On the other hand, when students are explicitly taught how to formulate a meaningful question, they are able to undertake purposeful, directed research. In order to answer their question, they have to make numerous decisions about the relevance, quality, bias, and objectivity of the information they find. To illustrate, contrast the following "topics" with their corresponding INTUs:

Figure 2	
Topic	**INTU**
Testing Consumer Products on Animals	I need to understand both sides of the debate concerning whether it is right to test consumer products on animals.
Video Gaming	I need to understand whether video gaming is helpful or harmful to learning for teenagers.
Downloading Music	I need to understand the arguments for and against downloading music made by consumers, record companies, and artists.

When Freddie and Anna asked their teacher if they could research pit bull terriers, she agreed and then helped them to formulate their INTU:

> *Teacher: What is it about pit bulls that interests you?*
> *Anna: I want to find out why they attack people.*
> *Teacher: But are all pit bulls dangerous?*
> *Freddie: No way! My neighbour has one and it's never attacked anyone.*
> *Teacher: Why are pit bulls in the news so much at the moment?*
> *Anna: Because lots of people want them banned.*
> *Teacher: Freddie, how do you think your neighbour would feel if they were banned?*
> *Freddie: He'd fight it!*
> *Teacher: So it seems that we have two sides to this issue.*
> *Anna: So I guess we need to look at both sides.*

Teacher: Right. So what might your INTU be?

Anna: How about, "I need to understand why some people want to ban pit bull terriers, while other people don't"?

Teacher: Freddie, what do you think?

Freddie: Sounds good to me.

PHASE 2: FORMULATING A RESEARCH PLAN

Once students have a well-written INTU, they learn how to break it down into subtopics and then how to develop a key research question for each subtopic. Figure 3 shows a useful template for helping students with this step. You can see how Freddie and Anna moved from their INTU, to subtopics, and then, with support from their teacher, developed a series of key research questions.

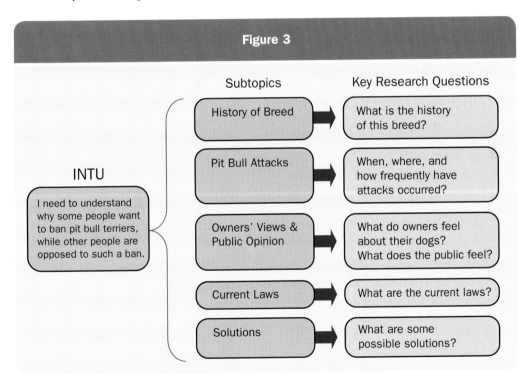

Figure 3

PHASE 3: LOCATING, RECORDING, EXAMINING, AND ORGANIZING THE INFORMATION

Gone are the days when a lack of information to answer research questions was a problem. Largely due to advances in information technology, the greatest research challenge facing students is how to sift and sort through the vast amount of information that is available to them. For this reason, teachers need to approach the information-accessing and organization elements of an INTU with care and careful planning. One source of confusion for students is the way that the Internet has blurred the distinction between primary and secondary resources. When students use a search engine, there is no built-in quality control filter. Their Google search will simultaneously produce legitimate resources as well as numerous individual websites that are fraught with bias.

To help deal with this problem, teachers may require students to locate information from several other sources *before* permitting them to go to the Internet. For example, Anna and Freddie's teacher provided the following guidelines to ensure that her students learned how to access a variety of information sources, including the Internet.

Student Guidelines for Locating and Gathering Information

1. You must draw information for your INTU from the following sources:

    - At least 4 print sources—books, newspapers, magazines, brochures
    - A student-developed public opinion survey administered to a sample of peer and adults (sample size to be negotiated with the teacher)
    - At least 4 Internet sources

2. You will receive an orientation to these sources from the school librarian before beginning your project.
3. All of your sources must be recorded on the Note-Making Sheets that I will provide.

As students locate and accumulate large amounts of information, the teacher moves from group to group, listening and observing. She is able to assess *for* learning by providing feedback, reminding students of the importance of their key research questions in focusing their research and ultimately in answering their INTU. The following conversation illustrates the depth of thinking that occurs as students examine information:

> *Freddie: Anna, look at this website! One hundred and twelve pit bull owners and not one attack!*
> *Anna: Of course! It's a website created by pit bull owners. They're not going to tell you about attacks, even if they know they've occurred.*
> *Freddie: So does that mean we can't use this site?*
> *Anna: I think we can but we have to explain that it only represents one side of the issue. I've found this newspaper article reporting on a homeowners group that is collecting signatures supporting a ban.*

To be effective, assessment must occur throughout the INTU project. Students learn about bias, objectivity, and reliability of information as they and the teacher/assessor work through the research process. The teacher's role is to be a roving facilitator, answering students' questions by posing more questions, asking them to explain and justify their decisions, and often causing them to rethink their current direction and consider alternatives. In this way, the teacher is able to "assess on the fly," noting which students are increasing their understanding of the research process as "messy learning," and which students are still tending to believe everything they read. Assessment *for* learning involves feedback to students *as they work,* helping them to internalize a vision of highly skilled performance and to move ever closer to mastery.

To aid assessment *for* learning, many teachers use a research skills rubric to provide students with specific feedback on their progress.

Figure 4. Partial Research Process Rubric

Criteria	Level 1	Level 2	Level 3	Level 4
Planning	• has difficulty formulating INTU, subtopics, and key research questions	• formulates INTU, subtopics, and key research questions that require significant revision	• formulates workable INTU, subtopics, and key research questions	• formulates insightful INTU, subtopics, and key research questions
Locating Information	• has difficulty locating relevant information • has difficulty distinguishing between fact and opinion	• locates relevant information from some of the required media but requires support for others • locates information from a limited perspective	• locates relevant information from all of the required media • collects information which represents different points of view	• locates information that reflects a sophisticated understanding of the issue • collects information which represents all relevant points of view

Effective use of such a rubric involves pointing out the indicators that describe what students are currently doing, and what they need to do to enhance their skills. It does NOT involve telling them the level at which they are operating. Ascribing a performance level need only occur once the research process is over and students receive a summary grade to indicate their level of achievement. In short, assessment *for* learning focuses on what the student is doing well, what the student is struggling with, and what the student needs to do to improve; assessment *of* learning occurs once the task has been completed and indicates to the student his/her current level of achievement, relative to a known standard.

PHASE 4: PREPARING, SHARING, AND ASSESSING OUR RESEARCH

As we have seen, the INTU structure is extremely rich in terms of the range of essential skills that can be taught and assessed. Preparing, self-assessing, and delivering oral presentations are among these essential skills. The widespread availability and use of presentation software has recently added another layer of complexity to the classroom presentation. A glitzy PowerPoint presentation will not compensate for a student's deficient oral communication skills, but without skilful teacher intervention, many students believe it will. Anna and Freddie's teacher decided to introduce the "Presentation" skills section of the INTU by delivering a dreadful presentation herself and inviting her students to brainstorm everything that was wrong with it. Apart from being a wonderful opportunity for her students to see her make a fool of herself and to share some good laughs, she was able to generate a rich class discussion about what an exemplary presentation *should* look like.

When working with presentation software, the medium can take precedence over the quality of the content. For example, technically savvy students will, if permitted, get carried away by the sound and animation possibilities inherent in the technology. As always, the teacher's ability to focus students' attention on what is important, as opposed to what is most fun, is critical. For example, students may be instructed that a basic set of slides, corresponding to each of their key research questions, must be completed before any time is spent on slideshow format and special effects.

As in each of the previous phases, the teacher conducts assessment *for* learning *while* students are preparing their presentations. This may take the form of commenting and asking questions while moving from group to group, or could even involve students doing a "trial run-through" of their entire presentation, either for the teacher or for a small group of "critical friends" (peer assessors). This would be an opportunity for students to receive feedback and to fine-tune their presentation prior to the formal presentation to the class and invited guests. Assessment has truly been successful when students ask, *"Miss, I'm pretty sure I'm ready to present. What do you think?"*

When it is time for the INTU presentations to occur, the teacher has a number of options, depending on time available and the number of students in the class. In a small class of twelve students such as Anna and Freddie's learning strategies class, the teacher may opt to have groups present their work to the whole class, with every student being responsible for assessing the quality of each presentation. In a large class, this approach may consume too much class time, so the teacher may split a class of thirty students into three groups: each group then presents its research to just eight peers, and each peer is responsible for assessing only one third of the class projects. The teacher roves from group to group to ensure that things go smoothly. Since the teacher will have assessed each group while they were working on their INTU and will also receive each group's slide presentation and written report, she doesn't need to hear each group's presentation in its entirety.

Planning for effective peer assessment is crucial if students are to provide meaningful feedback to their classmates. Notice that I said "feedback." There is little or no point in having students assign marks to the work presented by their peers—such marks are notoriously unreliable and serve no useful purpose. Instead, equipped with the same rubric that was distributed to all students, outlining the criteria for oral presentations, students observe, listen, and ask questions during each presentation, take several moments to reflect on the presentation, and then provide immediate, face-to-face feedback to the researchers in terms of what they did well, what they did poorly, and constructive suggestions for how to improve the presentation.

The INTU approach to student-directed research is highly effective because it promotes rich thinking and learning, while enabling teachers to integrate assessment with instruction. It is a model that is popular with students because it is engaging and self-directed; it is popular with teachers because it addresses a vast array of essential skills that are germane to all core subject areas. Furthermore, it is a model that may be utilized with students across a wide range of abilities. Anna and Freddie both have severe learning disabilities and were members of a segregated special education class. Speaking of them, it is appropriate that our two students have the last word, so what did Anna and Freddie conclude by the end of their INTU?

Our Conclusions

- *We think that pit bulls should be banned because they are dangerous and unpredictable.*
- *If our province bans pit bulls, we think other provinces will start discussing a ban because all other provinces are having this trouble.*

Note: pseudonyms have been used for the students.

accommodations strategies and supports applied to at-grade-level curriculum, assessment strategies, and/or instruction to enable students to be successful; providing extra time, different resources, and/or an alternative mode of demonstrating learning are all examples of accommodations (see also *modifications*)

achievement demonstrated student learning at a given point in time

affective domain feelings, attitudes, and emotions that may affect student learning

analytic rubric a rubric that breaks down a given product or performance into a set of criteria and identifies discrete indicators for each criterion

anchor a sample of student work that is matched, or "anchored," to a specific level of performance on a rubric (see also *exemplar*)

anecdotal record ongoing written observations about students' performance or work samples, collected over time

assessment gathering data about student knowledge and/or skills, either through informal methods, such as observation, or formal methods, such as testing

assessment *as* learning assessment as a metacognitive process involving students setting their own learning goals and reflecting on and adjusting their own learning

assessment *for* learning assessment designed primarily to promote learning. Assessment *for* learning includes both initial, or diagnostic, assessment and formative assessment. Early drafts, first tries, and practice assignments are all examples of assessment *for* learning.

assessment *of* learning assessment designed primarily to determine student achievement at a given point in time. Summative assessments are assessments *of* learning. Report card grades should be based on a summary of data from assessments of learning.

authentic tasks performance assessments, such as simulations and role-plays, that imitate real-world tasks

backward design a curriculum planning process with three stages: identifying essential learning, assessing essential learning, and planning instruction: developed by Grant Wiggins and Jay McTighe

balanced assessment assessment that includes an appropriate balance of oral, performance, and written evidence

checklist a list of specific skills to be demonstrated during a performance task or attributes to be included in a product

cloze procedure a diagnostic reading assessment technique in which readers use context and vocabulary clues to fill in missing words from a passage of text

content standards concepts and skills that students are expected to acquire and demonstrate

criterion-referenced assessment assessment that measures students' performance against a set of predetermined performance criteria

critical evidence a sample of work demonstrating that student has learned the essential concepts and skills associated with a given unit or course

culminating task an assessment task that requires students to synthesize learning at the end of a unit or other instructional period

diagnostic assessment described as "initial assessment" in some jurisdictions, it is assessment to determine appropriate starting points for instruction; one element of assessment *for* learning

differentiated instruction utilizing a range of alternative teaching and learning activities and grouping methods to meet the diverse needs of students.

enduring understandings the underlying and most important concepts and ideas that students are expected to acquire during a unit or course

essential skills critical competencies that students are expected to demonstrate with proficiency by the end of a unit or course

evaluation making judgments about student-demonstrated knowledge and/or skills

exemplar a sample of student work that represents either the best or expected level of performance on a given task (see also *anchor*)

formative assessment assessment that occurs during the learning process and provides feedback to both students and teachers to help improve learning; one element of assessment *for* learning

frequency scale a scale used to measure how frequently a desired behaviour or attribute occurs

grading summarizing assessment data for reporting purposes in the form of a letter or numerical grade

Glossary

holistic rubric a rubric that uses a general set of indicators to describe each achievement level; holistic rubrics are useful for scoring but of little use for instructional purposes

initial assessment see *diagnostic assessment*

inquiry-based learning a teaching approach that encourages students to create their own focused questions for investigation in subject areas; students are actively engaged in their own learning rather than receiving teacher-directed instruction

INTU an acronym for "I need to understand," referring to student-developed inquiry questions; developed by Carl Bereiter, Ontario Institute for Studies in Education

levels of performance a scale, often ranging from 1 to 4, used on many criterion-referenced assessment tools

mean the sum of a set of values divided by the number of values; also the arithmetic mean, or average

median the central or middle point of a set of values

mode the value that occurs most often in a set of values

moderated marking collaborative marking; teachers of the same course design a common assessment task and rubric and then meet to assess student work

modifications changes made to the curriculum to enable a student to be successful; permitting a student to work at a different grade level is an example of a modification (see also *accommodations*)

norm-referenced assessment assessment that compares students' performance with a normed sample of student performance; achievement is measured by comparing one student's work with the work of other students

pegged scale a grading scale in which the 100-point (percentage) scale is reduced to a 12- to 15-point scale

percentile ranking a measure of relative standing within a defined group in which scores range from 1 to 99: This type of score is not to be confused with percent scores; 35 percent correct on a test may indicate serious problems, while a percentile rank of 35 indicates that the student has done better than more than one-third of the group.

performance assessment assessment based on observing students demonstrating activities in which they apply their knowledge and skills; assessment that requires students to perform a task as opposed to merely writing about it

performance standards predetermined statements that describe expected levels of performance on an assessment task; a rubric is a tool that communicates performance standards to students and parents

rating scale a scale that assigns a numerical value to one or more assessment criteria

reciprocal teaching an instructional approach involving a dialogue between the teacher and a group of students as they talk their way through a text; group members check their understanding of what they are reading by stopping to ask questions, summarize, and predict

reliability a measure of the confidence the assessor has about the conclusions drawn from an assessment

rubric an assessment tool that includes a set of performance indicators, often organized into several levels, for a given task or set of skills; a qualitative tool, used when the product, process, or performance task is complex and has multiple criteria

scoring guide a precise explanation of how marks are awarded for specific questions on a test or for specific performance indicators on a product

standardized test an empirically developed test that includes specific directions for administering and scoring; test includes evidence of reliability and validity and information about how the test was normed

standards-based test a test that is based on a set of curriculum and/or performance standards, such as those developed by provincial ministries

substitution in differentiated learning, learning targets that are developed for individual students and that substitute for mandated curriculum

summative assessment assessment that occurs at the end of a significant period of learning and summarizes student achievement of that learning

triangulated data having at least three pieces of evidence on which to base a grade for each major learning target

validity a measure of how well an assessment instrument measures what it is intended to measure

Assessment Reform Group. (1999). *Assessment for learning: Beyond the black box.* Cambridge, UK: University of Cambridge School of Education.

Bereiter, C., & Scardamalia, M. (1996). *Rethinking learning.* Cambridge, MA: Basil Blackwell.

Black, P., & Wiliam, D. (1998, October). Inside the black box: raising standards through classroom assessment. *Phi Delta Kappan, 80*(2), 139–148.

Black, P., Harrison, C., Lee, C., Marshall, B., & Wiliam, D. (2004). *Assessment for learning: Putting it into practice.* Maidenhead, Berkshire, UK: McGraw-Hill Education/ Open University Press.

Bloom, B., Engelhart, M., Furst, E., Hill, W., & Krathwohl, D. (1972). *Taxonomy of educational objectives: The classification of educational goals.* New York: David McKay Company, Inc.

Chung Wei, R., Andree, A., & Darling-Hammond, L. (2009, February). How nations invest in teachers. *Educational Leadership, 66*(5), 28–33.

Cooper, D. (2007). *Talk about assessment: Strategies and tools to improve learning.* Toronto: Thomson Nelson.

Cooper, D., & O'Connor, K. (2009, February). Redefining fair: Assessment and grading for the 21st century. *Changing Perspectives,* 27–31. Ontario Association for Supervision and Curriculum Development.

Covey, S. *The seven habits of highly effective people.* NY: Fireside, 1990.

Davies, A. (2000). *Making classroom assessment work.* Merville, BC.: Classroom Connections.

Doctorow, R., Bodiam, M., & McGowan, H. (2003) *CASI 7-8 Reading Assessment Teacher's Guide.* Toronto: Thomson Nelson.

DuFour, R. (2004, May). What is a "professional learning community"? *Educational Leadership, 61*(8), 6–11.

DuFour, R., & Eaker, R. (1998). *Professional learning communities at work: Best practices for enhancing student achievement.* Bloomington, IN: National Education Service.

Earl, L. (2003). *Assessment as learning: Using classroom assessment to maximize student learning.* Thousand Oaks, CA: Corwin Press.

Fiedler, E., Lange, R., & Winebrenner., S. (2002). In search of reality: Unraveling the myths about tracking, ability grouping, and the gifted. *Roeper Review, 24*(3), 108–111.

Flewelling, G., with Higginson, W. (2000). *A handbook on rich learning tasks.* Kingston, ON: Centre for Mathematics, Science and Technology Education, Faculty of Education, Queen's University.

Fullan, M. (2001). *Leading in a culture of change.* Hoboken, NJ: Wiley/Jossey-Bass, Inc.

Fullan, M. (2001). *The new meaning of educational change.* Toronto: Irwin.

Gillet, J. W., Temple, C., & Crawford, A. (2008). *Understanding reading problems: Assessment and instruction* (7th ed.). Boston: Pearson Education, Inc.

Gregg, L. A. (2007). Crossing the canyon: Helping students with special needs achieve proficiency. In D. Reeves (Ed.), *Ahead of the curve: The power of assessment to transform teaching and learning* (pp. 183–206). Bloomington, IN: Solution Tree.

Guskey, T. R., & Bailey, J. M. (2001). *Developing grading and reporting systems for student learning.* Thousand Oaks, CA: Corwin Press.

Hall, T., Strangman, N., & Meyer, A. (2003). *Differentiated instruction and implications for UDL implementation.* National Center on Accessing the General Curriculum. Retrieved October 21, 2004, from www.cast.org/ncac/ downloads/DI_UDL.pdf.

Halton District School Board. (1998). *Guidelines for assessing the reading skills of your students.* Internal resource.

Hargreaves, A. (2003). *Teaching in the knowledge society: Education in the age of insecurity.* NY: Teachers College Press.

Hargreaves, A. (2004). "Cultures, Contracts and Change." Keynote address, Canadian Teachers' Federation Conference. Ottawa, ON.

Hattie, J. A. (1992, April). Measuring the effects of schooling. *Australian Journal of Education, 36*(1), 5–13.

Johnson, S. (ch. 5). Personal communication, 2008.

Kagan, S. (1994). *Cooperative learning.* San Clemente, CA: Kagan Publishing.

Leahy, S., Lyon, C., Thompson, M., & Wiliam, D. (2005, November). Classroom assessment: minute by minute, day by day. *Educational Leadership, 63*(3), pp. 18–25.

Marzano, R. (1992). *Implementing dimensions of learning.* Alexandria, VA: Association for Supervision and Curriculum Development.

Marzano, R. (2006). *Classroom assessment & grading that work.* Alexandria, VA: Association for Supervision and Curriculum Development.

Marzano, R. (2007). *The art and science of teaching: A comprehensive framework for effective instruction.* Alexandria, VA: Association for Supervision and Curriculum Development.

Marzano, R., Pickering, D., & McTighe, J. (1993). *Assessing student outcomes: Performance assessment using the dimensions of learning model.* Alexandria, VA: Association for Supervision and Curriculum Development.

National Strategy for School Improvement. (2007). The leadership and management of whole school change. *Assessment for learning: 8 schools project report.* UK: Department for Education and Skills.

References

Nova Scotia Department of Education and Culture. (1997). *Atlantic Canada English language arts curriculum guide, grades 10–12.* Nova Scotia: Department of Education and Culture.

O'Connor, K. (2002). *How to grade for learning: Linking grades to standards.* Thousand Oaks, CA: Corwin Press.

O'Connor, K. (2007). *A repair kit for grading: 15 fixes for broken grades.* Princeton, NJ: Educational Testing Service.

Ontario Ministry of Education. (1999). *The Ontario curriculum grades 9 and 10: Technological Education.* Toronto: Queen's Printer for Ontario.

Ontario Ministry of Education. (2000). *The Ontario curriculum grades 9 to 12: Program planning and assessment.* Toronto: Queen's Printer for Ontario.

Ontario Ministry of Education. (2004). *Leading math success: Mathematical literacy grades 7–12.* Toronto: Queen's Printer for Ontario.

Ontario Ministry of Education. (2005). *The Ontario curriculum grades 9 and 10: Canadian and world studies.* Toronto: Queen's Printer for Ontario.

Ontario Ministry of Education. (2005). *The Ontario curriculum grades 11 and 12: Canadian and world studies.* Toronto: Queen's Printer for Ontario.

Ontario Ministry of Education. (2006). *The Ontario curriculum grades 9 and 10: English.* Toronto: Queen's Printer for Ontario.

Ontario Ministry of Education. (2008). *The Ontario curriculum grades 9 and 10: Science.* Toronto: Queen's Printer for Ontario.

Ontario Ministry of Education. *Provincial report card, grades 9–12.* Toronto: Queen's Printer for Ontario.

Palinscar, A., & Brown, A. (1984). Reciprocal teaching of comprehension-fostering and comprehension-monitoring activities. *Cognition and Instruction, 1,* 117–175.

Popham, W. J. (2006, November). Phony Formative Assessments: Buyer Beware! *Educational Leadership, 64*(3), 86–87.

Reeves, D. B. (2004, December). The case against the zero. *Phi Delta Kappan, 86*(4), 324–325.

Reeves, D. B., & Allison, E. (2009). *Renewal coaching: Sustainable change for individuals and organizations.* Hoboken, NJ: Wiley/Jossey-Bass.

Saskatchewan Ministry of Education. *English language arts 10 teaching and learning strategies: Writing—assessment of writing.* Regina: Government of Saskatchewan.

Scardamalia, M., & Bereiter, C. (1996). Computer support for knowledge-building communities. In T. Koschmann (Ed.), *CSCL: Theory and practice of an emerging paradigm* (pp. 249–268). Mahwah, NJ: Lawrence Erlbaum Associates.

Schmoker, M. (2001). *The results fieldbook: Practical strategies from dramatically improved schools.* Alexandria, VA: Association for Supervision and Curriculum Development.

Stafford, J. (2006, Summer). "The importance of educational research in the teaching of history." *Canadian Social Studies, 40* (1).

Sternberg, R. (2008, October). Excellence for all. *Educational Leadership, 66*(2), 14–19.

Stiggins, R., Arter, J., Chappuis, J., & Chappuis, S. (2004). *Classroom assessment for student learning: Doing it right—using it well.* Portland, OR: Assessment Training Institute.

Stiggins, Rick. Personal communication, 2007.

Sutton, R. (2001). Unpublished document.

Tomlinson, C. A. (2000). Reconcilable differences? Standards-based teaching and differentiation. *Educational Leadership, 58*(1), 6–11.

Tomlinson, C. A. (2001). *How to differentiate instruction in mixed-ability classrooms* (2nd ed.). Alexandria, VA: Association for Supervision and Curriculum Development.

Vygotsky, L. (1978). Interaction between learning and development. In M. Cole (Trans.), *Mind in society* (pp. 79–91). Cambridge, MA: Harvard University Press.

Western and Northern Canadian Protocol. (2008). *The common curriculum framework, grades 10–12 mathematics.* Western and Northern Canadian Protocol.

Wiggins, G. (1993). *Assessing student performance: Exploring the purpose and limits of testing.* Hoboken, NJ: Wiley/Jossey-Bass Inc.

Wiggins, G. (1994). "Standards, not standardization." *A video and print curriculum on performance-based student assessment.* Genesee, NY: CLASS.

Wiggins, G. (1998). *Educative assessment: Designing assessments to inform and improve student performance.* Hoboken, NJ: Wiley/Jossey-Bass Inc.

Wiggins, G. (1999). "Understanding by Design." Workshop. Cherry Hills, NJ.

Wiggins, G., & McTighe, J. (1998). *Understanding by design.* Alexandria, VA: Association for Supervision and Curriculum Development.

Wiggins, G., & McTighe, J. (2005) *Understanding by design* (2nd ed.). Alexandria, VA: Association for Supervision and Curriculum Development.

Wiliam, D. (2001, Autumn). What is wrong with our educational assessments and what can be done about it? *Education Review, 15*(1).

Wiliam, D. (2007). Content *then* process: Teacher learning communities in the service of formative assessment. In D. Reeves (Ed.), *Ahead of the curve: The power of assessment to transform teaching and learning* (pp. 183–206). Bloomington, IN: Solution Tree.

Wiliam, D. (2008, August). "Using Assessment to Improve Learning: Why? What? and How?" Keynote address, Summer Leadership Conference. Penticton, BC.

Wormeli, R. (2006). *Fair isn't always equal: Assessing and grading in the differentiated classroom.* Portland, ME: Stenhouse Publishers.

We have made every effort to trace the ownership of all copyrighted material and to secure permission from copyright holders. In the event of any question arising as to the use of any material, we will be pleased to make the necessary corrections in future printings. Thanks are due to the following for permission to use the material indicated.

Except where indicated, interior photos ©Nelson Education Ltd.

Section 1: Assessment Today

Chapter 2

Photos: 13: © Miodrag Gajic/Shutterstock; **17:** © Simone van den Berg/Shutterstock; **22:** © iStockphoto.com/Arthur Kwiatkowski

Section 2: Planning Assessment of Learning

Chapter 3

Photo: 45: © Elena Elisseeva/Shutterstock

Text: 27, 35, 42: Source: From Understanding by Design, Expanded 2nd Edition (Figure 1.1, p. 18), by Grant Wiggins and Jay McTighe, Alexandria, VA: ASCD. © 2005 by ASCD. Adapted with permission. Learn more about ASCD at www. ascd.org; **28:** Source: From *Understanding by Design*, Expanded 2nd Edition (Figure 7.11, p. 170), by Grant Wiggins and Jay McTighe, Alexandria, VA: ASCD. © 2005 by ASCD. Adapted with permission. Learn more about ASCD at www.ascd.org; **36-37:** Adapted from Joseph Stafford, "The Importance of Educational Research in the Teaching of History," *Canadian Social Studies* Vol. 40, 1, 2006; **39-41:** Adapted from *Teaching With Rich Learning Tasks, A Handbook*, 2nd edition, 2005, Examples 3 & 4, pp 60-61, by Gary Flewelling with William Higginson. Published by The Australian Association of Mathematics Teachers Inc. http://www.aamt.edu.au

Chapter 4

Text: 60: Source: From *Understanding by Design*, Expanded 2nd Edition (Figure 3.3, p. 71), by Grant Wiggins and Jay McTighe, Alexandria, VA: ASCD. © 2005 by ASCD. Adapted with permission. Learn more about ASCD at www.ascd.org

Section 3: Assessment that Promotes Learning

Chapter 5

Photos: 72: © iStockphoto.com/Chris Schmidt; **75:** © JustASC/Shutterstock; **90:** © Layland Masuda/ Shutterstock

Text: 78: Adapted from "Guidelines for Assessing the Reading Skills of Your Students." Internal resource, Halton District School Board, 1998; **81:** From TORONTO DISTRICT SCHOOL BD. CASI: Program Guide, 1E. ©2003 Nelson Education Ltd. Reproduced by permission. www.cengage.com/ permissions; **82:** From TORONTO DISTRICT SCHOOL BD. CASI: Program Guide, 1E. ©2003 Nelson Education Ltd. Reproduced by permission. www.cengage.com/ permissions; **84-85:** From Jean Wallace Gillet, Charles Temple, Et Al. *Understanding Reading Problems: Assessment And Instruction*, 7e. Published by Allyn and Bacon/Merrill Education, Boston, MA. Copyright ©2008 by Pearson Education. Reprinted/translated by permission of the publisher; **87:** From *TORONTO DISTRICT SCHOOL BD. CASI: Program Guide*, 1E. ©2003 Nelson Education Ltd. Reproduced by permission. www.cengage.com/permissions

Chapter 6

Photos: 93: © iStockphoto.com/Chris Schmidt; **119:** © Laurence Gough/Shutterstock; **120:** © 2009 Jupiterimages Corporation

Text: 97: From GIBB. *Nelson Science and Technology 7*. © 1999 Nelson Education Ltd. Reproduced by permission. www.cengage.com/permissions; **117:** From BARRY/ ANDERSON. *Literature and Media 11*. © 2002 Nelson Education Ltd. Reproduced by permission. www.cengage.com/ permissions; **121:** From COOPER. *Talk About Assessment*, 1E. © 2006 Nelson Education Ltd. Reproduced by permission. www.cengage.com/permissions;

Chapter 7

Photos: 125: © Andrey Shadrin/Shutterstock; **133:** © iStockphoto.com/Lorraine Swanson

Text: 129: From DAVIES. *Between the Lines 12*, 1E. © 2002 Nelson Education Ltd. Reproduced by permission. www. cengage.com/permissions; **142-143:** ©Darlene Bowles, Educational Assistant; **145:** From COOPER. *Talk About Assessment*, 1E. © 2006 Nelson Education Ltd. Reproduced by permission. www.cengage.com/permissions

Section 4: Communicating About Achievement

Chapter 8

Photo: 179: © 2009 Jupiterimages Corporation

Text: 154: Source: From *Understanding by Design*, Expanded 2nd Edition (Figure 3.3, p. 71), by Grant Wiggins and Jay McTighe, Alexandria, VA: ASCD. © 2005 by ASCD. Adapted with permission. Learn more about ASCD at www. ascd.org; **156:** From AKER/HODGKINSON. *Language and*

Writing 11. © 2002 Nelson Education Ltd. Reproduced by permission. www.cengage.com/permissions; **157-158:** From Fielding/Evans. *Canada: Our Century, Our Story*. © 2001 Nelson Education Ltd. Reproduced by permission. www.cengage.com/permissions; **160:**

Saskatchewan Ministry of Education. Reproduced by permission, 2009; **164:** From COOPER. *Talk About Assessment*, 1E. © 2006 Nelson Education Ltd. Reproduced by permission. www.cengage.com/permissions

Chapter 9

Photos: 209: © iStockphoto.com/Chris Schmidt

Text: 191: © Queen's Printer for Ontario, 1999. Reproduced with permission; **207:** Excerpt from Douglas B. Reeves, "The Case Against the Zero," *Phi Delta Kappan*, Volume 86, December 2004, pp. 324-325. Reprinted with permission of Phi Delta Kappa International, www.pdkintl.org, 2009. All rights reserved.

Section 5: Implementing Change

Chapter 10

Photo: 7: © iStockphoto.com/bonnie jacobs

Text: 12-13: Jennifer Adams ED.d., Superintendent of Curriculum, Ottawa-Carleton District School Board; **15:** From COOPER. *Talk About Assessment*, 1E. © 2006 Nelson Education Ltd. Reproduced by permission. www.cengage.com/permissions

Tools

1.3-1.5, 1.7, 1.8, 3.4, 3.5, 4.1-4.5: From COOPER. *Talk About Assessment*, 1E. © 2006 Nelson Education Ltd. Reproduced by permission. www.cengage.com/permissions;

4.6: © Jeff Catania; **4.7:** © Nancy Wakeman; **5.1-5.5:** From DAVIES. *Between the Lines 12*, 1E. © 2002 Nelson Education Ltd. Reproduced by permission. www.cengage.com/permissions; **5.6:** From BARRY/ANDERSON. *Literature and Media 11*. © 2002 Nelson Education Ltd. Reproduced by permission. www.cengage.com/permissions; **5.7, 5.8:** From AKER/HODGKINSON. *Language and Writing 11*. © 2002 Nelson Education Ltd. Reproduced by permission. www.cengage.com/permissions; **5.9:** Halton District School Board; **5.10:** © Brad Volkman, Assistant Superintendent, Prairie Rose School Division No. 8. Reproduced by permission of the author; **5.11:** Reproduced by permission of Rachel Skillen, Mathematics Teacher; **5.12-5.15:** © Jeff Catania; **5.16:** From GIBB. *Nelson Science and Technology 7*. © 1999 Nelson Education Ltd. Reproduced by permission. www.cengage.com/permissions; **5.18 [top]:** Source: Andrew Bigham and Samantha Goodwin, **5.18 [bottom]:** From COOPER. *Talk About Assessment*, 1E. © 2006 Nelson Education Ltd. Reproduced by permission. www.cengage.com/permissions; **5.19-5.21:** Reproduced by permission of Julia Cale, Department Head of Social Sciences, St. Anne's Catholic Secondary School, Clinton, Ontario; **5.22:** Iroquois Ridge High School Grade 10 History Team; **5.25-5.26:** Jeff Boulton, Business Studies Teacher, Iroquois Ridge High School; **5.27:** First page adapted from OJEN'S resource, *Making the Case: Mock Hearing Toolkit*, available at www.ojen.ca, second page by Brenda R.M. Celi, Secondary Teacher, BCHS; **5.28:** Source: Brenda R.M. Celi, Secondary Teacher, BCHS; **5.29:** Source: Krista Caron, White Oaks Secondary School Teacher, along with HDSB; **5.30:** Source: Brenda R.M. Celi, Secondary Teacher, BCHS; **Appendix:** © Damian Cooper, Plan-Teach-Assess, 2005

Index